THEY ESCAPED FROM THE MIDDLE CLASS WITH
THE PARK AVENUE MONEY DIET!

"Dan's money diet is the greatest! It's done more for our finances than all the investment counselors in Beverly Hills could do."
Irv and Georgia Smith

"What I like best about Dan's program is that he used it himself. He didn't make it up just to write a book and make a lot of money. It's a program I plan to spend the rest of my life on."
Joan Schmidt

"We've been on Dan's program for almost five years now. It's changed our lives. We've learned how to save and spend money more wisely. We've learned how to invest. We're accomplishing financial goals we never thought possible."
Jim and Larri Lee Hooper

"Dan's marvelous book should be required reading in every high school and college. Dan tells it like it is. His program puts emphasis on the mind and the pocketbook.
Cokie Mingelli

THE PARK AVENUE MONEY DIET
"really works because Dan really cares. It would be hard not to respond to such commitment. Dan deserves a medal."
Richard Hildebrand

THE PARK AVENUE MONEY DIET

How to Escape from the Middle Class Forever
By Investing in Residential Rental Real Estate

DAN BAUMGARTNER

FAWCETT COLUMBINE • NEW YORK

A Fawcett Columbine Book
Published by Ballantine Books
Copyright © 1983, 1984 by Daniel Baumgartner

Library of Congress Catalog Card Number: 84-90840

ISBN 0-449-90139-4

This edition published by arrangement with the author. Originally self-published in
hardcover

Manufactured in the United States of America

First Ballantine Books Edition: October 1984

10 9 8 7 6 5 4 3 2 1

I dedicate this book to all the wonderful people
who took the time to help me with my research;
and to you, the reader. Here's hoping this book will
help you escape from the middle class forever.

ACKNOWLEDGMENTS

Thanks—

To my wife and partner, Billie—for love, help, and understanding.
To my daughter, Jessica—for new joy and inspiration.

WARNING . . .

Reading this book in a room where a television set is turned on can make some of the words drop right off the page. It is the policy of the publisher, and your bookstore, not to be responsible in such cases.

C O N T E N T S

C H A P T E R

+ _ RICH

0 _ MIDDLE CLASS

– _ POOR

This book, which offers to help you escape from the middle class, begins with Chapter 0; because on a scale from rich to poor, where rich is a plus and poor is a minus, being average and middle class is (yawn!) a zero. Being average and middle class is not making it, and it's not *not* making it. It's the economic median floating somewhere between privilege and deprivation, affluence and poverty.

The lines between the classes in a democratic society are not always clearly drawn; however, an average middle-class person is generally assumed to be: a white-collar worker, a professional person, a well paid blue-collar worker, a small business owner, a successful farmer, a teacher, or a government employee.

A middle-class person is anyone who is not wealthy; who is not impoverished; who does not have a high paying, secure job which allows him to live well and put aside a substantial amount of money into savings; or who does not have a substantial amount of independent investment income.

The depression of the 1930s, the recession of the 1980s, and four or five recessions in between, have made it clear that average middle-class people can become poor people overnight. Many individuals in high paying jobs, including managers and corporate executives, from time to time find themselves out of work and out on the street. In fact, ordinary people who never lose their jobs are occasionally counted among the poor as a result of medical or other emergencies.

On the other hand, average middle-class people are only a few small steps away from being wealthy. Wealthy people normally survive depressions, layoffs, and medical or other emergencies. They seldom lose their assets, their incomes, or their social positions.

Wealthy people are the people who come to mind when Park Avenue is mentioned. Park Avenue is a street where rich people live, work, and play. This book is called *The Park Avenue Money Diet* because Park Avenue is synonymous with fabulous wealth and success.

The Park Avenue Money Diet is a tried and proven three-part plan that shows you a way to achieve Park Avenue affluence for yourself and your family. It's a program which will help you escape your lean existence in the middle class and make you fat where it really counts—in your wallet, in your bank account, and in the ownership of real property.

The basic elements of *The Park Avenue Money Diet* are the three M's: (1) the method, (2) the means, and (3) the motivation. The program is simple, it's basic, and it works.

The Method

The method is investing in residential rental properties. Residential rental properties are the finest investment vehicle available to the average person today whereby you can actually build a fortune without incurring an inordinate amount of down-side risk!

The reason is simple. Residential rental properties offer a package of benefits unavailable in any other investment today. The package includes: safety and stability, appreciation potential, income, substantial tax shelter, pride of ownership (which still counts for something!), and opportunities for high loan-to-value leverage. This complete package of benefits makes residential rental properties the most powerful tool available for the wealth seeker today, without exception!

You'll learn basics of investing in residential properties. I'll show you how to find the best properties, what to expect once you've committed yourself to a Ten Year Real Estate Investment Program, and where to get the money to get started.

The Means

Personal financial record keeping. This is the soapbox issue in *The Park Avenue Money Diet.* Accounting for yourself. Committing yourself to the day-to-day detailed habits so necessary if you are ever to get a handle on your financial life.

If there is one thing that self-made wealthy people know that most of us don't know, it's that liberty is the product of order. They're organized! They organize not only what they have, but who they are, and how they think. They're sticklers for detail. Successful people do those things that most people don't want to do, and one of those things is keeping their books. They monitor their progress.

The Park Avenue Money Diet Personal Accounting System is a simple, step-by-step program for regaining and maintaining control of your financial life. It's a means for laying out and cementing the solid foundation of your plan for financial freedom. It's a specific program for finding out and keeping track of what you have, what you owe, and what you're worth. It's a blueprint for detailing your income and expenses and projecting them out into the future. It's a specific financial goal-setting formula.

The Motivation _____

Finally we're going to talk a lot about what I call prosperous thinking . . . learning to think like the rich people think. Prosperous thinking is the intangible behind the tangible which makes the tangible possible.

Prosperous thinking is motivation. No, not this business of jumping up and down and getting excited, but rather motivation which will allow you to make a commitment and stick with it. A lot of motivators of the earth are going to motivate you to get you started. I'm not peddling that kind of motivation. I think wishing can get you started. Real motivation to me is motivation which keeps a person "keeping on"—one hour a day, two hours a day, day after day.

Prosperous thinking involves concentrated efforts, acquired habits, positive thoughts, desire, faith, and specific goals. It's the mind-set required if you ever want to make big money.

But before we get into the actual *Park Avenue Money Diet* program, we're going to spend a few pages getting to know one another and getting to know ourselves. Let's take a long, hard look at what it really means to be middle class in an affluent society.

Let me warn you: you are going to come across a bunch of quizzes and tests which I'll ask you to take. They're not hard. Actually they're kind of fun to take and score, and I know that most people who have been taking them have been going, "Uh-huh! Yep! I hear what you're saying Dan, I do that, too!"

The Park Avenue Money Diet has been written for all the average middle-class people who do not wish to continue to live zero-based lives simply because that's the way their "ball bounced" or their "cookie crumbled." It's been written for you . . . to show you how to put your economic life back into your own capable hands . . . to challenge you to take it upon yourself to become far more than just the average middle-class person you are today.

C H A P T E R 1

OCTOBER 1971

I remember it was a Saturday morning. Billie and I had just returned from having breakfast at our favorite restaurant on the beach at Waikiki when we received a long distance telephone call from Billie's mother in Texas. She was excited. An oil company was drilling a well near a small tract of ranchland that Billie had inherited from her father. Billie's mom had been told that the land was going to be included in the production pool if they made a well.

That was all we heard for awhile. Then one day, two months later, we received the fantastic news. The oil company had completed a good oil and natural gas well.

And that should be the end of this book. Fortunately for you and me—

you because you just put out a lot of money for this book, and me because I would still be teaching and living an average middle-class life—it's not.

I once was a high school music teacher. I thought I'd better mention that right up front, because having been a teacher, I have credentials to present myself as a former member of the middle class.

But that's not the real beginning of the story. I actually started out being middle class as the direct result of growing up in an average middle-class family in Lake Mahopac, New York. My father owned a consulting and experimental nursery business there. My mother was a housewife. My sister was a cheerleader. My brother was perfect. He could have been Beaver Cleaver.

I knew from a young age that I was a member of a middle-class family. Well, at least I knew we weren't rich. It was obvious. We drove Fords and Chevies and lived in Lake Mahopac all year 'round. Rich people only lived in Mahopac in the summertime. They came up from the city every year in June, July, and August. They drove Cadillacs, Continentals, and sports cars. They stayed at the fancy hotels, or in their summer homes on the lake. Rich people lived in New York City most of the time.

Growing up as a member of a middle-class family in Mahopac, New York, appeared to me at the time to be no problem. Actually, I thought it was great! It seemed to me to be demonstrably preferable to living in New York City.

I grew up doing ordinary middle-class things. I played children's games like cowboys and Indians. I was a Cub Scout and a Boy Scout. I took piano lessons and I played the trombone in the marching band. I played football and ran track in high school.

My career ambitions were middle class. I wanted to be an employee. At various times, I considered becoming an airline pilot, a rocket scientist, and a commmercial artist . . . all employee positions.

I spent twelve years in school (thirteen, counting kindergarten!). I watched TV, worked as a caddy at the country club, and hung out with the boys and girls at the Chicken-in-the-Basket! My major goal as a teenager was to get my driver's license. Now you can't be more middle class than that, can you?

There was never any question about the fact that I would go to college when I graduated from high school. My folks had both gone to college, and it was always assumed that my brother and sister and I would go, too.

Besides, I'd been shown that chart in the ninth grade social studies textbook. Do you remember seeing it? It had two little blue men of different sizes. Alas, the littlest blue man didn't have a college education. He would only earn $250,000 in his lifetime. (This was 1957!) He was represented on the chart as being less than two-thirds the size of the bigger blue man. The bigger blue man had a feather in his cap. The feather in his cap was a college education. The big blue man could expect to earn $400,000 during his working years.

Of course, everyone in my class wanted to be like the bigger blue man with the feather in his cap. I was no exception. So, I spent four years studying liberal arts at one of the finest small colleges in the Southwest, Texas Lutheran College.

At TLC (don't you love it!) I learned to recognize, analyze, and criticize. By the time I finished, I could recognize, analyze, and criticize some of the finest things in life: Shakespeare, Picasso, Mozart, Lone Star beer, and German sausage. However, to be perfectly candid, after four years of studying and having a pretty good time, I'd acquired no moneymaking skills. Curiously, I was no better off than the little blue man.

At the time I graduated from college, I had not escaped from the middle class. (To be fair, escaping from the middle class wasn't really a goal of mine at the time!) I did, however, accomplish something very worthwhile at Texas Lutheran. I fell in love with and married a wonderful girl, Billie Dawn Spies.

But where, I wondered, was the occupation that was supposed to greet me at graduation, acknowledge my skills of recognizing, analyzing, and criticizing, and pay me suitable compensation?

My problem should have been immediately obvious to me, but it wasn't. I had assumed, or had been led to believe, that the liberal arts curriculum was somehow supposed to put me on the direct road to riches. (So much for my skills of recognizing, analyzing, and criticizing!) I hadn't even attempted to get a teaching certificate at TLC. You see, I'd found out that teachers didn't get paid very much.

Anyway, now all of a sudden school was out. I was about to get married, and it seemed to me to be about time I tried to do something practical. Unfortunately, the only practical thing I knew how to do was to climb back up on the side of the chart with the big blue man with the feather in his cap again. I went to Los Angeles and enrolled in the University of Southern California School of Music. I was hired as a teaching assistant, which helped to pay my way through graduate school.

Billie and I took up residence in an apartment building on campus. Billie taught high school to support us. When we weren't working or studying, we nurtured our average middle-class time and money habits. For reasons which were unclear to me at the time, but which are clear now, we had a compulsive desire to get away . . . to kill time!

As soon as we could afford it, we bought a TV. I loved that TV! It was turned on whenever we were in the apartment. Two or three times a week, we went out. We'd get a hamburger, go bowling, play miniature golf, or see a movie. At other times, we'd go to shopping centers and walk around. During the summer months, we'd spend one day a week at the beach. (It didn't cost anything!) Once or maybe twice a year, we'd take a trip to Disneyland, Magic Mountain, Knott's Berry Farm, or the zoo. Our weekends were spent driving all over Southern California. When we socialized with other people (all middle-class) we did exactly the same sorts of things.

Looking back now, I can see that killing time helped to shelter us from having to face our middle-class problem. In fact, killing time was a major part of our middle-class problem.

Money was a constant concern of ours. It was always just barely in adequate supply. We'd get to the end of each month and be five or ten dollars ahead or fifty to a hundred dollars short . . . the latter more often than the former, which often left us with the problem of deciding which credit card bill to let slide.

We tried ineptly to find ways of making some money. We invested several hundred dollars (money we couldn't afford to lose!) in the stock market, and lost it. I tried without success to write and sell popular songs. We went to high-pressure meetings held by land brokers, insurance salesmen, and cleaning products distributors. We even tried to get on a TV game show. Getting rich quick was not in our cards at this time.

I earned both a Master of Music Degree and a Teaching Certificate at USC. Through the patronage of one of my professors, I took my first real job as the Interim Director of Choral Music at Punahou High School in Honolulu, Hawaii.

For card-carrying members of the middle class, the job at Punahou was an enlightening and enjoyable experience. But the Hawaiian Islands, the islands themselves, had the effect on Billie and me of enhancing all that was negative and middle class in our lives.

After the initial excitement of being in the South Pacific, we began to feel confined. We began to think of Oahu Island as "the rock." We couldn't afford to get away by flying back to the Mainland, and even a trip to one of the other islands, because of the expense of the air fare and hotels, was only an occasional reprieve from our confinement. Billie and I rented a three-room apartment, lived on borrowed and secondhand furniture, and drove a Volkswagen bus. We scrimped and saved in middle-class fashion to make ends meet.

We killed time in Hawaii the same way we had killed time in Los Angeles. Mostly we walked around, we drove around, and we watched TV.

Our daily entertainment included an occasional hour or two at the beach. Once or twice a week, after school, we'd go down to one of the hotels on Waikiki for a beer and peanuts. On weekends, we'd go shopping. We would spend hours walking around the Ala Moana Shopping Center. We ate out at least once or twice a week, and we saw a lot of movies.

One of our favorite pastimes was going out to the airport after dinner to watch the 747s fly back to the Mainland. Another favorite getaway was driving the 140 miles around Oahu Island, clockwise. One day we decided that that was old hat, so we began driving around the island counterclockwise! Had we stayed on the island much longer, we might have figured out a way to drive around the island in a figure eight pattern.

Fortunately, the job at Punahou was more exciting than the way we spent our spare time.

Punahou is a private high school set up by Protestant missionaries to Hawaii in the nineteenth century. As James Michener mentioned several times in his book *Hawaii,* Punahou is an educational haven for the offspring of the well-to-do. The waiting list to get in is long. In some cases, wealthy Hawaiian children are actually enrolled at Punahou before they are born. (Admirals and generals stationed on the Islands, and Hollywood movie stars stationed in California, can generally get special dispensation to send their kids there on shorter notice!) The school also accepts and offers scholarships to particularly bright or talented members of other segments of Hawaiian society.

The quality of the education available to the students at Punahou is decidedly better than the education available to the average middle-class public school student. Everything required by the faculty to teach their classes is provided at a moment's notice. The teachers at Punahou are exceptional. I was able to watch students at Punahou make contacts which not only guaranteed them entrance to the best colleges on the Mainland, but which practically assured them their success in their chosen fields later in life.

At Punahou, I was given a limited glimpse of how the money class lives; but a limited glimpse was all it took to make me realize rich was better.

And that brings us back to where we began this story—back to that Saturday morning when Billie's mom called to tell us about the oil company drilling the well.

We didn't know at first how much money, if any, the well was going to generate. I can tell you, our expectations exceeded the actual results. Nevertheless, even before the news of the actual strike, the well did wonderful things for us. All of a sudden, with just the news of the drilling activity, our lives changed. The world became a different, more exciting place. Our potential opportunities seemed to be without limit. The air was cleaner, the grass was greener, and the ocean was more beautiful. We acquired fabulous feelings of freedom, security, and well-being. As it turned out, our enhanced senses and those good feelings were among the best things the well produced.

The tract of land that Billie had inherited from her father was not very big, and since the production pool was spread out over many neighboring acres, our share of the production turned out to be only one-eighth of one-eighth of the total. Right at first this amounted to $650 a month. In comparison to what some of the royalty owners received, it was not very much, but to us it was a lot of money. After all, I was only taking home a little more than $650 a month from my teaching job.

We were satisfied from the beginning, but as time went by, things got better. Soon after the Arab oil embargo, the price of oil and natural gas started rising. We started receiving checks for over $1,000 a month. A year later we were taking in $2,000 a month.

Then one day we received word that the oil company had set up a new derrick across the road from the first well and was drilling a second well. As you might imagine, it started getting downright euphoric around our house. Since the existing well was producing over $2,000 a month, we assumed the next one should bring in at least an equal amount . . . maybe more.

Our lives couldn't have been much more exciting. Still, everything was not all dewberries and cream. There was a sour side to what was happening to us.

We were becoming responsible for an increasingly heavy income tax burden. Having paid a hefty income tax the preceding couple of years, it now looked like we were going to have to start paying substantially more. We were making about $24,000 a year from the first well. With the new well about to come on line, we were projecting an income of $48,000. By adding our teaching salaries to that, we anticipated a combined income of over $70,000, a lot of money back then. The tax on an unprotected income of $70,000 was (and still is!) staggering.

Making a lot of money is not generally a part of the average middle-class experience; so naturally, like other middle-class people who come into a lot of money without being prepared for it, we were overwhelmed by our lack of knowledge about money and taxes.

We knew we had to do something, and not knowing any better, we did the worst possible thing. We consulted several of our average middle-class friends and colleagues. Unfortunately, they didn't know any more than we did about high finance . . . but since we'd asked, they offered us their advice.

You know the only thing that's worse than asking for average middle-class financial advice, don't you? You guessed it! It's following that advice! And that's just exactly what we did.

After counseling with our middle-class confrères, we concluded that the universal middle-class solution to our tax problem was to quit making so much money. We couldn't figure out a way to stop the oil and gas money from coming in, so we decided to quit our jobs.

Thanks a lot! With tax planning like that, who needs H & R Block? But that's not all! There's more!

Whenever we did something overtly middle class (that is, when we tried to do something that was beyond the bounds of our knowledge or experience!) we tended to overdo it. This time we really overdid it. We assumed our income potential without our teaching salaries still to be in the neighborhood of $48,000 annually. We figured we still faced a hefty tax burden.

Like a rabbit out of a hat, we pulled another great tax shelter idea from our most recent income tax experience. The interest we'd been paying on the home we'd purchased was the biggest annual income tax deduction we'd been taking. Why not, we thought, find a way to pay more interest?

We decided to buy another piece of real estate so we could pay a lot of interest and write it off our taxes. We even considered paying prepaid interest! (Talk about your middle-class Bozos!)

We bought a beautiful 400-acre Texas cattle ranch for $250,000. I don't know if the rancher who sold it to us saw us coming, if he had more faith in the longevity of oil and natural gas wells than he should have, or if he was just marvelously intuitive! But whatever his reasons were, we are indebted to him. (In more ways than one!)

We put $5,000 of our savings down, along with $20,000 borrowed against the land pooled with the oil and natural gas wells. The rest of the purchase price was financed through the rancher. We determined that we'd have payments of $32,000 a year, almost $16,000 of which was deductible interest! This left us approximately $16,000 of the $48,000 we projected the two wells would produce to live on.

In addition, we were to get $4,000 a year by leasing the ranch back to the rancher who sold it to us. The income remaining after the mortgage payments appeared to be more than enough for a middle-class couple to live on! But remember, the second well hadn't been turned on yet.

Guess what. Our prowess at tax planning paled in comparison to our ability to forecast the future. The oil company never started producing the second well. What's more, several months after we'd closed the deal on the ranch, the oil company cut off the first well.

After some careful thought, it occurred to us that we had a couple of problems. Here we had quit our jobs, bought the most beautiful ranch in Texas (acquiring enough debt in the process, it seemed, to float a small country), and found ourselves with little more than our savings to use to make the annual ranch mortgage payments and defray our living expenses.

Mercifully, the gravity of the situation didn't hit us immediately. We'd saved enough money over the previous years so that we knew we'd be able to meet the first annual payment on the ranch. We figured the oil company would turn the production of the oil and gas wells on by the time the next ranch payment came due.

We tried not to think about any of the other alternatives, like losing the money we'd already invested in the ranch, or having to call the school administrators to tell them we were just kidding around, and plead for our teaching jobs back.

In the meantime, our lack of knowledge about money and taxes began to disturb me. Nothing in my background had prepared me for making a lot of money. I decided to learn something about it. I wanted to be ready when they turned the wells back on.

I started reading a lot, which had the added benefit of keeping my mind off the sizable payments which were coming due on the new ranch. Occasionally I read for as long as twelve hours a day. I kept it up for almost nine months. It was an interesting time, and as it turned out, a very important one. I read about money, accounting, tax shelters, and wealthy people.

I learned a lot, especially the fact that simply paying interest is not tax shelter at all—in fact, you can get enough tax shelter to go bankrupt out of simply paying interest. I began to learn about the wonders of capital gains, investment tax credits, and depreciation. I learned about how wealthy people create and protect fortunes by investing in residential rental real estate. I learned about stocks and bonds. I found out the difference between term and whole life insurance, and I found out that like most average middle-class people, I had been sold the worst kind of insurance.

Another thing I learned was that my liberal arts education was never intended to help me increase my earning power. Liberal arts educations, I found out, were created for the already wealthy (originally European nobility) to educate them to recognize, analyze, and criticize the finer things in life . . . finer things which actually were a part of their lives.

In the eighteenth century, wealthy landowners, industrialists, and well-to-do merchants, believing themselves to be democracy's noblemen, adopted the practice of sending their youngsters off to acquire liberal arts educations, too. It became sort of a status symbol. The practice spread to and throughout much of the middle class (never a group to miss out on a status symbol!) and the practice has continued to the present day.

Of course, so long as the kids can come home and work in the family business, or so long as Dad can have them placed in good professional positions, or so long as they marry into money or housework, a middle-class liberal arts education, in an esoteric sense, can be said to enhance the quality of a person's life.

The problem arises when that person attempts to find actual gainful (that is, profitable!) employment (which also might enhance the quality of a person's life; and which rules out teaching, government work, secretarial, and bottom-rung corporate positions!) on the strength of that liberal arts education. It's only then that many a graduate has found out that liberal arts educations, in most situations, are not particularly remunerative.

I also learned the principles of accounting, and I set up a detailed set of books, which I credit with being instrumental to my success in staying afloat in bad times and for getting ahead in good.

In the meantime, the oil and gas wells remained off. We made the first annual mortgage payment on the ranch, and came within a couple of thousand dollars of depleting our savings reserve.

After completing my reading program, and after about three more months of waiting for the oil company to get its act together and turn on the wells, fear began to settle in. My faith in my own providence and the gas wells evaporated. I started looking around for a way to salvage the situation.

One day Billie and I heard a radio ad for a real estate school. We investigated and decided to get our California real estate licenses. (We'd moved back to the Southern California mainland by this time!) We studied for two months, passed at least the required 105 out of 150 multiple choice questions, and found ourselves immediately qualified to put other people in debt for thirty years. What an amazing world we live in, we mused.

Not satisifed that the licensing course had taught us the practical skills we needed to be competent real estate sales agents, we found and participated in a course taught by Tommy Hopkins. This course focused on how to sell real estate and provide services for our clients like champions. Then we went back to work—selling real estate.

By working twelve- to eighteen-hour days, seven days a week; by being innovative; and by careful budgeting, we were able to earn enough money in real estate sales, not only to make a living, but also to make the second mortgage payment on our ranch. (Unlike the teaching profession, the real estate profession let us begin paying ourselves what we were actually worth!)

We continued to study the finer points of our new profession. We attended seminars and classes at USC and UCLA. We read a lot. Through study and through experience, we learned that no matter how hard we worked, and no matter how many transactions we put together, we weren't really going to get ahead just working for commissions. (Commissions, fees, and salaries normally work out to be just adequate to cover adjusted living expenses!) The way to make a lot of money, we discovered, was by investing.

We started buying and selling small investment properties, mostly single family houses, and trading them up for bigger and more profitable ones as opportunities arose. Within several years, we were able to buy our first large apartment building, which was in Oklahoma City. It was a twenty-nine-unit apartment building, which we purchased for $290,000 with $29,000 down. We made a number of improvements to the property, and within two and a half years we were able to sell it for $450,000. After costs, we cleared $135,000.

We purchased a second, thirty-three-unit, apartment building in Oklahoma a year later for $450,000, putting $90,000 down. We still own that property. It's providing us with income and becoming more and more valuable every day.

The rest of the money from our first apartment deal and some of the money we got from the sale of our first home was used to buy a twenty-five-unit apartment complex from a builder in Dallas, Texas for $775,000. We sold the project a year and a half later for $1,028,000 — a profit, after costs, of over $200,000.

I mention these deals to point out that we've made, and continue to make, considerably more money (through both good times and bad!) in real estate investing than we ever made from the oil and gas well.

Of course, there are many plateaus of wealth. By some standards, we're not wealthy yet; however, I subscribe to the standard that says you're wealthy if you own income-producing real property, earn enough money to live well, and have enough left over to continue to save and invest for your future. By that standard, Billie and I are at least on or above the first plateau, beyond middle class, and we're climbing up.

There wouldn't be much sense in my writing a book telling you how to escape the middle class and get rich if my first instruction to you was to drill an oil and natural gas well out in your backyard, would there? I might, however, tell you to go buy a cattle ranch you can't afford, and, believe it or not, that would make sense. So pay close attention!

As things turned out, the oil and gas wells were only catalysts for us. First, they woke us up to the real, wonderful world of money. Then they taught us the value of setting goals by getting us into a traumatic situation (buying the cattle ranch) which, once the wells were shut off, became a goal we had to strive for! Thanks to the wells being shut off, we'd been set up to accomplish something we'd never have tried without that little outside push.

Making payments on a quarter-of-a-million-dollar loan gave us something big to aim our middle-class sights on. The annual payment was constantly on our minds. In order to make the payments, we found ourselves making decisions that would have been entirely different (and in some cases less painful!) had that great big beautiful carrot not been dangling out there in front of us.

The decisions we made in connection with accomplishing the cattle ranch goal opened the door for our escape from the middle class. This was because these decisions had numerous beneficial consequences affecting every aspect of our personal, professional, and financial lives. The effects went far beyond the achievement of that one specific goal. And that, we discovered, is more often than not the nature and effect of a worthwhile goal.

By the way, even though the payments on the ranch have become easier now that we're making more money, they're still a yearly challenge. If you're wondering if the struggle has been worth it, it has. The ranch is presently worth nearly a million dollars.

I suggest that you can let this book act as your catalyst. It can be your oil and natural gas well. It can open your eyes to the possibilities for wealth all around you just as our oil and gas well opened our eyes. It can help you establish your goals. Remember, it took the wells to wake us up to the fact that there is a lot more money out there in the world than we'd ever realized. They alerted us to the fact that we, as easily as anyone else, could really get our share of it. That's what this book should do for you.

While I was beginning to earn substantial sums from real estate investing, I began to develop a course to teach our real estate clients to do the same thing. Through study and experience, I discovered a correlation between investing in real estate, accounting, and mental attitude in their effects on the effort to achieve wealth and financial independence. I slowly began to devise a plan that would combine these three elements in a safe, effective, and rewarding success formula. I began to think I had a really great idea. After more study I found out that, in reality, the idea is as old as the hills. The idea is gospel to the most successful entrepreneurs. It's just that those guys weren't telling you and me.

I first wanted to make sure that all of my ideas applied to the people I was working with . . . average middle-class people. So I started asking my clients questions about themselves. It took me no time at all to discover that most average middle-class people had literally no idea what they were doing with their finances, and they had little financial restraint while they were doing it. I was challenged. I felt a real need to help them discover what I'd discovered.

I started with a few homeowners and talked them into trying my plan on a small scale. Most of them borrowed money on the equities they'd built up in their homes—their first real estate investments. They bought income-producing residential rental properties—single family homes, duplexes, and fourplexes. Each of these investors noticed an immediate and dramatic decrease in the amount of income tax they had to pay. As their equities in each property increased, they either borrowed on the rental properties, or sold them, and bought other, more expensive properties. Some of these investors are becoming quite well off.

These were real people who needed my help. I took an interest in them—the stock market investor who always bought at the top of the market and sold out at the bottom; the school teacher besieged by insurance agents and credit unions to set up savings accounts or to buy annuity plans that she didn't understand; the executive who realized he'd never be the chairman of the board, but who wanted the benefits and a semblance of the top man's prestige and security anyway; the widow with no marketable skills, some money from her husband's estate, but no knowledge of how to best put it to work for herself and her family; the young doctor who was seeing little benefit from his personal corporation and pension fund, but whose attorney was accumulating large sums by setting them up and keeping track of them for him.

For all these people, I suggested the regimen of a Ten Year Real Estate Investment Schedule, a Personal Accounting Process, and a method for developing a Prosperous Mental Attitude, all three of which embodied the idea of financial goal setting. It worked. I became so interested in the idea of being able to help average middle-class people with ideas they'd never considered before that I started investigating the spending, saving, and investing habits of every person I met. I became increasingly convinced that, through the basic truths and common threads of shared experience which all average middle-class people share, I could create beautiful butterflies out of the world's financial caterpillars—the middle class.

I questioned everyone who walked through the door of my office.

"Excuse me, Mr. and Mrs. Wilson, but do you know exactly how much money the government takes out of your paycheck each month, including federal withholding, state withholding, unemployment compensation, Social Security . . .? Did you know that you have the right to keep most of that money and use it today, not just when you receive your tax refund, to improve your personal financial situation?"

"Pardon me for asking, Joe, but have your written down your goals for the next five years of your life?"

"Mrs. Green, would you be offended if I told you that because of inflation and the tax laws, the money in your certificates of deposit is only earning a fraction of what you think it is; and that money could be making you a much better before and after tax return?"

Next, I prepared a financial questionnaire which I distributed all over the country by way of friends, relatives, and associates. I received detailed information on the spending and investing habits of a large cross section of average middle-class people: what they bought, how they bought, how much they saved, how much they spent on frivolity, how much they paid in taxes. When I completed the survey, I had thousands of survey sheets on my living room floor. I called them The Average Middle-Class Financial Survey.

It became apparent to me that in spite of the fact that we are supposedly a nation of democratic affluence, very few of us know the basics of money-making, and we are living lives that reflect it. I saw that what most people were going through was similar to what I'd been through. But they hadn't experienced that one remarkable event which would enable them to see past the flimsy restraints that were binding them, break out, and liberate themselves from the middle class.

As I looked down at the survey sheets, I became determined to publish my ideas. I purchased every book ever written on money, accounting, and motivation; even ones from underground presses put together in someone's basement and distributed through direct mail outlets. I studied the other plans. I tried some of them and compared the results with my plan. I found out what worked, what was safe, and what was too risky. I discovered ones which looked safe but were full of hidden dangers. I worked with more and more clients who agreed to try my ideas.

Finally, after six years of research and testing, I completed my work. It's a simple system which I believe to be revolutionary in comparison to the money and investment habits of most average middle-class people. It is not a quick or easy plan, but it is relatively painless. You won't get overnight results and instant riches, but you won't get Pac Man (eat you up alive!) investment headaches, either.

I don't have a magic wand or a simple Great Truth that will automatically change your life. Instead, I have an aggressive, while at the same time conservative, plan that will increase your net worth, augment and stabilize your finances, open your mind, and change your life forever. It will make you money and help you keep it. It combines three important ingredients that must all work together.

- A Ten Year Real Estate Investment Schedule.
- A Personal Accounting Process to allow you to keep track of your assets, liabilities, net worth, income, expenses, profits, and cash flows.
- A Prosperous Mental Attitude, including exercises to keep your mind in shape from here on out.

The Park Avenue Money Diet will shuffle and redeal the cards you've been playing with. It is a safe program, and it's good for you. It's fun. You won't start off and then quit several months or several years down the road because it's boring. I promise you, you'll be a much happier and more secure person by following *The Park Avenue Money Diet.*

CHAPTER 2

INTRODUCTION I

The average middle-class person sleeps seven hours a night; makes between fifteen and fifty thousand dollars a year (before deductions); has a family; one dog, a cat, or a bird; two color television sets; at least two credit cards; an economy car . . . maybe two; and a nagging feeling that he or she will never have the opportunity to "make it rich." Yet this ordinary person also believes "his ship" (guided by mysterious forces totally beyond his understanding and control) "is coming in."

It may seems like there's a contradiction at the end of that last paragraph, but there's not! Recognized or not, there are opportunities to "make it rich" all around us every day. Hoping a "ship will come in" is a less likely prospect.

Don't misunderstand me . . . ships do come in. They cross hundreds of miles of ocean, sail up narrow channels, and arrive at dockside with predictable regularity. But these ships "come in" to strong, goal oriented individuals who are *making* their ships come in . . . they're "*making* it rich!" They know exactly where their ships are at any given moment, where their ships are headed, and how long it's going to take them to arrive at their destination.

Sure! Occasionally, even vessels belonging to wishful thinkers, daydreamers, and unlikely hopers make it into port. Once in a while one will approach the coast, escape the miles and miles of sandbars, coral reefs, and rocky shorelines, and drift into a safe harbor. As a rule, however, these ships twist and turn, rudderless on the high seas, leaving their captains waiting at the dock, continuing to live their *chronically* average lives.

In our society, simply being average and middle class is the only social and economic goal we are normally expected to achieve. Society as a whole is dependent on its strong middle class. So we've been told, and so it's true. We endeavor to become middle class and that's it. That's as far as most of us go. And then we rally ourselves to be inordinately proud of that modest achievement.

Few of us ever see the rest of the social and economic picture. We never get a clear idea of what being middle class in an affluent society really means to us. We are never told, and seldom discover, the real truth: that being average and middle class is a handicap and a menace to our daily existence. Being average and middle class affects our self-image, our relationships with our families and friends, our health, our security, and the horizons of our possibilities. It adversely affects every aspect of our lives—from the jobs we need, do, or don't get, to the happiness, love, and security we feel or never receive.

The fact is, the only thing worse than being average and middle class is being poor. What's not so obvious, but true, nevertheless, is that most average middle-class people, because of their middle-class money habits and mindsets, are closer to being poor than they are close to being anything else.

Of course, we all really know that there's something more than just being average and middle class, because we've all tried one or more ways to improve our situation. We've taken risks either in the casinos or the stock markets, with all the other gamblers. We've listened to get-rich schemes, tax shelter promotions, pyramid selling programs, and insurance policy presentations. We've been conned into purchasing meretricious items which are "guaranteed" to make us happier, sexier, skinnier, wealthier, and healthier, but which in effect only postpone the day when we can really begin to improve our situations.

But despite all of our best efforts, we've all failed time after time to break through those flimsy barriers between being average and middle class, and being financially independent. Or, if you're reading this book, you've failed *thus far.*

The difference between you and me is that you've failed thus far, and I quit failing a few years ago. I used to work as a school teacher. I had a salary which came to me once a month, complete with, or should I say, came incomplete because of, withholding taxes, Social Security taxes, automatic withdrawals for annuity plans, etc. I used to be average, middle class, and miserable, and I didn't like it; but I had a remarkable event occur in my life that caused me to find a way to beat the system and come out on the side of the winners. And, in the process, I discovered where you've gone wrong and why you've failed so far.

You've failed simply and honestly because you have never attempted to approach your average middle-class problem from the right direction and with the proper amount of determination. The regrettable fact is, you may not have even realized you had a problem. After all, why should you know? Everyone around you is average and middle class, and they all have the same problem. As a result, you probably never noticed. At least you've never really attempted to tackle your *real* problem, despite your dreaming and hoping, your stocks and bonds, your whole life insurance plans, and your dedication to new trends and fads. You may have looked your associates and competitors in the eye and stared them down, but you've never looked yourself in the eye and come away with the dedication to change your life for the better, and forever.

True Confession

Let's begin at what should always be the starting point. Yourself! No skipping ahead, now. Before we go any farther, let's get your problem out where we can see it. Let's discuss it openly and honestly. Admit that you're average and middle class. Confess to yourself that being middle class and average is a problem. Don't just look away, shrug your shoulders, or caress your big screen projection TV. Don't get depressed or upset, and don't rush out and throw yourself under your neighbor's new fuel-efficient 35 mpg highway and

28 mpg city automobile in shame or embarrassment. Calmly look at that mirror, and deep into your baby blues. Admit you are average and middle class, and commit yourself, body and soul, to doing something about it. Something now. Something permanent. For yourself. For your family. Forever. Because you and they deserve it.

One of the first things you're going to have to do is stop feeling sorry for yourself, stop hoping for that elusive day when "your ship will come in." Own up to being caught in a pattern of being average and middle class. Let me hear you say it. I'm average. I'm middle class. I've allowed myself to get trapped in a situation not of my making. My life has not turned out the way I always thought it would. I no longer have the dreams and goals I once had. Shout it! Go ahead. Shout it out!

Now there, don't you feel a lot better?

Now that we've gotten that off your chest, let's get down to brass tacks and start making some positive changes in your situation. Slap your cheeks a couple of times—time to snap out of it, fella! You've been in a trance, in a state of false (and I mean false!) security, in average middle-class Nirvana. Grab those middle-class ideals that have been making your decisions for you and toss them across the room. Wait a minute. Don't kick them out the back door just yet. You might want to keep a few of them around just for awhile, at least until you get some new habits established; but at lease let them know who's boss. Let them know you're the one taking charge of your own life now, and their days are numbered.

Take Charge

By now your average middle-class problem, no matter how average and middle-class, or slightly upper or lower average and middle-class, should be out in the open. At this point you should begin to realize, if it's not already apparent, that being average and middle class is a slow, destructive state of affairs that continually attacks every part of your life. Once you understand that, and realize that this is not what or where you really want to be, you will be ready to face up to a program that will change your situation; a program that will wipe away all of those end-of-the-month "minimum payment due" nightmares and change your life forever.

You should know right from the beginning. There are a couple of definite responsibilities and fears involved in becoming captain of your own ship. You need to learn what they are *now* and prepare yourself to handle them.

For many people, not being born rich is a catchall excuse for everything that is messed up in their lives. If they have no friends or the wrong friends, don't get promotions, and can't make ends meet, they look over and around and blame it on their "fate," or on the fact that their parents weren't rich. If they were wealthy and had similar problems, they would have to look to themselves for solutions, and that can often be much too agonizing to contemplate.

"Everyone tells me that I'm wasting my time in my present position, that I'd have a real future if I went out and accomplished something on my own; but that really scares me, because what if I did start making my own financial decisions, and what if I were to start making more money and then nothing happens? No beauty queens? No terrific new horizons? No new friends? Nothing changed? Then what?"

The entire middle class has this "what if" complex it uses as a delaying tactic. A well-timed "what if" can postpone having to make a decision indefinitely. Well, what if you never make any real money, and what if you continue in your headlong race into mediocrity along with your neighbors? So let's stop all the *what ifs* and start facing the world and your future as it really is.

Hey, chin up now. Don't you know? There's a real, dynamic person inside of you. An interesting, exciting, well informed, wealthy, dynamic person. Aren't you just a little bit curious about who that is? It's easier than you think to find out. You're just going to have to take a few chances, establish a few new patterns, and that's it. Don't stop now—don't settle for anything short of greatness; of what will make you happy; of what will make you money—prove to yourself that you can do it!

The Status WHOA! _____

"Don't be such a show-off, Daniel! You've taken more than your share! Just sit there and be quiet! Act like the good little gentleman we know you can be. For goodness sake, don't do anything to draw attention to yourself."

From day one, you were urged to conform. To be average! To be middle class! Conformity was taught to you from your earliest childhood days as certainly as you were taught to read and write. Can't you hear your mother, your father, and your second grade teacher pleading: "Sit up straight, Danny" . . . "Be on time" . . . "Do it this way, everyone else does!" . . . "Polish your shoes, keep your shirt tucked in" . . . "If you want a gold star, you've got to do it this way."

In the beginning, your insides were crying out "NO, THAT'S NOT WHAT I WANT TO DO! THAT'S NOT THE WAY I WANT TO DO IT! PLEASE LEAVE ME ALONE!" But demands for conformity kept coming at you. Finally the pressure became too great. You began accepting their way as the "right way." The middle-class way! After all, you found out, it's easier to let someone else make the decisions for you than to make them yourself. And so you ended up like everyone else, patterning your behavior according to the average middle-class norm and asking, "What's my next reward?"

But we're going to try and change all that, aren't we? Before you reach for that next reward, whether it's a merit badge, a promotion, or another Jack Daniels on the rocks, here are some facts about being average and middle class you ought to know.

1. *Your mind has a limitless capacity to provide you with creative and profitable ideas. This capacity does not function well when it is forced to comply with mindless middle-class conformity.* Since we've already determined that you are average and middle class, you must now accept the fact that in most important ways you've been a conformist. Your mind accepted the goals and desires of other people, and as it did, it found it necessary to elbow your inclination to be your own person out of its way. Your mind became accustomed to working on other people's projects and living with other people's values. It was easier and safer for your mind to do this than to come up with projects and values of its own!

"They offer me the same sense of accomplishment."

"It puts bread on my table."

"It gives me status."

You learned patterns of acceptance which put you into your present (temporary?) average middle-class predicament. The layers of conformity you've acquired may have crept up on you quietly, without your notice, until suddenly you realized (if you realized at all!) you'd been transformed.

Or you may have given in immediately. Perhaps you recognized and appreciated the simplicity of following a pretested schoolbook-to-nursing home set of instructions which promised to protect you from the danger and the unexpected experiences that should be a part of your life.

Slowly and methodically, or suddenly, as if you were inspired, you became an average person, a company man. You became one of them, one of the attractive, successful, acceptable, average middle-class people. It wasn't all bad. In fact, there were many tangible benefits. Your self-image improved. You grew in stature among those around you. Your life acquired a direction.

But believe it or not, your ultimate well-being suffered.

2. *Embarrassment, shyness, and certain amounts of social withdrawal are abiding companions of most average middle-class people.*

"I have trouble meeting people. We hardly know the neighbors. There always seems to be a competitive wall between us."

"My major social contacts are the people I work with at the office."

"Anyone who appears to have more money or status immediately has one up on me."

"I feel inferior, which is a terrible feeling."

Being excluded because of one's station in life is not fair, but it happens. It's a common occurence on a business and professional level.

"But who am I to complain?"

3. *As an average middle-class person, you are hung up on the use of status symbols which lack substance, and which can sometimes make fried zucchini out of your self-image.* Your jewelry, the clothes you wear, the car you drive, etc., tend to identify you as a member of a particular group. But these things can also be used as a form of social and economic deception (and intimidation!). It's typical of most average middle-class people to try to present public images which project a somewhat higher station in life than where they actually belong. This practice is generally considered acceptable in middle-class society, but it can occasionally be an expensive and disappointing charade.

"I really wanted to impress them at my ten-year reunion. I dressed as though I'd really made it. A $300 suit, my gold watch, my college ring, the works. Everything went great until this clod who'd dropped out of high school our senior year showed up at the bar where our reunion was being held. He was wearing sneakers, a sweat shirt, and dungarees.

"I nudged another old classmate. 'Old Bob's not much for fashion, is he? What's he doing?'

" 'Bob? Oh yeah. You remember. He fooled around for awhile after dropping out of school. Then when we went off to college, he went to work picking up garbage for United Disposal Co. I understand he bought a garbage truck of his own a year later, hired a couple of guys, and got a contract with the city to service the north end of town. He bought more trucks, hired more people, and kept expanding his business as the new subdivisions went in. Someone told me he sold out a couple of years back for over a million bucks. He's into real estate in a big way now. Dumb luck!'

" 'You'd never know it to look at him, would you?'

" 'I don't think I could pick up someone else's garbage. Could you?' "

4. *The normal state of affairs for average middle-class people is "having problems making ends meet."*

"Every raise I get is already earmarked to cover a new time payment, or some expense for something I only recently found we couldn't live without."

Money problems adversely affect people's jobs, their marriages, their health, and the conduct of their daily lives.

"All I can think about is the payment that's due at the end of this week. I can't keep my mind on my work."

"All my husband and I do is fight about money!"

"You know, I think all this worrying about money is making me ill. The doctor said my blood pressure is way up."

"If I could only afford to take some time off and really relax."

"I drink too much."

5. *The medical facts. Given the fact that the average middle-class person has money problems, and the fact that money problems can lead to other problems such as stress, working at hazardous jobs, and not getting proper medical attention when one needs it, being average and middle class isn't good medical practice.* People who are not in control of their lives experience high degrees of stress and have a tendency to have high blood pressure. They also experience a high incidence of alcoholism and drug abuse.

Stress, high blood pressure, and alcoholism are responsible for related illnesses including cirrhosis of the liver, kidney trouble, heart disease, circulatory disorders, diabetes, and respiratory ailments, to mention just a few.

But the list doesn't stop there. Lung cancer as a result of cigarette smoking, accidents, suicides, and homicides kill proportionally more average middle-class people each year than they do members of more affluent segments of our society. To make matters worse, average middle-class people don't spend the money on medical care and regular checkups that they should.

Do you want this made any clearer? Do you want horror stories about arteries hardening up in young and middle-aged men and women, leading to heart attacks, or cutting off blood to the brain, precipitating strokes? Do you want four-color graphics? Or do you get the picture?

Television's Average Man

Not only have middle-class traditions of averageness been rooted in our youth, our daily lives, and in the makeup of our society over generations, but for the past three and a half decades these average traditions have been potently reinforced by television. The television medium has made traditions of averageness extremely hard to ignore . . . even if they're seldom related to good thinking, logic, or common sense.

Prime time television has introduced us to a host of charming friends who do nothing but make us laugh and induce us to be middle class and average. Who are these TV heroes? Why, super average middle-class people, of course. There are a host of typical parents, working divorcees, and a bunch of basically good kids. These super middle classers constantly get themselves into happy, healthy, only slightly risky situations that everyone understands, and which tend to make our real-life, everyday problems seem small in comparison.

First there were Lucy and Desi and the Nelsons, followed by Mary Richards and Bob Hartley (now all in reruns!). Then we had the Cunningham family on *Happy Days*, and Mork (an average middle-class alien!) and Mindy. Today we have the gals and guys on *Give Me a Break*, *Joanie Loves Chachi*, the variety of threesomes on *Three's Company*, the "girls" on *9 to 5*, Mr. Jefferson, Archie Bunker, and Sidney . . . all good people, for the most part, who live in apartments or in modest homes, and are extraordinarily happy.

I hear what you're saying. What about J. R. Ewing on *Dallas*? The rich guy that all the world loves to hate? Well, he's not good people. I'll grant you that. The problem is he's not very funny, and he's a character with money. Television is a medium used primarily to stroke, entertain, and sell products and ideas to average middle-class people, so you can understand why, if a television character has any money at all, he will usually be portrayed as a villain. That's the way average middle-class people like to think about rich people.

Of course, we'd all like to emulate J. R.'s wealth, and some of us would even like to be as nasty as he is; but the truth is, as a way to become a rich man, J. R. Ewing is a lousy role model. He functions well, though, in the role he was designed to play, a video punching bag for the ordinary man.

In real life, J. R. would be lucky to own a townhouse in Bulverde, much less a palatial ranch estate in Dallas. Despite common folklore, wealthy people seldom get or stay wealthy by cheating and trying to destroy other people. And, contrary to prevalent popular thought, studies have shown that most second and third generation wealth is soon dissipated.

The Are Rich People Miserable? Quiz ⸻

We've all been told that rich people are unhappy people. We've heard that it's much better to stop and smell the roses. (As though the rich only stop to smell the *Wall Street Journal*!)

Despite what you may have heard, there is absolutely nothing miserable about having a lot of money. (Now forget about fictional characters like Scrooge or that other literary character who was so rich and unhappy he went home one night and put a bullet through his head!) Is it miserable to be able to spend an extra half hour in bed if you want to? Is it miserable to have someone else clean the house or do the gardening? Is it miserable to fly to Switzerland for your vacation and stay an extra week because you feel you need the extra time? Is it miserable to choose anything you want from a restaurant menu without noticing or being influenced by the price? Is it miserable to fly your own plane or sail your own yacht? Is it miserable to have the ear of your local politicians? Of course it isn't!

If you are still not convinced, just ask yourself these simple questions and then remember what Mom and Dad told you about rich people being miserable. The folks sort of misled you, don't you think?

1. Giving up all hope of attending the college of my choice because I can't afford it is *not miserable*.

    True _____   False _____

2. Dying ten years earlier than necessary is *not miserable*.

    True _____   False _____

3. Having twice as many emotional problems as rich people is *not miserable*.

    True _____   False _____

4. Having no direct line to the people who can help me get a better education, a more profitable position, or a bank loan, is *not miserable*.

    True _____   False _____

5. Being treated by waiters, clerks, and highway patrolmen as someone with about as much clout as a Koala bear is *not miserable*.

    True _____   False _____

Now see? Erase the connection between rich and miserable and proceed (without going out and purchasing the newest electronic video game) to finding out more about what you've been really missing.

Average Middle-Class Folks I've Known _____

Most of the average middle-class people I've known seem to be coping with their situations by trying to lose themselves in one way or another. The ones I've known can be categorized as one or a combination of the following:

1. *The Sports.* These are the average middle-class people who live and die for the good times. The drinkers, the drug users, the TV soap opera watchers, the carousers. They're all trying to find meaning for their lives in chemically, electronically, or sexually induced ways. They live in a sort of perpetual adolescence, "experiencing" today, spending last week's paycheck, and hoping tomorrow will take care of itself.

2. *The Dead Reckoners.* These are the folks who have found a way to lose themselves in the details of decision making. They're the perfectionists. They carefully consider every detail of everything they do, no matter how trivial. (Never mind the fact that they drive those around them to distraction!) They become so involved in the details of their assigned projects that they seldom look up to see the whole picture. Their powers of concentration are phenomenal. (Imagine what they could accomplish if they'd use their powers to concentrate on their own personal goals and objectives!) The Dead Reckoners reward themselves with crossword puzzles, ham radio sets, and Rubik's cubes.

3. *The Accessories.* These are helpful, amiable, and generous people. They'll do anything and everything they're asked, providing it doesn't appear to be for a selfish motive. They're always available to work for the Boy Scouts, the P.T.A., the Women's Circle, the Little League, the Garden Club, the car pool, and you name it. They'll do anything to keep busy, to get approval, and to be noticed. These average middle-class people (the accessories) are in essence bored, unhappy people, trying to lose themselves in a do-gooders' amusement park. They are totally involved in everything but themselves. It keeps them from having to consider or do anything about the bankrupt quality of their own lives.

4. *The Don Quixotes.* The average middle-class Don Quixote tries to either do nothing or do everything . . . a little of this and some or none of that. Now mix it all up. The Don Quixote never reads the directions before assembling, and he always has three screws and a nut remaining after it's

all together. He tries not to miss anything, but in his haste, or because he's not paying close attention, he misses it all. He's like a dull lawn mower, knocking the grass over but failing to cut it off. He's impatient, often giving up in frustration before completing a project that requires his concentration. He watches a lot of TV and takes a lot of naps. A Don Quixote's opinions are generally verbatim from the evening news or the Johnny Carson show.

5. *The Fussbudgets.* These are the anarchists. They are average middle-class people who despise themselves, their jobs, and the people around them. They deal with their middle-class problem by complaining in a variety of ways about it; by being fussy. Instead of building on what they already have, they abandon themselves, and everything else, to negativism, and end up going the wrong way. Their goal is to retire to a desert island or a mountain cabin and look for sea shells or acorns. To them, having less is often better than being average. They are self-destructive and potentially socially destructive. At best, they end up disillusioned and alone. At worst, they blow up buildings and kill people. They are the net losers in our social and economic class system.

* * *

"The rich people have all the money. I'll never get any."

"All the good ideas have been taken."

"I'd much rather be poor and happy, than rich and miserable."

These three sentences could be the average middle-class people's national anthem. So how do you know you're average and middle class? It's simple.

1. When the biggest financial risk you've ever taken has been to move your savings out of a passbook account to a certificate of deposit.

2. When you have to decide between eating out at McDonald's or Burger King, and then realize it doesn't make any difference.

3. When you're able to make a major purchase only by arranging installment payments equal to the amount of your next monthly raise in salary.

4. When you look forward to Friday afternoon and dread Monday morning.

5. When you hate your job but stay at it because the company you work for has a good dental plan.

And the clincher is:

6. When you allow your salary to be ravished by withholding taxes and then feel grateful when you get money back in the form of your annual income tax refund.

The Who Are You Kidding Now? Quiz _____

This is a very simple test to see if you really are ready to leave your average middle-class life behind, or if you're just reading this book because you'd heard it discussed at your last nude encounter group meeting. Take out your pen—that's right, pen. Not pencil. Pens are more believable than pencils because you can't erase what you write with pens as easily—and fill in this space. Just answer this single question:

Who are you?

Finished already? That was really easy. All right, let's you and I take a good look at your answer. Reread what you wrote. Did you give an honest answer to the question? Did you tell me what your occupation was? Did you tell me about your appearance? Did you tell me about your hidden self? Did you tell me about what you hope (or had hoped!) you would be? Did you describe yourself in relation to another person—your spouse, your child, your mother? I hope you didn't tell me your sign! Of the hundreds of people who responded to this question in the Average Middle Class Financial Survey, most completely avoided the question. If I got an answer, it was a response such as:

"I'm a small businessman. I'm very happy, and I make a comfortable living."

"I have brown hair and blue eyes."

"I was voted most likely to succeed in college."

"I'm an engineer for NASA."

"I'm a housewife and mother."

"I'm a Virgo."

Another group answered with other people's opinions of who they were, rather than with their self perceptions:

"My girlfriend says I'm a real fun person."

"My mom says I get along good with people."

"The coach says I've got a real future in athletics."

Few of these people ever look at themselves in their mirrors with their eyes wide open. They've never really taken stock of who they actually are. Many didn't attempt to answer the question. Most described themselves as their jobs, the groups they belong to, or in terms of their physical appearance.

Describing one's self in terms of one's outward appearance is important, but it's only a fraction of the job. The rest of the job is to describe one's self in terms of one's beliefs, one's ideals, one's economic status, the way one sees oneself relating to the world around us, and one's plans for the future.

I'm not saying don't judge your book by the dust jacket it's wearing. I am saying don't *only* see yourself as your dust jacket. I am saying that one's dust jacket is often deceiving. I am saying that if you don't know exactly who you are without reference to some outside person or thing, then you haven't come to grips with one of your average middle-class problems, and until you do you will not be in a position to take charge of your life.

Now let's try it again. This time I want you to give a wide-awake, thoughtful, painfully honest answer. Tell me everything. I want to know who you really are. And no copying.

(*Oh, no you don't.* Don't you dare read any further until you've finished!)

*   *   *

Now let's look at what you've written this time. Do your beliefs, ideals, and goals in any way resemble those of your parents, your friends, and your associates? Do they resemble those of the organization or person you work for? Do your beliefs, ideals, and goals include any selfishness? Something of major benefit to yourself? (They ought to!) Are these beliefs, ideals, and goals the same ones you might have written down five, ten, twenty years ago? Bigger? Better? Smaller?

If they're bigger or better, and of your own choosing, great! Your only question might be, are they big enough? If they're smaller and less impressive, we're going to try to secure some real big ones for you as we get closer to the end of the book.

The Self-Worth Very Honest Image Test _____

Oh, I can guess what you're thinking now—when you bought this book you didn't realize you were going to have to take a bunch of dumb tests, right? (Do you mean to tell me you didn't thumb through the book before you bought it?) Well, tough luck. That's actually what the first half of this whole book is. I'm testing you so that you'll begin questioning yourself:

1. To see what you know about who you are and where you, as an average middle-class person, really fit in to the economic scheme of things,

2. To make you aware that you could be accomplishing and experiencing much more,

3. To give you the tools and the knowledge and the encouragement to acquire the money it requires to be the very best person you can be.

*   *   *

So stop bellyaching and get with the program!

(*Check off your selection*)

1. When you think about your life five years from now, are you:

   a. You've never thought about it?

   b. In about the same situation you're in right now?

   c. Better off?

   d. A lot better off?

2. In your opinion, if your parents could compare their lives to the life you're living today, would they think you were:

   a. Worse off than they were at your age?

   b. About the same as they were at your age?

   c. Better off than they were at your age?

   d. Substantially better off than they were at your age?

3. In relation to your closest neighbor, do you think you are:

   a. Economically worse off?

   b. Economically about the same?

   c. Better off?

   d. Without a doubt, much better off?

4. When shopping for clothes, do you:

    a. Shop for bargains?

    b. Consider the probable opinions of another person or group?

    c. Shop for the latest fashions?

    d. Adopt your own style?

5. When you're in unfamiliar surroundings, do you:

    a. Try to make yourself invisible?

    b. Pretend that you've been there before?

    c. Hope that someone talks to you?

    d. Introduce yourself to the first person who comes along?

6. In making decisions, do you:

    a. Give up and go take a nap?

    b. Change your mind constantly?

    c. Always defer to someone else's "better judgment"?

    d. Decide immediately and stick to your decision?

7. When a friend asks you for a favor which will require quite a bit of time or effort on your part, do you:

    a. Agree because you're afraid to turn them down?

    b. Agree because you have nothing better to do?

    c. Agree to please them?

    d. Agree or turn them down, depending on your interest?

8. Do you drink or take drugs at home, or spend your free hours in front of the TV, because:

    a. It's a nervous habit?

    b. It's something to do?

    c. You need to get away from the tensions of the day?

    d. You enjoy it?

9. Knowing what you know now, if you could start your life over again, would you:

   a. Choose new parents?

   b. Choose a new career?

   (c.) Do the same things, but start earlier?

   d. Not change a thing?

10. If your doctor told you that you only had a month to live, would you:

    a. Spend more time being depressed?

    b. Hope for the best?

    c. "Grab for all the gusto you can"?

    (d.) Get a second opinion?

11. You drive downtown for an appointment. What do you do with your car when you get there:

    a. Drive around the block until you find a parking space?

    (b.) Park in a cheap parking lot six blocks away?

    c. Pay a premium to park across the street from your appointment?

    d. Use the valet parking service in the building where you have your appointment?

12. You've had expenses on a business trip. For income tax purposes, do you:

    a. Assume most of the expenses are not deductible?

    b. Use the short form?

    c. Deduct some, but not all, of the expenses because you're embarrassed?

    (d.) Deduct everything?

YOU HAVE FINISHED THE TEST

How To Score:

For each (a) answer you checked, give yourself 4 points.

(b) answer you checked, give yourself 3 points.

(c) answer you checked, give yourself 2 points.

(d) answer you checked, give yourself 1 point.

Total your score. Hold on now...no cheating here. This is really important.

High Self-Image (10 – 15 points)

You are either delighted with yourself as a member of the average middle class and are planning to enter yourself as the spokesperson for motherhood, apple pie, and Chevrolet; or you bought this book by mistake. Perhaps you could give it to your aerobic exercise teacher?

Maybe So, Maybe Not Self-Image (16 – 35 points)

You're not admitting you have the average middle-class problem, but you're going to read a little further just in case. If there is a problem, you want the solution. You think you know the answers as to who you are and where you're going in life, but you can also accept that there is an off chance you could be wrong. (Boy, do I know the feeling!)

Low Self-Image (36 – 48 Points)

Hold on now. What's the matter with you? You don't think you're some kind of bug, do you? Your very true self has been buried underneath layers and layers of conformity; of doing what anyone else wants you to do— probably since childhood. You don't know there's a completely different way to live. And I don't mean "dropping out." You think you're doing everything you're supposed to do, but you keep missing the boat. You're insecure, not very sure of yourself, and feel like the most worthless person around. Go back and read this chapter again, and buy a copy of this book for every member of your family!

CHAPTER 3

INTRODUCTION II

I spent most of my life as an average middle-class person. Like you, I had it in the back of my head that someday I would stumble over a rock and find a discarded sack of money. Or I expected to do something about inventing that better mousetrap. I just knew that one day I'd look out my window to discover that the world had beaten down a path to my door. I expected to be rich one day, but that was never one day certain. It was always some nebulous day in the future; that wonderful day when my ship would come in.

It amazes me to think of it now, but do you know, I never really understood exaclty why I would be better off if I were rich. Sure, there were thoughts of the obvious glitter—a sports car, a bigger house, a trip to Europe;

but I never really understood that the amount of money and property I had would have a direct and profound bearing on every aspect of my life—in the way I relate to people, to the way they relate to me, to every decision I make, to the way I spend my day. It seemed irrational to me to think that people might like me better because I was better off. After all, my financial situation had nothing to do with the type of person I was, and I knew full well, deep down inside, that I was really a great guy. It seemed inconceivable that I could get or do a better job simply because I was affluent. But then, why should I have conceived of it? What could be a more rewarding job than teaching music to high school students? (We're not talking money here!)

Still, I remember I had this desire for a bigger slice of the wealth pie. As an average middle-class person, I seldom came in direct contact with the more affluent in our society. But I knew, because everybody said it was true, that people with a lot of money had the world dangling on a string—or whatever it is you dangle the world with.

It wasn't until after I had experienced the possibility of making some real money that I began to fully realize its significance. Nor did I begin to understand the dangers to the human spirit that being mired in the murkiness of the middle class can do to a human being. It was only after my personal financial picture improved that I could sort out the truths and fictions about having and not having money; having or not having financial independence or dependence (or whatever the opposite of financial independence is); and begin to understand how and why it is that people let themselves get trapped in the middle class.

Being average and middle class is a really lousy thing to do to yourself. It wreaks chaos on your personal relationships. It limits you to mediocre life experiences. It fogs up your windows. And, it can be detrimental to your health. There are a few other not-so-wonderful pitfalls to being a middle-class cipher.

The Time of Your Life Is Not Your Own _____

The alarm clock buzzes in your ear. You and your wife jump out of bed, both half asleep. She runs to wake the kids and then to the kitchen to start the coffee and breakfast. You trip over the dog and stub your toe on the bathroom scale. You shower, shave, brush your teeth, dress, and quickly swallow breakfast. Hurry now. You can't afford to be late. It's off to work—on time again. Whoops, don't forget to kiss the wife and your kids good-by. You hop into your turbo-charged Subaru, back out of the driveway, and off you go into the crowded 6:45 commuter traffic.

Your wife sends the kids off to school. She takes a fast cold shower (you used up all the hot water, you crumb!). Brushes her teeth. Gets dressed. And it's off to her job. She takes the economical diesel station wagon.

In the meantime, your day progresses predictably. You spend half an hour to an hour on the freeway. Eight hours working at your job. Then more time on the road again. Your wife hands you a drink as you come in the door—don't ask how she does it! You sit down to a dinner of warmed up "take-home Chinese or Polish"; and then collapse, too tired or uninspired to do anything but sit in front of the TV for four to five hours.

Stimulating day, wouldn't you say? Nice, heartwarming family life, am I right? Frantic maybe. But stimulating, or nice . . . Well, not the way it could be.

Ask yourself these questions. Does this hectic existence leave you much time to consider your own financial and personal situation, to ponder your predicaments and find solutions, or to take account of the direction your life is taking? Go to your room if you answered no. The answer, as we'll see later, is yes.

The alarm clock buzzes in your ear again, and you begin the process all over—five times a week, two hundred and fifty times a year.

The Checking Account Is Always Overdrawn _____

"At least once every couple of months, the bank calls to tell me that I've overdrawn my checking account as well as my overdraft protection, again. Sometimes they just call, other times they tell me that they had to send back several checks and charged my account a penalty. If they sent back any checks, you can bet several things are about to happen.

"First, the butcher, the manager of the food market, or someone from one of the utility companies will be calling or waiting for me the next time I come in, to threaten me with severe bodily harm and to impose their unsympathetic returned-check penalty policies on me. The whole situation will normally precipitate a fight with my husband, who tends to write checks out of sequence, and forgets to record them (or mention them to me so I can record them!), causing the checks I write to bounce.

"Following the fight, we'll agree that the family will be put on a strict budget. (Our budgets normally last the weekend!) Finally, since what little money we've saved is in a 180-day c. d., and since it's not the middle or end of the month when we get paid, we'll have to look to see if there is someone else in the family whose earning power we can tap to redeem our check writing privileges with the offended party."

Sound familiar? It does to me. I once considered putting the family dog out to stud to pay a middle-of-the-month bill. I put an ad in the paper, but unfortunately for our creditor, and Macho (that was our dog!), no one answered the ad. Poor Macho! He was never the same after that.

Meretricious Consumption at the "Company Store" —

It doesn't matter how much money the average middle-class person makes—fifteen thousand a year or fifty thousand a year or more—he will normally find a way to stretch his purchasing power beyond the bounds of his finances, up to and often beyond the limit of his ability to borrow. The MasterCard, Visa, and American Express are always at or near their credit limits. The overdraft protection on the checking account is always at work for the bank at 22 percent + or − interest.

Average middle-class people are extended credit unmercifully.

So what's wrong with that, you're asking. After all, our country was built on credit—the use of other people's money (OPM), right? Not exactly; yes and no. There is a distinction that we have to make between using credit as leverage to improve one's financial situation, and using credit only as a means of hurrying up one's consumption rate. Average middle-class people generally only use credit as an aid to consuming.

Most middle-class people don't really use credit. They are *used by* credit, in much the same manner as the coal miners and the migrant workers were during the '30s depression. The coal miners and the migrant workers, before going to work, would have to buy their necessities of life—food and clothing—paying exorbitant prices at the "Company Store." The Company Store was usually owned by their employer. The workers bought on credit secured by the following week's wages. It was part of a system to keep them in debt and on the job.

Today, the necessities (?) of life for average middle-class people are not food and clothing—those are taken pretty much for granted—but rather those big ticket items which are always slightly above and beyond reach: TVs that are also telephones, video disc players, swimming pools, a closet full of designer outfits, etc. Those big ticket items don't make anyone any better off in any measurable or appreciable sense. They're quickie "fixes." They make people feel better for a short period of time . . . until they need another fix.

These products may last longer than the good feelings they produce, but they don't add to anyone's financial security, and they don't make anyone rich. The best they do is make people appear to be rich.

How do average middle-class people buy these "quickie fixes"? They charge them. They borrow the money from the bank or run up the account balances on their plastic credit cards. They mortgage away their futures for oversized trinkets, and in the process they're charmed into accepting as their song Tennessee Ernie Ford's old hit, "I owe my soul to the Company Store."

The Company Store today is not as closely tied to the place where people work as the original Company Store was; and there are many more goods available for purchase today than there used to be. However, when you consider the predominance of nationally franchised retailers in and around the malls where average middle-class people shop, you realize that there is a similar lack of variety of choice in available merchandise and merchandise suppliers.

Today's Company Store is a nationwide consumer network offering a system of unlimited, electronically verifiable credit. This is a system best characterized by the thousands of identical brightly lit multi-storied covered shopping centers; crammed from below ground level to the skylight with identical nationally franchised shops; offering shelves and aisles full of nearly identical chargeable meretricious goods.

If you haven't look it up for yourself yet, I'll give you Webster's definition of meretricious:

Meretricious, a. [L. *Meretricius*, from *meretrix*, a prostitute.]
1. originally, of, like, or characteristic of a prostitute.
2. alluring by false, showy charms; speciously attractive; fleshy; tawdry.
    —Noah Webster L.L.D.

The migrant workers, farm hands, and coal miners of the '30s are today's average middle-class people. Armed to the teeth with plastic charge cards, they purchase their way through neighborhood shopping malls and then go off to the office-mines and the factory-farms next door, to earn the money to pay the end of the month bills when they arrive. (Anyone feel like picking a few grapes?)

Born Free—Taxed to Death

Not only do you pay proportionately more taxes than most people with money, but you probably pay them sooner. And you don't exactly pay income tax. What you pay is called withholding tax. It's a tax that is withheld from your monthly salary. There was even an effort by Congress to withhold taxes from interest and dividends. Luckily, that measure was defeated in April of 1983; but you can bet the government will try to push it through again. Demeaning when you think about it, isn't it? Do you think your Uncle Sam doesn't trust you?

Let's talk about income tax refunds. You probably get money back from the IRS each year after you file your return. Isn't that great? Just about as great as using your hard-earned dollar bills to wipe up spilled milk. Every dollar the government collects early or holds in excess of the taxes you owe is held with no interest accruing to you. The government has the use of your money for that whole time; you haven't. And you're not even given a minimum interest payment. What's your feeling when they finally give your own money back to you? You're grateful!

"Oh boy, it's just enough to pay for that weekend vacation in Palm Springs we wanted to take. Thank you, Uncle Sam."

Did you know, most independently wealthy people only pay their taxes once every three months, or just once a year, if at all! Did you know that in some cases, people with money pay no taxes at all! They hang on to every penny they take in, and they do it with the government's blessing. Do you think they're disappointed at not being eligible to receive an income tax refund? Hardly! Wouldn't you like to know how they do that? Keep reading.

So How Did a Nice Guy Like You Get Trapped in the Middle Class? _____

It's obvious to me that you're a nice person. After all, you bought my book, didn't you? That makes you a nice person. You may be small potatoes, but you know, I understand that kind of thing. I used to be small potatoes myself. We both know that given the chance, you could be much more. How did you get into this situation? Why have you been drifting all your life, and never reaching or even setting your goals? Why have you been working and achieving all your life and never accomplishing anything of greater lasting value for yourself and your family than your home? (Don't tell me you're a tenant!) Just how in this world did you ever come to be so average, middle class, and miserable?

There's a whole bunch of answers to this question. I'll bet you've already formulated your favorite, the one you've been telling anyone who would listen—including yourself—over and over again:

"I'm average because I believe there's more to life than just chasing the almighty dollar."

"I'm average because I couldn't afford to go to college."

"I'm average because I was a liberal arts student. I should have studied to be a brain surgeon."

"I'm average because I think it's more important for me to spend time with my family than working all the time just to get ahead."

Your answer or answers may be good or bad—we'd have to judge them individually—but chances are your answers are really just excuses. And your excuses are based on misinformation and mythical nonsense.

There is no excuse in the world for you to be so average today. If you wouldn't mind taking this little quiz, we'll separate the facts from the fallacies of your life and move on to divorcing you and your average middle-class self from the misinformation which has been keeping you from your affluent destiny.

The Average Middle-Class Cop-Out Quiz————————

Reasons why I'm stuck in neutral:

(Circle those which apply to you)

1. I'm not a money slave. I've got better things to worry about than the almighty buck.

2. I'm stupid. It's beyond my understanding. My heredity has done me in.

3. My whole family is average. Why should I be any different?

4. We do everything for the kids. We don't do anything for ourselves.

5. I do what I'm told. It keeps me out of trouble.

6. Neither a borrower nor a lender be.

7. It's a man's world. What's a girl to do?

8. I'm too old. It's too late for me to be taking any chances. Besides, I deserve a rest.

9. All rich people are so worried about losing their money that they never have any fun.

10. My job's secure. I've got my retirement and Social Security. Why make the effort?

Okay, let's take them one at a time and see if you really have a good reason for being so average, or if you're just fooling yourself.

1. Naturally there are more important things in life than money. But to experience and really appreciate many of the "more important things in life," one often needs the freedom of having some money first. The idea that money is nonessential to a free life-style is silly. Many people actually believe that the ultimate freedom is to have nothing left to lose. (Sounds to me like they'd be left standing out in the cold! What do you think?) I don't think that's the kind of freedom I'd ever want to strive for.

I think, if given the chance, anyone would prefer the kind of freedom expressed by a friend of mine who said, "If you've got enough money, honey, everything is free."

2. If you're smart enough to have read this far in my book, you're smart enough to finish the book. I guarantee you that by the time you finish the book, you will have learned some secrets that can make you wealthier than the smartest person you know. By the time you finish this book, you'll probably consider *yourself* to be one of the smartest people you know.

3. This is a more serious problem for many people than it sounds like, but its solution is simple. It's to recognize the problem and face it. We all need the love and approval of someone, especially close family members. Most of us are frightened about doing things in a different manner than our "kinfolk" have always done. We don't like being different, and we are rightly afraid of arousing jealousies. We were all brought up to like and dislike the same people, things, and ideas our parents did. To live a life which is more affluent and fulfilling can seem like disloyalty—like joining the other side. If this is your problem, it's a tough one. You may have to make some difficult choices.

4. Do your kids a big favor and save them the burden of your martyrdom. You can also save them from their own inevitable average middle-class future at the same time. Your attitude is probably the same attitude your parents had towards you, and their parents had towards them. Why don't you be the one to break the chain? Make a break with tradition, and try and create some real money. Believe me, if your kids miss out on a new "Ronnie the Robot" or "Betty the Busty" so that they can have a better college education, or dress better, or have a brighter outlook on the world, they're going to benefit from your decision. They're also going to have a better feeling for you than if you continue setting them up for a "we sacrificed everything for you" guilt trip.

    Hold that thought for just a moment. Could it be you *want* your kids to feel responsible for you in your old age? Come on now, you don't really want that, do you? Wouldn't you rather have your freedom, as well as the love and respect of your children? I'm going to show you a way to build yourself up financially so that you needn't be dependent on anyone but yourself in your old age. It doesn't matter how old you are right now. Take charge and start to change your life today.

5. *A very basic problem.* Decisions have been made for you all your life. What brand of paper towel to squeeze. What clothes to wear. What school to go to and what classes to take. Where to go and what to do when you get there. There are literally millions of people in this country who are middle-class, do-it-by-the-book go-fors. They function well in our society. The system, to be sure, depends on the middle-class go-fors; but it has greater rewards for those people who can throw the book away and take an occasional risk.

   My purpose in writing this book is to encourage you to make just one financial decision; to watch it, nurture it, and do whatever is necessary to make it become successful. Once you've worked through the consequences of your decision and succeeded, you'll never want to operate any differently. That first step is the only really difficult one. I encourage you to find something in this book that will help you take that first step. It's in here. You won't have to look any farther.

6. This very old saying, attributed to Benjamin Franklin, is best used on a person with no collateral, someone you consider to be a bad risk, and who has just asked you to lend him some money. Be sure to put your right hand over your heart, your left hand over your wallet, use a properly disdainful tone of voice, and assume an air of virtue and pomposity. In all other cases, don't use this old saying.

   Lending money is a good way to make money. When you lend money, charge interest and secure the loan with something of greater value than the amount of your investment.

   Borrowing money is an even better way to make money, provided that you reasonably assure yourself in advance that you can make a profit using the funds you borrow. The use of OPM, other people's money, is the sacred creed of every entrepreneur.

7. It may still be a man's world. I don't know. It seems to me that the pendulum has swung quite a ways the other way in recent years. But be that as it may, it's a man's world only if you insist on playing strictly by men's rules and on men's courts. Build your own court, establish your own house rules, and see who starts making most of the points. My

advice to men is exactly the same! It's the whole point of this book, and an essential ingredient in your program for achieving financial independence.

8. If I get to be fifty-five to sixty-five and see one of those savings and loan commercials which tell me to put my money away in a risk-free savings account (which they avoid mentioning won't even keep up with the devastating combination of even moderate inflation and taxation) because "Well, there just isn't time to earn it again," I think I'll burn my passbook.

    I know that I can do better. I won't go out and buy any cattle in the Bahamas, or copper mines in Peru. I won't put anything in the stock market. But I will invest in something that I am knowledgeable about, that is relatively risk-free and secure, like well-located market-value income-producing residential real estate. After all, even discounting pride of ownership, which is still worth something, and occasional periods of time when real estate is not easily converted to cash, there will always be a better chance of getting a substantial return on my money in real estate than in an interest bearing savings account. And there's always the chance that I can outsmart the savings and loan and live till I'm one hundred.

    I know there are a lot of financial planners who would disagree with me, maybe even yours; but most of the financial planners I've listened to look at their clients' financial lives as being plotted on a bell curve, curving up in the middle years, and then curving back down again. Even if I were starting out at sixty-five, I'd prefer to think of my financial life as being plotted on a compound interest curve, starting out in the lower left-hand corner, bending slowly upward, then rising faster and faster till it shoots straight up and off the page at the upper right-hand corner. Don't you agree?

9. *Malarkey.* Assuming we are not talking about some inheritors of wealth, most rich people are very familiar with the wealth formula presented in this book. They got where they are not by sticking their heads in the sand (you make a bigger target that way!), but rather by moving around, looking for opportunities. You can't get very far in this world if you're not willing to make some decisions and take some risks. Rich people know this, and they know that they can lose everything they have today

and go back to work tomorrow and rebuild their fortunes all over again. After all, if you can't use it, enjoy it, and make it grow, why have it?

10. You bought the wrong book. You must have been looking for something in the gardening section.

Who Taught You to Be Average and Middle Class, Anyway? _____

"Everything in my world is valued by how it measures up to middle-class normal."

> —*The Average Middle-Class Financial Survey*

As the song goes, "You've got to be carefully taught. Before you are six or seven or eight, to hate all the people your relatives hate. . . ." It also makes perfect sense that you've got to be taught at a very early age to fit in to the society you live in, as your parents and teachers see it. Good or bad—habits of medocrity were pounded into your cute little ears during your formative years. You grew up not knowing so much what's actually best for you, but rather, what's right and wrong, spotlighted by your parents' and teachers' middle-class perceptions of what it takes to get along in their world.

People learn about being average and middle class the way they learn about everything else—through subtle and not-so-subtle reinforcement. For our discussion, if your Dad works from nine to five, you too will likely work from nine to five. If he works with his hands, you'll probably work with your hands. Or, if he works in an office, you'll probably work in an office. If Mom is a housewife and mother, you'll probably be a housewife and mother. If she's a professional person, you'll be a professional person. It's the exceptional child who breaks out of his parents' mold.

With allowances for change in style and technology, you probably live in a neighborhood very much like the one your parents live in, and drive a car that's very similar to the one they have. If your folks vacation at the beach, you and your family most likely vacation at the beach.

Your educational level is probably very close to that of your parents.

You or your marriage partner may have even been the rebel star, the black sheep, or your family's closet skeleton; but if you were to sit down and compare the similarities and differences between your life and the lives of your parents, it's a pretty good bet you'll find many more likenesses than differences. You don't think you inherited your parents' likes and dislikes, do you? You didn't. You inherited their middle-class values and preferences, but not through genetics—through exposure.

Your parents and teachers only reflected the values and preferences of their parents and teachers, and their parents and teachers, and their parents and teachers before them, and many of these hand-me-down values resulted from an industrial society which has demanded certain things from its middle class for centuries.

Three hundred years ago, rural society moved out of the fields and into the factories of the industrializing cities. One of these rural transplants was named Andy.

Andy moved his family into the city because he'd heard of all the wonderful things that were happening there. He especially like the stories of the money he could make in the fabric mills. Once there, Andy's enthusiasm for city life began to moderate. The poor guy had an inner clock which was set to tell him, to the day, when to plant and harvest his crops. Andy's seasonal clock was less than useless, however, in helping him show up at the factory on time. He became frustrated because he was constantly being bawled out by his supervisors.

While Andy's problems with punctuality and other factory disciplines were difficult for Andy, they were Excedrin headache #4 for the factory owners. The looms needed disciplined workers.

It was determined in a morning meeting of the FOAGCTGATWOT (Factory Owners And Governmental Committee To Get Andy To Work On Time) that it was too late for Andy to learn the factory disciplines. But if their industrial revolution were going to get off the ground, young people like Andy's son, George, would have to be prefitted to the factory system in order to ease their problems with industrial discipline. Out of this meeting the concept of mass public education was born, patterned after the factory model.

Andy didn't know what to think about the idea of George getting some education. Actually, he thought it sounded like one highfahlut'n waste of time. But the FOAGCTGATWOT had made the education thing compulsory, and besides, Andy's wife Emma was overjoyed at the prospect of getting the no-neck monster out of the house for a couple of hours a day. So George went off to school.

George was taught to read, and to write, and to do some arithmetic. He was also given a smattering of history and other subjects, but his real curriculum was more fundamental. It consisted of three subjects . . . punctuality, obedience, and brutally repetitious rote work. The factories demanded workers who were prefitted to the industrial necessities of showing up on time, taking orders from management without question, and working away at machines on assembly lines or in offices, doing painfully repetitive tasks.

Mass public education was clearly a civilizing force. But equally important, the factories profited from the increased human efficiency. The demand for compulsory education spread from country to country. George's son, Clyde, started school at a younger age than did his father, and Clyde's son's school year was extended longer into the calendar year.

At the beginning of the twentieth century (what with child labor laws, increased mechanization, and the advent of powerful labor unions), the need for Andy's descendants to enter the work force at an early age disappeared. A new problem resulted. Something had to be done about all of the laborers and office workers being graduated from the schools who were unable to find jobs.

A meeting of the Patriotic Sons and Daughters of the FOAGCTGATWOT was called to find an answer. Their solution was predictable. Keep the students in school even longer. Children soon were spending twelve to thirteen years in the public schools.

Not counting new courses covering three centuries of world history and technology, the mass education curriculum of today has changed very little from the time of Andy. The covert studies of punctuality, obedience, and adaptation to monotony remain basic to the system. Despite its humanizing qualities, public education has been responsible for transforming generation after generation of Andy's descendants into a pliable, regimented, and accepting work force, the largest percentage of which we today call the middle class.

If all this historical stuff is a little too far removed for you, I'll bring it all back home. You were born into this world naked, messy, and demanding. I see you don't remember this part too well, so I'll clue you in. You ate when you wanted to, went to the bathroom when and where you wanted to, talked when you wanted to, slept when you wanted to, and pretty much had everything your own way.

Mommy and Daddy tolerated this for awhile, until you make the mistake of showing more than a glimmer of awareness. Then the real struggle began. Because you weren't really prepared for the contest, and because you were a lot smaller, and because Mommy and Daddy were a lot smarter, you began to lose your penchant for independent action. Mommy and Daddy took seriously the job of teaching you the accepted methods of fitting into middle-class society. Mommy and Daddy were pretty clever teachers, don't you agree? Think back and see if you can remember some of their tactics.

The Direct Physical Method

You had finally gotten to that pretty round object on Mommy's coffee table. Suddenly it fell over, spilling water and dirt and a stick and some leaves all over you and the rug. You thought that was great . . . until you heard those loud noises coming out of Mommy and felt that stinging sensation on your backside.

You heard the same loud noises and felt the same pain when you stuck your finger into Cousin Joey's eye. This time, only some of the loud noises were coming from Mommy. A few of the loud noises were coming from Cousin Joey! It began to occur to you that Mommy and some of the other people around you weren't always going to be totally pleased with everything you did. You started giving some serious thought to what Mommy and Cousin Joey might do in response to your personal educational excursions.

The Comparison Technique

"Cousin Joey's a good little boy. Joey wouldn't spread peanut butter all over his dog. Don't you want to be like Cousin Joey?"

Sure you did! Nice Cousin Joey became your first role model.

The Guilt Trip

"Shame on you, leaving your room in such a mess! Mommy works hard all

day. She shouldn't have to clean up your room, too. You don't want Mommy
to get old and die just because you didn't clean up your room, do you?"

Imagine what the newspapers would say. "Ungrateful Child Slays Mom
with Messy Room."

Threats

"You've got until the count of three to let your little sister out of that box, and
I mean it, or you'll stay in your room 'til you're forty-five years old. Do you
hear me!"

Gamesmanship

"Now you and Daddy are going to play in the garden. Daddy will pull one
weed, and then you pull one weed, then Daddy will pull two weeds . . . no,
no, no, not the pansies!" (The name of this game turned out to be "Work"!)

Pleading

"All you have to do is take that snake out of the bathtub, and put him back
outside where you found him. That's all I ask. Please! Please! Please! Now,
Mommy has to go and take a Miltown and lie down."

Martyr Method

"Your mother and father have sacrificed everything for you. And what do we
get in return? A kid who wants to join the circus. Is that fair?"

*   *   *

Of course, all this at-home learning was pretty important . . . even necessary. If only it didn't leave you with all those unfortunate middle-class side
effects.

The trouble was, unless someone became so exasperated with you that
they gave up on you, no one ever told you, "Okay, do it your own way." That,
of course, would have left you with the guilty feeling that it probably wasn't

okay to do it your own way. The trouble was, no one ever said that guilt and love and doing things the way everyone else does them have nothing to do with each other. Instead, you were fitted with a pair of conformity antennae which helped you search out acceptable, if only modest, behavior patterns— patterns that guaranteed you the most love, and the least amount of guilt, and that guided you timidly through your school years and modestly on through your middle-class life. I know! I developed a set of antennae which would have made a honeybee proud.

Imitation is a child's way of adjusting to the world around him. I began to do things the way I thought my parents would do them. You probably did, too.

"Oh my, Leroy, come look at what your son and daughter are doing! Where did you learn that, Heather? That's disgusting. Now, Jason, look at me! Stop that this instant!"

What were Heather and Jason doing? Sitting out behind the garage, smoking one of Mom's cigarettes, sharing a can of beer, and playing cards. Jason and Heather were real quick to pick up on the way Mom would light up a cigarette and Dad would drink a beer to relax. Mom played bridge with the girls and Dad played poker with the boys, and Heather and Jason were doing their best to emulate them. What else do Jasons's and Heather's antennae pick up?

1. How Dad brags about having $150 bet on the Miami Dolphins, loses it, and complains that the family is spending too much money.

2. How Mom proudly wears fancy clothes, an imitation fur coat, and costume jewelry whenever they go out to dinner or to parties.

3. How Dad is always a little nervous and very polite when he talks to his boss on the phone; then calls him a jerk when he hangs up.

4. How big brother Bill takes his whole $30 allowance and spends it playing Space Invaders after school at the video game arcade at the shopping mall.

5. How the whole family always seems to be mad at rich people: bankers, baseball players, doctors, lawyers, landlords, and anybody named Rockefeller.

The children observing this family at home are picking up behavior patterns that will stay with them the rest of their lives. Dad works hard to get by, and gambles on dreams in the unrealistic hope that his gambling will keep him in the game and deliver him from his medial circumstances. We've got a Mom and Dad who consume much of what they purchase just to impress the neighbors. They blame others for their own shortcomings.

Here are a couple of kids who probably get most of what they request, from the latest electronic gadget to the breakfast cereals they see advertised on Saturday morning television. These are kids who are learning that money is best used to buy relaxation and entertainment. These kids are developing into adults who one day will go off into the real world handicapped with prejudice, financial ignorance, and misinformation. They'll begin a life of doing as little as possible, hoping for a salary as big as possible. These are children who are preconditioned to mediocrity. They will see themselves at odds with their employers, superiors, and anyone else who appears to have more or be more than they are. They will position themselves on the opposite side of the fence from people who actually have, or are perceived to have, money and prestige—people they should try to get to know.

Did uninspired role models, bad information, and a false understanding of the nature and value of money get you into the bind you're in now? It could be . . . but maybe not. One way to find out is to take this little test. Honest answers, now. No cheating. We're not going to score this test, so relax and be as truthful as possible. Then read the answers and see if you're not ready to make some substantive changes in your life.

The Economic Awareness Test ————————————

1. How did you choose your present occupation?

   a. I became interested while in school.
   b. It was suggested by a friend or parent.
   c. It was the only job I could find.
   d. It's what I always wanted to do.

2. What are your chances for making a lot of money in the next five years?

 a. I've never thought about it.
 b. None.
 c. Slim.
 (d.) Good.

3. What type of life insurance do you own?

 (a.) I don't own a life insurance policy.
 b. Whatever my insurance agent sold me.
 c. Whole life.
 d. Term.

4. What percentage of your income did you pay to the government in income taxes last year?

 a. Don't know.
 (b.) 00–15 percent.
 c. 16–30 percent.
 d. 31–50 percent.

5. Do you know the total present value of your assets?

 a. No.
 (b.) Yes. Write it down. $ 210,000

6. Do you know the total of your present liabilities (debts)?

 a. No.
 (b.) Yes. Write it down. $ 138,000

7. Do you know your present net worth (total assets, minus total liabilities)?

 a. No.
 (b.) Yes. Write it down. $ 70,000

8. Do you know how much money you will make in the next twelve months?

   a. No.
   (b) Yes. Write it down. $___86,000___

9. Do you know how much money you will spend in the next twelve months?

   (a.) No.
   b. Yes. Write it down. $_____

10. When was the last time you took a class or attended a seminar of your own choosing?

   a. In high school.
   b. In college.
   c. Within the last five years. What was it? _____
   (d.) Within the last twelve months. What was it? ___work (Ojai)___

11. Your evenings and weekends are spent:

   a. At leisure.
   b. Working on projects for the boss.
   (c.) Working at self-improvement.
   d. Working on financial matters.

12. When you purchase something, you:

   a. Buy the most economical and least expensive.
   b. Buy secondhand.
   (c.) Buy better than average.
   d. Buy the best.

Here are the answers.

1. It's often an interesting and valuable lesson to look back and see the circumstances which led to major decisions in your life like choosing a career. People often make the decision to enter a particular occupation on little more than a whim, before they really understand what the occupation will require of them, or what it will do for them.

   It's not unusual to find that a person has chosen an occupation because its starting pay was good; because it was recommended by a friend or relative; or simply because the person was out of work, needed a job, and took the first thing that came along. It may not be until several years down the road that he realizes he's on a road to Commonplace, or worse, is on a dead end street. But by that time he's established in the firm, hooked by the retirement and dental plans, and fearful of making any drastic changes which might upset his average middle-class apple cart.

2. I'll bet you've never seriously considered the possibility of actually making a lot of money in the next five years. Like most average middle-class people, you've probably only thought of increasing your income through annual "cost of living" salary increases, and promotions. Ignoring for the moment your dream of tripping over a discarded bag of cash, you might think it seems improper or greedy to think of making lots of money, especially when you put a time frame around when you expect to achieve it.

   Don't feel bad, and don't deny it. It's not your fault. You've been taught to think that way. When you start looking for it, you're going to find that there is so much money out there, actually available to you in the real world, that you will have trouble accepting it. To begin to picture some of that money as yours, you need simply to use your imagination. The first step in making a lot of money is to believe it's there and that you can get it. This is where the average middle-class person first stumbles.

3. **Study insurance.** Don't take anybody's word for what type of insurance is best for you. Having said that, my advice to someone who is planning to get rich is to buy term and invest the difference.

4. **Study the income tax laws.** There are plenty of informative books around that will teach you the basics painlessly. If you paid more than

15 percent of your income to the government in taxes, you paid more than your share. (*Note:* That's not necessarily by the IRS's standards!) It doesn't matter if you made $20,000, or $150,000. The more money you make, the easier it is to shelter, legally. You say you want to know how to do that right this minute? Take a speed reading course, and hurry up and get to Chapter 7.

5., 6., 7., 8., 9. Study accounting. It is critical to the wealth formula for you to begin (right now!) to keep track of your finances. Get the numbers down in black and white. You should reevaluate your financial position at least once every three months. If you didn't respond to these five questions with five "yes" answers, putting down the exact dollar amounts, because you don't know how to figure them, I'll show you a simple method later in this book. Believe me, detailed accounting is critical to becoming and staying wealthy. It is not unusual for the average middle-class person not to know the answers to these five questions, but you will. Remember, successful people do what failures don't want to do, and keeping accurate records is one thing all successful people do.

10. Your local community high school or college probably has night school courses in accounting, taxes, real estate, general business, personal financial planning, etc. These classes can make you money. Why not take an evening off each week and, instead of watching TV, get some practical education. Watch your local paper for announcements and advertisements of financial seminars. One of them could change your life.

11. Are you a disciplined person when you're on your job, working for someone else? I'll bet you are. It probably seems only natural, then, for you to want to relax and rejuvenate yourself by going totally berzerk or inert on your own time. Maybe you like to kill time by sitting in front of a movie screen or a TV set, or you may attempt to kill yourself by sitting on a motorcycle, a snowmobile, or a bar stool. If I just hit one of your hot buttons, and if you want to become a member of the money class any time soon, an attitude change on your part regarding your own time is in order.

You need to use your own time to plan your escape from the middle class. You'll find the plans and the tools you'll need to escape here in this book. All you need to do is invest some of your free time and effort to make them work. I think you'll find that using your own time profitably is more refreshing in the long run than wasting precious evening and weekend hours trying to simply escape the realities and the "no great shakes" of your life.

12. Once you've initiated your own *Park Avenue Money Diet,* you will want to start living like you've already got money. Go with the "top o' the line" every chance you get. This is a part of the plan. Recognize and accept the fact that a Cadillac really is a much better car than a Chevrolet. Gold is more valuable than gold plate. Flying first class is more fun than traveling coach. Don't accept any rationale that makes you accept second best.

Expensive things will make you feel good about yourself and will give you a competitive edge. If you feel good about yourself, you'll do a better job; you'll make more money; and you'll be able to afford even more expensive stuff.

I Can't Afford to Save and Invest

A lot of people really think they can't afford to save money and invest.

"Do you know how hard it is to stretch a dollar these days? I can hardly budget for the necessities of life like food and clothing. Do you know what our utility bill was last month? My gosh!"

Whether you make two hundred or three thousand dollars a week, your income has nothing to do with your inability to save money. As a middle-class person today, you are practically obliged to increase your spending to equal or exceed your income. Whatever your income level, the first step on your get-rich plan might be to learn to live *beneath* your means for awhile.

I know! A few paragraphs ago I told you to start going first class, and now all of a sudden I'm suggesting that you might want to cut back a little. Several paragraphs ago, I was talking about motivating yourself personally and financially once you're established in *The Park Avenue Money Diet* program. But right now, we're talking about the practical business of getting started. Don't get the two confused, or the results could be catastrophic. It will take money for you to make money, and if you don't have any extra money at the moment, and can't arrange to borrow it, you're going to need to save some.

I shop at shopping centers once or twice a month, and I wait behind people at checkout counters who are buying more inconsequential crap than I can believe. Some people seem to be totally obsessed with purchasing all the latest "in vogue" fads, and all the latest disposable items of convenience: plastic knick-knacks, pet rocks, message T-shirts, electric vegetable slicers, vibrating foot baths, etc. Today's consumer is faced with aisles and counters full of beautifully packaged products which are only, more or less, expensive imitations of the real things. Their limited usefulness is matched only by their limited lives (except for the pet rock, who should be useful and live forever!); and they are all terribly expensive. Why not? All those development costs, market research costs (to see if you'll pay money for it, and how much), advertising costs (to insure that you *will* buy it), and all those synthetic materials have to be paid for.

The truth is that many of your average middle-class, hard-earned dollars are being spent for strange-shaped plastic and semi-plastic whatnots which are of little value other than to perk you up, give you a false sense of economy, and convince you that you're better off than you really are. You may think you're a wise shopper but, at the point of sale, when you're buying one of these foolish articles, you really aren't shopping wisely.

You buy these meretricious items because they make you feel good, and after a hard week's work you deserve to feel good; or because they're supposed time-savers, and you never have enough time; or because you think they are of real value and will make you a better or a more important person.

As the hair coloring ad says, "Sure, it costs more, but I buy it because I'm worth it." What is that ad really saying? Is it saying that this is a more valuable product and therefore it costs more? It may be a product that's better or more valuable than its competition, but my point is, that's not what the advertising pitch is. The ad is saying, because you're vain enough to believe you're really something special, you're willing to pay more. It's a sad appeal to people in our society who have a limited sense of personal worth. It's not telling you that the product's a better product. You hope it is, but you feel better about buying the product because the ad tells you that you as a "special individual" deserve to pay more. Never mind the fact that you may not be able to fill the car up with gas next week.

Talk about your mental acrobatics!

What about cars? Is your Volkswagen Rabbit really a wolf in sheep's clothing? (That's a strange looking animal!) Does it really combine the speed and excitement of a racing car with the economy and comfort of a sedate European sedan? You let Madison Avenue do this to you, and you wonder why you never have any money left at the end of the month.

If you have any of the following items lying around the house, in the kitchen or garage, you have typical middle-class spending—and wasting—habits. In some cases, you're spending too much for too little, and in others you're not spending enough.

1. Does someone's name, a fancy pocket design, and a slick advertising campaign really make a $15 pair of slacks worth $40, $50, or $100? Please don't tell me you have more than one pair of designer jeans in your closet. Well, okay, maybe two pair, but that's it, right? No! You're not really the type that when you get a few dollars ahead you buy some Calvins, and then if there's any left you pay the rent, are you? How embarrassing! Tough luck for you *and* your landlord.

2. An "artist clearance" painting, print, or sculpture. This is the stuff you buy at so-called discount art stores and auctions. You may have thought you were ripping off some bohemian artist somewhere, while at the same time giving him a few dollars to feed his family. In reality, the artwork(?) is only worth little more than the cost of the materials used to create it, and you're only really helping out a smart businessman.

    That so-called "discount art" is mass-produced according to formulas by salaried workmen in assembly line fashion. The paintings may have value to you because they have colors or shapes which look good with your furniture, but they will never have the aesthetic value of a real work of art, and they will never increase in value, thereby increasing your net worth. The same goes for unsigned, unnumbered, mass-produced prints and sculptures, except that instead of being done by hand, they are simply run off or molded on machines.

3. Have you noticed that impulse purchase items such as the knick-knacks, gossip magazines, horoscope books, romance books, and yum-yums, have taken over the checkout stand at the grocery and department stores? It's because these items have taken over your life. Managers who decide these things know: If it's there you'll buy it on impulse, and you'll be willing to pay plenty for it, too.

4. Clever magazine and television advertising and fancy package designs make you remember brand names, but they all add to the costs of the products you buy. Take vitamins, for instance. You can almost always save a considerable amount of money by buying a generic item rather than a nationally advertised brand, and still get the identical product. And what about bottles of imported carbonated water?

5. A little economy car. They are dangerous. How much money would you have to save on the price of the car or on the cost of gasoline to make up for the loss of a family member, or an arm or a leg, as the result of a collision with a vehicle of larger size at 55 mph? It's only common sense to realize you are much safer with your seat belt on, snug inside a full-sized car. And safety in a dangerous environment like the highway should be your primary concern, not economy.

6. A lawn mower, a hedge trimmer, a vacuum cleaner, or a dust mop. You can hire helpers who have their own equipment. They can operate more efficiently than you can, and you can use your time, if you spend it profitably, more valuably than wasting it puttering around the house.

*   *   *

Whether you are a middle-class member of the jet set or the Chevrolet set, there are intelligent ways to balance your budget and spend money. Always look first for quality—the most quality for X amount of dollars. Quality will always have value. Take some extra time and make wiser purchasing decisions. Plan your purchases, use a shopping list, and don't buy on impulse. You can afford to spend intelligently. You can't afford not to.

Some Economic Social Studies

Many average middle-class people, particularly those approaching the top rungs of the middle-class ladder, say they can't save money or invest because their jobs or life-styles demand that they show off by spending a large amount of their income on pretentious entertaining to impress and influence other people. They have to live beyond their means in order to put themselves forward.

They must throw or attend functions properly attired, have the right kind of car, own the right kind of home in the right neighborhood, have the right kind of kids in the right private school, and the list goes on and on. These people are living high on the hog, but they're no more independent, no less middle class, or no more capable of reaching financial independence than the family who spends their last twenty dollars each month on dinner out at the corner fast food franchise.

You know you've got a social problem if you:

1. Really don't have fun at parties but go because you think "it's important to be seen"! This is especially true if you have to buy a new suit, rent a fur coat, or emboss the word "Gucci" on your penny loafers; and Visa or MasterCard has to send you one of their impertinent reminders telling you that you've exceeded your credit limit again.

2. Visit an associate's home and within the first five minutes after arriving, explore the house to see if they've got some new gadget or amenity which you don't have. If they don't, you're relieved. If they do, you make plans to get a bigger and better one. This exploratory work is done under the guise of "Mind if I use the john?"

3. Buy all new furniture and wallpaper the den before you're willing to throw a party.

4. Interrogate your host about the price of the dining room chandelier, the cost of her new dress, and the average price of a meal at their favorite restaurant.

*   *   *

Don't feel paranoid or intimidated. This is typical average upper middle-class person socializing. Technically, it might be called the comparative method of being social. Like, "Darling, I'll show you mine and I sure hope you can't show me yours." Most average middle-class social events are arranged not so much to have a good time, but to give the host a chance to show off. It's only when you start adding up what it costs you to throw or attend all of those upper-middle-class exhibition cocktail parties, picnics, dinners, theater evenings, sporting events, and reunions that you realize how expensive middle-class status socializing can be.

"After working my way through college, finding my first job, and starting to make some money, I decided it was time to start doing all of those things I had dreamed of. I could go to fancy restaurants, entertain, take cruise vacations, and drink as much as I wanted. I work hard and I deserve the trappings of success."

Even success can lead to money problems. There are many examples around to prove it. But a really successful person can learn to say, "No thanks." The willpower that it took for him to get up the ladder in business is going to be needed to make him watch his spending habits if he ever plans to reach real financial indepdendence . . . which is really what success is all about anyway, right?

There are many joys and profits to be had from entertaining and being social. But there's no good reason why people should have to hock the family jewels to be able to afford to throw or attend a social gathering. People should be able to get together, have a good time, do a little business, and still spend their money sensibly.

The Middle-Class Merry-Go-Round _____

Being average and middle class is the most pernicious of all possible Catch 22s. It follows this script:

1. Middle-class people don't have the money they need to escape the middle class, so they find ways of accepting themselves as being middle class.

2. Middle-class people find ways to accept themselves as middle class by spending money on various forms of specious entertainment and by making meretricious purchases.

3. Middle-class people spend their money on various forms of specious entertainment and by making meretricious purchases, so they don't have the money they need to escape the middle class.

You move through your life like a wooden horse attached to an amusement park ride. You work hard to earn money; you spend your money on goodies or on diversions which are quickly consumed, or which have limited value; you wonder where the money goes; you go back to work to earn more money; you spend your money on more goodies; and you never break out of the cycle long enough to see what's really happening to you. You never seem to find an end to your problems, and you never take the time to figure out what you need to do to get off the ride.

You know everyone has problems. Just being alive in today's complicated world is a problem. But some people find a way to take charge of their lives and solve their problems. They catch the brass ring and get off the circus ride without bringing calamity down upon themselves. Why can't you? That is the real problem we're facing here, you know! We both know other people have done it—why can't you!

Some people nod and say, "I know the problem is me." But they never really accept what it is about themselves or the way they do things that creates the problem. Others say "I'm my own problem, all right, but I'm this way because I'm all that's ever been expected of me." They continue going 'round and 'round and 'round, doing only what is expected of them.

Very few people realize that they can expect more of themselves. That they can recognize their own problems, take charge, and cure them. That's why very few people ever attempt to earn any real money or ever try to achieve real financial independence.

If you're totally hung up on remaining average, you may need some professional help. Don't be shy. There's nothing wrong with seeing a shrink or a psychologist or joining an encounter group if it does the trick for you. I happen to believe you can make a lot of your own changes yourself . . . if you really want to change   if you get the correct information you need, like the information you'll get out of this book . . . if you like yourself enough and know you are truly worth the effort.

Let's face another fact. You and a lot of other people have a lot of time on your hands which you are wasting. You don't have the slightest idea how to organize yourself or your time. You're bored at work and you're bored when you're not at work. When you're bored, you look for some form of entertainment to pull you out of your boredom. You'll do anything and everything that on the surface looks like fun, providing it requires little thought and less effort.

But if you sincerely want to escape from the middle class, you've got to know where you're going and why; how to get there and when; and what to do when you get there. You need to know how to keep from getting bogged down in nonessentials; how to keep from being bored, depressed, and lonely.

It's time to face the music. It's time to grow up. It's time to stop this escapism and face your problems head on. Don't turn to your fancy new food processor and expect love and affection. Whatever is bothering you needs some fresh air—but not a ride on the newest attraction at the average middle-class amusement park. Let your average middle-class problems become verbal ones. Talk them out. Shout them out, if you need to. Discuss them with your friend, your pet, your doctor, or your television set. Figure out what events in your life got you to where you are today. Find out why you are average and middle class and frustrated. Begin to look for a solution to your problems.

You must do something if you expect to change. And you must change, because your present situation is unhealthy. In fact, maintaining your present situation could be considered an unconscious death wish. Did I tell you? I'll kill you if you die before you finish reading my book.

CHAPTER 4

WASTED OPPORTUNITY

I've heard that love is the answer to most of our problems. I disagree. Love is a wonderful happy thing, but it won't do a thing to cure our average middle-class problems. Face it, a lot of average middle-class people are in love, but they still have problems. The answer to most middle-class problems is money. Money is a lot of fun, exciting, and very gratifying. There's no small talk involved, not a chance of getting pregnant, and believe me, money is a lot easier to get hold of than love is.

How many times have you heard one of your average middle-class friends or neighbors say, "Money isn't everything. There are plenty of things in life that don't cost a lot of money"?

Presumably they're talking about love, the moon, the stars, the flowers and the trees, the birds that sing and fish that swim. Do you think they mean that you won't want to continue to enjoy these things if you have some money? Where is the logic there? No one wants to give up the free things in life. To do that would be to lower the return on our investment in living.

One of the reasons average middle-class people are stuck in the holding patterns they're in, is because they present themselves as easy marks to promoters who want to introduce them to their versions of "the investment of the decade," the one sure vehicle to transport every average middle-class person from mediocrity to instant riches.

Investment salesmen, working on commissions that would allow morons to make a good living (often 20 percent of the investors' money up front, and occasionally 50 percent or more!), play on a particularly unfortunate weakness of ordinary people . . . their lack of patience and their desire for instant wealth.

The fact is, many middle-class investors won't consider a proposition unless it promises to double their money in the blink of an eye or two shakes of a lamb's tail. The way they analyze investments is simple. An investment that guarantees to double their money in six months is decidedly better than one that guarantees to double their money in twelve months.

The predictable outcome of most of these miracle investments is that the investor is seldom able to get his original investments back in a reasonable amount of time, if at all, much less double his money.

We're not talking about "off the wall" investments here, either. We're talking about real estate "deals"; stocks and commodities; precious metals, gems, and other collectibles; tax shelter schemes (these are the worst!); oil and gas promotions; research and development projects; annuity plans, IRAs, Keogh plans, and other pension plans; and whole life insurance "investments." Most of these so-called investments are conceived with the primary goal of making the promoter, the company, the bank, or the salesman a few bucks by relieving the middle-class pigeon of the excess cash he has left over after his meretricious shopping sprees.

But what am I telling you this for? You've probably bought one or more of these so-called investments already, right? You're the expert. You tell me the disservice these schemes have done to your future. You tell me about the way you've been talked into yoyo-ing your financial life and your savings away on these miserable, misguided ventures.

Take another look at your local bookstore. The country has gone investment crazy. Every week or so there seem to be twenty-five new money books, all geared to one scheme or strategy or another, especially tailored to make you an overnight millionaire. Their main purpose, of course, is to make the author some more money. Magazines on the newsstands offer you articles on how to build your immediate personal fortune: *The Omega Strategy, The Negotiation Strategy, The Three-Year Strategy, The Technical Strategy, The Japanese Strategy.* My favorites are the get-rich schemes you can send away for from mail order post office boxes.

"New! Self-Made Millionaire Reveals Wealth Formula. Revealed to him while climbing the mountains of Nebraska. Yes-sirree-Bob, folks, he risked his life to find the secret, and now it can be yours. Send check or money order for $25.95. Please hurry, this is a one-time offer."

So you cut out coupons, tear out pages, and send away for these cheaply printed books and pamphlets that promise "riches in twenty-four hours or less." I've still got so many of those books describing schemes and magic potions that I could probably open up a retail bookstore. Some of the people who answered my survey admitted the same.

"You name it and I've bought it and tried it. A girl friend of mine once told me, 'Sharon, by the time you retire you'll be the leading authority on get-rich formulas and still be out of pocket money.' "

How to Make a Killing in the Stock Market _____

Our subtitle, and best and favorite method ought to be, shoot the stockbroker.

One of the most popular ways for ordinary people to invest their money is in the stock market.

So-called stock market investors are divided into two camps: the "insiders," and the "little guy off the street." Custom has it that the average middle-class person gets to play the part of the "little guy off the street." It's always the "little guy off the street" who gets to take it in the shorts. He's conned into the market after stock prices have been rising (like hot air balloons!) for several months. He's invited to participate just when it looks like the market is about to go out of sight.

Perhaps he wakes up one morning in time to hear street hype in the form of a newsworthy interview on one of the early morning news and commentary shows. It's all about the phenomenal riches being made by a fourteen-year-old kid from Provincetown, Massachusetts, who has developed a secret system which involves the use of a dart board, his girl friend's tube top, and the financial pages of his local paper. Or maybe he hears the exaggerated bragging of a friend who has been lucky enough to win a few bucks in the market because of a "tip" from his "insider" friend. He may have been told stories about IBM and Xerox increasing to ten, fifty, one hundred times their original value back in the glamour years. For whatever reason, he gets hooked.

"This is what I've been waiting for," he shouts loud enough to be heard three blocks away. In a state of euphoria, he calls a stockbroker. He listens to some more hype about airlines, high technology, or oil stocks, depending on what's in the *Wall Street Journal* that day; and he buys something. Next . . . he becomes an expert. He learns to read the stock tables in the paper, buys a book, picks up some of the lingo, and subscribes to a newsletter or a charting service.

Unfortunately, the "little guy off the street" gets hooked just when the gondola of the market's hot air balloon is rising on its last blast of hot air; when it's about ready to descend. He jumps in on the strength of the street hype of those "insider" speculators who were looking for a way out. As usual, the "little guy off the street" gets the privilege of riding the stock market's gondola all the way down until the balloon collapses on top of him, again!

Let's take a good look at what it is an investor invests in when he buys a share of stock. Where did it come from? What is it, how secure is it, what does he expect it to do for him, and who benefits most when he buys it?

A share of stock is a piece of paper issued by a corporation for the sole purpose of raising working capital. It is a miraculous moneymaking means by which an owner of a company supposedly sells his company to the public, and yet in most cases, by holding on to a controlling number of shares (in large corporations it only takes 5 percent to 15 percent of the outstanding shares to have a controlling interest), maintains control of the company. These guys (and the stockbrokers!) have a sure thing. Everyone else is gambling.

Then if the company prospers and the profits can't be absorbed by (or manipulated into!) higher management salaries, reserves for expansion and replacement, future development costs, and/or other accounting mumbo-jumbo, the shareholders will share in the prosperity of the company by receiving proportionate dividends. If a stock from a profitable company does not pay dividends, or can keep from having to pay dividends, it's often dubbed a "growth stock"! (Interpreted by the brokerage houses as "You may profit later . . . if you sell your stock, if the company grows, if the price of the stock goes up.")

Once the shares of stock are sold to the public, they complete their initial purpose for the company—that of raising working capital. They remain a liability to the corporation, however, because the stockholders are entitled to a proportionate share of the company's net profits (those net profits which can't be absorbed, as mentioned above!), and because the price of the stock becomes a reflection of the public's perception of the company's stability. Once sold to the public, the shares take on an entirely new character, one which is only remotely related to the parent company. Then the shares of stock become commodities in their own right—ones which are traded back and forth on a stock exchange.

Now the real fun and games begin. Technical analysts for brokerage houses begin to compile price data on the stock. They update and revise their data with speculative guesses, based on what they know about past history, as to which way they think the price will go. As the stock is traded back and forth, chart analysts draw straight lines between the stock's successive price highs and lows and profess to tell gullible investors when the stock is about ready to take off, or when it's about ready for a correction . . . whatever that is! (Does that mean the stock market made a mistake?)

It's insanity!

The value of the share of stock now no longer (necessarily) has any direct relation to the profitability or net worth of the company it represents. The solvency and the profitability of the parent company often become of only peripheral importance to the value of the stock. Of equal or greater importance are: unrelated happenings in Washington, D.C., the Middle East, European money markets, the imagination of you and your stockbroker, someone sneezing in Rangoon, earthquakes in California, and windstorms on the moon.

Strange things begin to happen. For instance, if someone sneezes in Rangoon, or if the wind on the moon is blowing from the east, your stockbroker might call you and suggest that you buy. You, believing him to be a knowledgeable expert, buy. If you already own that particular stock and the guy in Rangoon gets hold of some nasal spray, or the wind on the moon is blowing from the west, the stockbroker might advise you to sell. Again, since in your mind he's the expert, you sell. Since you're the "little guy off the street," you probably lose money either way. Too bad, the guy sneezing in Rangoon or the direction of the wind on the moon turned out to be of little importance to your particular stock that day.

What you may never find out is that your stockbroker's expertise, which you were relying on in making your buy/sell decisions, came from his ability to master a few multiple choice questions on a test. (That test does more to acquaint the aspiring stockbroker with the verbiage of his trade than it does to assure his competency!) He also got help from technical analysts employed by the brokerage house for the sole purpose of helping them sell stocks. He might even have picked something up from that morning's "brokerage house oracle," the *Wall Street Journal*.

Your expert advisor collects a commission each time you buy or sell, regardless of whether you win or lose. Obviously, it's to his advantage to keep your account active. For that reason alone, any advice he gives you should be considered suspect. The only thing a stock market investor can be sure of is that his stock and the market will either go up or down.

Another strange fact. The stock market is a "perfect" market. Sounds pretty good, don't you think? I mean, what can be better than a "perfect" market? A perfect market is one in which every product is of equal size, shape, consistency, and value. Each item is exactly like every other item. Samples are not printed in different colors (pink or blue), or cut into different shapes (circles or triangles), so that one might appeal more to one person and another might appeal to someone else. Stock certificates don't have a variety of uses so that a person with a different reason for buying it might be willing to pay more for a particular share of stock.

In a perfect market every buyer and seller has exactly the same information available about the same product at any given moment. The information is on the radio; it's on TV; it's printed in all the major newspapers; it's on ticker tapes; it's on cables; it's bouncing off of satellites; it's traveling around the world and out into space at the speed of light. If a share of stock is selling for $15 a share in New York City on October 28, at 11:30 a.m., the chances of it being worth $16.50 to someone anywhere in the world at that exact same time are pretty remote.

While the concept of the stock market being a perfect market sounds ideal on the surface, it works against the profit motives of all the "little guy off the street" speculators in the market.

Consider this scenario:

You look in the morning paper and see to your delight that the stock you bought the week before has gone up three dollars a share. At that exact moment, the other investors who own shares of that particular stock open their papers and feel that same feeling of elation. You and the other investors think optimistically, "If it went up today, it might go up again tomorrow." You decide to hold, or to buy more.

But the next day, your stock drops two dollars and fifty cents a share. An analyst on the local TV news comments that the stock market was reacting to some statement by the president, and that "stock market investors today participated in a democratic market and cast their votes in opposition to the president," causing a general stock market decline of ten points. (No kidding! Listen to those guys. You'll hear them say stuff like that all the time!)

Now, you and the other investors feel a churning sensation in the pits of your stomachs. "What if it's peaked out and . . . ?" You and most of the others decide not to think about it and hold on for another day. But a few stockholders decide to sell, take their profits, and run.

The stock declines again the next day, and the next, and the next. Your investment is in the red. Your stockbroker calls. You note the air of urgency in his voice. "I think we ought to vote, I mean sell!" (It's always *we* . . . not just you! Isn't it nice to know you're not in this mess alone? The poor guy's got a commission riding on your decision!)

"The man's a genuine psychic," you gasp to yourself. "I agree. I feel miserable. Let's sell!"

At the same time, other stockholders take a look at their charts and hear from their stockbrokers. Many of them make the same panicky decision you made. You've all lost money, but you can all say in unison: "At least I cut my losses."

The next day the stock goes back up again. Your broker calls and suggests you buy. You slam the phone down in his ear, right? Probably not. After all, he's the expert. Now that's a perfect market—a lousy way to invest—but a perfect market. What do you think?

The perfect stock market makes little sense to the studious investor. It's dominated by speculators, not investors, and speculators are governed by the emotional events of the moment rather than the trends of the long term. If the speculators are jittery, they sell. If they feel okay, they buy.

Why otherwise seemingly intelligent people venture into a market like the stock market, which is subject to such strange goings on and methods of analysis, is beyond me. Well, at least it's beyond me now. I used to buy stocks. It took a few tries, and a couple of good healthy losses, for me to realize that I'd been conned into playing a game devoid of rational rules, against dealers who had stacked the deck.

Big Brother Investments

If, for some reason, you just can't seem to stick to a savings or investment plan of your own, get out your copy of the Yellow Pages. You'll find hundreds of people and organizations who will offer to help you—of course, they're going to want a share of your cash in return. Investments are big business, as we've noted. Many of these folks, or experts (as they refer to themselves!), and organizations are national and international in scope, with branch offices in every major city in the country, perhaps the world.

The success of these experts and organizations is based on, among other things, the reluctance of middle-class people to take their own risks without "expert" advice, the belief that misery loves company, and in most cases, the famous quote attributed to Phineas Taylor (P. T.) Barnum, "There's a sucker born every minute."

Should you ever decide to use one of these financial experts, you should first ask yourself (don't ask them!), "Do I really need you, and if so, why?" The second question you should ask is, "What do your services cost me?" The answer to question number one should be, "You don't need them," and number two, "They can cost you your weight in paper dollars," for something you usually can do yourself by following the suggestions you'll find in the next few chapters of this book.

Let me introduce you to a representative sample of one of these "Big Brother Experts"—the syndicator.

The syndicator, as sinister as his name sounds, is an interesting fellow. He makes his living by raising money to put together group investments. He can be an accountant, a real estate broker, an oil and gas man, or he can be an organization, like a brokerage house or an investment firm.

Syndicators and their groups buy everything from single family houses to shopping centers, apartment buildings, car washes, office buildings, and large and small tracts of land. They arrange oil and gas drilling groups, research and development projects, and almost anything else that requires large pools of investment capital.

For his trouble, the syndicator or his company often collect:

1. A "front-end load"—a portion of the funds he raises, usually 10 to 50 percent

2. A "back-end load"—a share of the investor's profits when the investment is liquidated, again commonly 10 to 50 percent

3. A management fee—for watching over the investment

4. A commission on the sale, normally 6 to 20 percent (usually both going into and coming out of the investment)

(You can imagine how well the investment must have to do to pay off some of these syndicators, much less the investors!)

Probably the most common type of syndication is the limited partnership. A limited partnership is made up of one or more general partners, usually the syndicator(s), and any number of limited partners, usually ten to thirty-five, but there could be hundreds, and even thousands.

The limited partners (average middle-class people for our discussion) are so-called because their liability in the syndicated project is limited to the amount of their investment. They can lose that, and no more.

The syndicator is the general partner. He assumes all the risks inherent in the ownership and operation of the investment. This is usually a major selling point, but the truth of the matter is, a great deal of the general partner's liability is covered by insurance . . . paid for by the limited partners.

While undoubtedly there are good and bad "Big Brother" investments, average middle-class people should approach them all, especially the larger ones, with great care. The largest syndicators are the brokerage houses. They can usually be counted on to approach the "hog line" in determining their front-end, middle, and back-end loads.

In most cases, the single most distinguishing characteristic of the brokerage house "Big Brothers" is their ignorance of the product they're selling. Incredibly, their knowledge of the product seems to decrease with the size of the offering and the size of the organization making the offering. The salesmen in these organizations are used to selling stocks. They get confused when they try to talk about anything that is real.

A dead giveaway that you're dealing with a brokerage salesman who doesn't know what he's talking about is when you ask him a specific question about the property or the investment and he ignores you, hands you a beautiful four-color twenty-eight page brochure, and starts talking about tax shelter. (If he hands you a brochure, you're in luck. Forget about the investment and take two of the brochures. They should appreciate 200 percent!)

The rule with "Big Brother" investments, as with all investments, is always to investigate carefully. Know exactly what the expert is going to do for you, and how much what he's going to do for you is going to cost you. Be sure he's doing something for you that you're unable to do for yourself. Be absolutely certain that what he's doing is worth what it's going to cost. Syndicators have been known to have arranged for enough front-end, middle, and back-end expenses (usually in the name of tax shelter!) to eat up all of the profits.

The "Whole Life" Life Insurance Investment————

The average middle-class person, whether he understands what he's buying or not, buys life insurance. Nothing is more sacred in middle-class life than life insurance. And nothing is more bewildering than sitting across a table from a life insurance salesman.

The agent talks about what would happen to your family if "God forbid, you are removed from the scene," and presents you with a wide variety of insurance plans, none of which you or he understands, with the exception that he fully understands his commission schedule. He presents you with computer run outs and indecipherable policies until you give up and buy.

After all, you need to have insurance, and it all costs about the same, you suppose.

If that's what you suppose, you're wrong again. The insurance industry has come up with a bewildering array of different types of policies, all with different names and all with different prices. Nevertheless, they can all be broken down into only two types: whole life insurance—sometimes called cash value life insurance—and term insurance.

In reality, there is only one type of insurance—term insurance—because the other type, whole life, is just term insurance plus a savings account.

Term insurance is so named because it is written for a specific number of years, usually five. It's the least expensive type of insurance to buy, especially in a policy owner's early and middle years when the need for insurance is greatest. It becomes more expensive in the later years when the need for a lot of insurance is questionable.

Term insurance is a certain sum of money wagered by the insurance company against an event happening, in this case your untimely demise. ("Untimely" is defined by the insurance company as during that period of time, or term, for which they have you insured!) The insurance company bets that they will take in enough in premiums, and that they can make enough money by investing those premiums before you die, that they can afford to pay off your survivors, and still make a profit.

As to your part of the wager, your self-interest gets more than a little bit confused. You're supposed to put up a sum of money, called your insurance premium, which you bet against the house (the insurance company) that that certain event, namely your departing this life early, *will* happen while they've got you insured.

Term insurance is pure insurance. And although your insurance company will probably disagree (vehemently!), term insurance is all the insurance you really need or want, knowing as you do that you are capable of saving and investing on your own.

Whole life is the other kind of insurance available to average middle-class people. It was dreamt up in the middle of the last century and is promoted by your insurance company as being not only insurance, but a "safe and sound investment idea." Your insurance company's claim that whole life insurance is an *investment* is the sole reason we're discussing it here.

The basic idea behind whole life insurance, sometimes called cash value insurance, is to combine a savings plan with your term insurance. In this way, the insurance company is able to collect the term insurance premium plus an additional sum (usually substantial!) which they agree to hold for you as a savings account. Their argument for providing you with this method of forced savings is that you don't have the gumption to save and invest for yourself.

In later years, their rationale continues, when the rates for the term insurance portion of your whole life premiums increase substantially, you can pay the same premium amount for less insurance and have the savings account that you've built up in the policy act as the rest of the insurance policy. (This is your own money, mind you! The insurance company no longer has much, if anything, at risk!)

There is a major advantage to whole life policies which probably won't impress you very much, but they do pay the insurance salesmen a much larger commission—often 70 percent or more of the total amount of your first year's premium.

It is clear from their promotions that insurance companies don't like term insurance. Unlike the whole life policies, term insurance does not produce big surplus cash reserves for the insurance companies to invest for their own benefit.

My point is, why give the insurance companies your money to invest in real estate and other sound investments for their own benefit, when you can invest the same money and get as good a return as they do, and keep it for yourself? The obvious key difference here is that in the latter case, you come out much farther ahead.

If you can develop the self-discipline and the willpower to save and invest in your own investment program, outside of and completely separate from the insurance company, and if you can keep your hands off of your savings or investment capital, you and your survivors will be much better off. You can, and probably should, still protect your investment with one of the insurance company's less expensive term insurance policies.

The two charts on page 81 show graphically the advantages of buying decreasing term insurance and investing the difference, as opposed to buying whole life insurance and letting the life insurance companies decide how much interest your money is worth.

CASH VALUE INSURANCE

$100,000 $100,000

Cash value
(your money)

Decreasing term insurance

Age 25   Age 70

Large Premiums

TERM INSURANCE

∞

$100,000

Value of investments
bought with insurance
premium savings

Decreasing term insurance

Age 25   Age 70

Small Premiums (invest the difference)

IRAs (Individual Retirement Accounts) ————

A plan to encourage saving and investment, and at the same time help out the ailing savings and loan industry, is tax-free IRA (and Keogh) accounts. In allowing and promoting these accounts, I think the government may also be trying to soften the blow of admitting to the bankruptcy of the Social Security system by allowing average middle-class people to establish their own personal retirement funds.

  Under the IRA plan, you're allowed to invest up to $2,000 a year in one of these accounts or $4,000 for a family with two income earners. The money invested is deductible from the present year's income tax and is allowed to accumulate interest, tax-free, until the depositor retires.

  IRAs need not be limited to savings accounts in banks or savings and loans. They can be investments in money market funds, insurance annuities, mutual funds, credit unions, and self-directed brokerage accounts—which include almost any investment vehicle available. Furthermore, as far as the IRS is concerned you can change your IRA account from one investment to another whenever you want.

The institutions you invest with may not be so lenient. Some institutions promoting IRA accounts have stiff fees, brokerage commissions, and maintenance assessments. Some banks, savings and loans, and some credit unions have penalties for early withdrawal. The major problem with all of these accounts is that you cannot withdraw your money from the accounts, in most cases, until you are a minimum of fifty-nine and one-half years old. If you do, you're subject to tax on your initial investment, a tax on all of the interest the account has earned, plus a 10 percent penalty. This problem at the moment is potentially greater for twenty-five-year-olds than for fifty-eight-year-olds.

The savings and loan industry, of course, loves the IRA idea. It advertises that young savers, by adding to their accounts each year, can retire at the age of sixty-five as millionaires—a meaningless title when inflation is taken into account! One of the assumptions behind the IRA plan is that the taxpayer will be in a much lower tax bracket when the money is finally drawn out.

But, is it really a good idea for young people just starting out to dump their excess funds into a non-liquid IRA account? Wouldn't they actually be better off to save that money and use it as a down payment on a home to live in? They could buy a home now, live in it, enjoy it, improve it, and sell it in a few years at a profit. If they buy another home within two years of the time they sell their first home, the entire gain is tax-deferred. The law does not require that the entire profit from the first house be put into the new home. If the young couple can arrange for a low down payment on that next home, any excess tax-deferred profit that they have in cash could be used to buy a rental property.

By utilizing a very simple gimmick in the tax law called an exchange, a similar tax-deferred program of trading up can be started with the investment properties. A young couple who did this several times in their lifetime would probably exceed the return on any IRA account; be millionaires several times over when they retired (if even that means anything by that time!); get a one-time forgiveness of taxes on a portion of the gain (presently $125,000) on their primary residence; and be taxed at much lower capital gains rates on the remainder. And they would have had the enjoyment of the homes, the security of more liquid investments, and the satisfaction of having done it all themselves. We'll discuss a similar plan in more detail in Chapters 8 and 9.

Another consideration about IRA accounts is that in some states IRAs may be tax-free only as far as the federal income tax is concerned. Some states do not consider the initial money put into these accounts or the income they produce to be free from state income taxes, if the participant is also enrolled in a retirement plan at his work. While this may not be a problem right at first, in later years it could become one. If the accounts begin earning substantial sums, the tax could become painful. It would have to be paid for from earned income outside of the IRA plan itself. Be sure to check your state tax policy toward IRAs before investing.

Ding-Dong Tax Avoidance Schemes

Quite a number of the investments that you come in contact with are what I call ding-dong tax avoidance schemes. In these schemes, the promoter is the bell ringer, making beautiful music in the form of commissions. The investor is usually both the bell and the clapper. First, he often clobbers himself in the head by spending more money out of his pocket, hoping to avoid taxes, than he would have if he simply paid his taxes. Second, he occasionally rebounds to find that the IRS has disallowed his deduction because they find the whole promotion to be a sham. The promoter promises you riches and help in avoiding paying your taxes, but, in most cases, his schemes distinguish themselves as being only plain vanilla lousy investments.

I was recently approached by an accountant selling a research and development project which promised to give me a first-year write-off that was five times as large as the amount of money I invested with him. The idea was to invest in a new computer manufacturing company which, as my research determined, was not established enough to go public on the stock market and not a good enough risk for a straight commercial loan.

I was to be given the opportunity to invest $20,000 of my own money and sign a note for $80,000, allowing the computer company to get the $80,000 from the bank in my name. I would then get to write off $100,000 from my income tax because the money was being used for research and development. In a 50 percent tax bracket, the $100,000 write-off would have been worth $50,000 in actual, after-tax cash savings. In other words, I would invest $20,000 to save $50,000 which I would otherwise have to pay in income tax—a $30,000 profit.

Basic to the scheme was the fact that the note would not come due for five years when, according to the accountant, the computer company would be up and running and would pay off the note for me out of its profits. Of course, if the company was not up and running in a profitable fashion in five years—well, it was left to me to figure out who would get to pay off the note (plus the accumulated interest)!

Another popular tax shelter scheme, I understand, that was being promoted in the Midwest recently was to buy precious gems from a promoter one year for, say, $5,000. These same gems would be appraised by the same promoter a year later for $50,000. The plan called for the investor to give the gems which he had bought for $5,000 to a charity, using the appraiser's value of $50,000, and then take a charitable gift tax write-off of $50,000 on his income tax. In a 50 percent tax bracket, that tax write-off would be worth $25,000, or five times the $5,000 the gems originally cost. I understand the IRS has disallowed the deductions of the investors who tried to claim them under the guise of this precious-gem sham.

I personally think that investments that are sold strictly on the basis of being tax shelters stink. Whether it is or not, the concept of creating a loss for the sole purpose of saving on taxes seems counter-productive, if not just downright stupid and dangerous. I've been exposed to a lot of tax shelter investments, and I've come to the firm belief that you can't really live a productive investment life by searching out counter-productive investment ideas. I'd much rather participate in an investment that has the potential of making some real money—understanding that no one ever went broke making a profit—even if I had to be prepared to pay taxes on that profit. Of course, if you can get tax shelter as a side benefit to an otherwise sound investment, as in real estate, so much the better.

*   *   *

Now to answer the questions you've been asking yourself throughout this chapter.

"If he's so down on investments and investment promoters, what is he doing writing another investment book? Why does he think he's so smart? And why should I think his ideas are any better than the ones he's been knocking?"

Aha! I've got you there. The whole purpose behind this book, and the reason it's called *The Park Avenue Money Diet*, is that I'm trying to offer you a practical approach to living as an *economic person*. My plan goes way beyond the simple presentation of another warmed-over investment strategy. I believe in:

- Owning Real Property
- Personal Accounting
- A Prosperous Mental Attitude

Stick with me, Sweetheart. This is really the most meaningful investment book you're ever going to read.

The What's My Best Investment? Quiz

Okay, now, you've read about most of the major types of investments commonly offered to middle-class investors. But reading isn't going to reduce your susceptibility to a good investment pitch. You're going to have to practice what I'm preaching to you. When faced with an investment choice, you are the only one who will be able to decide whether to buy or not. So take this quiz and see how you do with real investment problems and in real investment situations which require some financial understanding.

If you get more than three wrong answers (including the trick questions), go back to the beginning. You must have been watching a TV movie while you were reading the last twenty pages, instead of paying attention. Just kidding. Actually, this next test is designed to give you a pinch of essential information which every investor should be aware of when considering different investment proposals.

1. Assuming you intended to withdraw your money after one year, which investment gives you the best return:

    a. $1,000 invested in a money market fund at 12 percent
    b. $1,000 invested in a certificate of deposit at a savings and loan at 12 percent
    c. $1,000 invested in an IRA account at a savings and loan at 12 percent

2. If you are in a 30 percent tax bracket, a $1,000 tax deduction is worth _____ in actual after-tax cash to you.

   a. $1,000
   b. $1,300
   c. $ 300

3. What is a "front-end load"?

   a. A heavy piece of equipment attached to the front end of a tractor
   b. A fee charged up front to an investor by a syndicator
   c. A stock dividend

4. Which is worth more?

   a. $1,000 given to you today
   b. $1,000 given to you in six months
   c. $1,000 given to you a year from now

5. What is worth more?

   a. $1,000 earned in the form of a capital gain
   b. $1,000 earned as ordinary income
   c. $1,000 received as an inheritance

6. Compared to term insurance, whole life (cash value) insurance premiums cost _____ times as much, in the early years of the insured, for the same dollar value of insurance.

   a. Two
   b. One and one-half
   c. Three to six

7. The best way to avoid losing money in the stock market is by:

   a. Technical analysis
   b. Charting
   c. Staying away from it

8. In the Hindu religion, the poor are rewarded for their obedience and complacency with the promise that they will be rewarded and that the rich will be punished, later. *Later* refers to:

   a. Later this month

   b. In a couple of years

   c. In the poor person's next lifetime

9. Which tax deductible expense leaves you with the most cash in your pocket after taxes?

   a. Property taxes

   b. Interest payments

   c. Cost recovery (depreciation)

10. Who can best determine the course you should follow to your own financial independence?

   a. Your stockbroker

   b. Your mother

   c. Yourself

The answers:

1. One thousand dollars invested in a certificate of deposit. If you invested the $1,000 in a money market fund, you would earn the same 12 percent, but you would have to pay a fee to start the account, as well as a yearly management fee, both of which would affect your nominal 12 percent rate of return.

    If the $1,000 were invested in an IRA account, you could actually end up losing money. If you withdrew your money at the end of the year and you're not fifty-nine and one-half years old, you would be subject to a federally mandated 10 percent or greater penalty. (That's not counting any penalties the institution you invested with might impose!) If inflation were any greater than 2 percent, you'd end up in the red.

2. The after-tax cash value of the $1,000 deduction to someone in the 30 percent tax bracket is $300. This points out a fallacy in some investment promotions which suggest that you spend $1,000 simply because it's tax deductible. You'd be better off to pay the $300 tax on the $1,000 and keep the $700 difference.

3. Of course the answer is the up-front money which compensates the syndicator for his efforts in raising the funds to put the project together. A 10 to 20 percent fee is common and fair. Anything above that is approaching the "hog line." Anytime you are approached by someone selling shares in a limited partnership investment, for tax-shelter purposes or otherwise, ask about the "front-end load," the "back-end load," the management fees, and the commissions due the promoters. Whatever is left after these deductions will be the portion of your investment which will work for you.

4. There is always time value to money. A dollar today is worth more than a dollar tomorrow. This is because if you had the dollar today, you could put it to work earning interest. Also, any dollars you receive after today will be worth less because they will have been reduced in value by whatever the inflation rate for that period of time happens to be.

5. If you receive $1,000 from an inheritance, you get to keep the whole thing. The taxes have already been paid on it. It is what remains of a larger sum from which your benefactor's estate may have had to pay an estate tax.

    The $1,000 earned in the form of a capital gain is tax-free for the first $600, or 60 percent of the gain. The remaining 40 percent of the gain, or $400, is added to the rest of your ordinary income for the year and is taxed at whatever tax bracket that total puts you into. If, for example, you are in a 30 percent tax bracket, the tax on the $400 is $120. So out of the $1,000 capital gain, you get to keep $880.

    The $1,000 dollars you earn from ordinary income is taxed the hardest. The whole $1,000 is subject to tax. In a 30 percent tax bracket, you'd pay out $300 to Uncle Sam, leaving you only $700 after taxes. In addition, your ordinary income may be subject to Social Security taxes, which both capital gains income and inheritance income are not.

6. Believe it or not, it's three to six times as expensive to pay the premium on whole life insurance in the early years as it is for term insurance.

7. Buying stocks in the stock market is one of the purest forms of gambling available to the average middle-class person outside of the casinos in Atlantic City and Las Vegas. Don't be taken in by the hype that you, the "little guy off the street," are a participant in economic democracy, or the backbone of our country's capital-raising mechanism.

Instead, listen to the insiders' back room whispers.

"Pay attention to 'the little guy off the street.' He's always wrong. What would we do without him? When we're ready to bail out, he's there to buy. When the market has bottomed out, he's ready to sell."

8. About the best the poor Hindu serf is going to get is a reward in his next lifetime. This philosophy of quiet suffering is a part of many religions and is partially responsible for keeping ordinary people in their places.

9. In a 50 percent tax bracket, a $1.00 deduction for any actual out-of-pocket expense like property taxes and interest costs you $1.00 to save $.50 on your taxes. After paying taxes, you're $.50 behind. A $1.00 deduction for cost recovery or depreciation is a paper write-off. It actually costs you nothing out of pocket, but still saves you $.50 in taxes; so you are a full $.50 ahead after paying your taxes. Your cash-in-hand difference between a $1.00 property tax or interest write-off and a $1.00 write-off for cost recovery or depreciation is, therefore, $1.00.

10. Good for you. It's yourself, of course.

CHAPTER 5

NICE PEOPLE DON'T TALK ABOUT MONEY

My financial education was characteristically average and middle class. None of my school classes ever really addressed themselves to money matters, other than as part of one of those apples-and-oranges math problems. I do remember my parents preached about thrift as being a good thing ("a penny saved is a penny earned" and the like), and they did insist on the importance of my working hard to make money. Other than that, it seemed the prevailing rule when talking about money was, "The less said, the better!"

There were, however, two major financial episodes in my early life.

The first of these occurred when I was about nine or ten years old. My mom and I went to the Mahopac First National Bank to open up my first savings account. The lady at the desk told me how wonderful it was that a young person like myself would think to open a savings account. (I pretended it was my idea!) She told me the bank was going to pay me 3 percent interest. I didn't think that sounded like a whole lot of interest, but I signed the papers, deposited three dollars, and sheepishly walked out of the bank with my first passbook in my pocket.

It was three years later when I learned the lesson of this financial event.

I guess I wasn't totally convinced that saving money was any better than spending it, and not being asked to do anything different, I never added any more money to that savings account. I withdrew my three dollars several years later when I was in junior high school. The principal plus the years of accumulated interest amounted to $3.25.

I never was much for putting my money in savings accounts after that.

The second major educational financial event in my young life occurred when I was a freshman in high school. My father decided that it was time I had some experience with the stock market. He offered to put up some money, and I was to buy two stocks: one that he would pick, and one of my own choosing. His idea was to show me the difference, as he saw it, between "investing" and "speculating" in the market.

He picked U.S. Steel as my "Blue Chip" stock from the New York Stock Exchange. I knew U.S. Steel was a big company and it appeared to both Dad and me to be a good conservative selection.

I had problems choosing my second stock. I decided to pick one from the American Stock Exchange, but after looking, I didn't recognize any of the company names. Eventually, I put the stock tables from the financial section of the paper on the dining room table, closed my eyes, and pointed. My finger landed on a cheap little stock called Thiakol.

Several weeks after we'd bought the stocks, the Russians launched the world's first satellite, *Sputnik*, and the space race between the USA and the USSR began in earnest.

Thiakol was the first company to make a solid rocket fuel. Our rocket scientists had been using liquid fuels, with disastrous results. After *Sputnik*, they decided to switch to solid fuels. As a result, Thiakol took off and climbed like one of the rocket ships it propelled. It ascended for the next twelve months, going from $30 a share up to $120 a share. Then it split two for one.

After the split, I had two shares of Thiakol. Those shares went from $60 a share back up to $120, and then those shares split three to one. I ended up with six shares of Thiakol worth $40 each, a total on paper of $240.

I couldn't believe it. This was my speculation stock. It could, of course, have gone either way. Or it could have gone nowhere! But this was better than anyone could have anticipated. Dad began to speak of me as his son, "the stock market wizard!" I was heartily congratulated by everyone who heard of my good fortune, although when I was asked, I was hard pressed to explain the system I'd used to choose the Thiakol stock. Still, I immodestly accepted all of the accolades.

For my part, on school days I couldn't wait for study hall so I could go to the library and check out the daily newspaper. On weekends, I would wait with anticipation for the family's trip to church and Robusto's General Store, where Dad would get his weekly copy of the Sunday *New York Times.* In each case, I'd go right for the financial pages and look up my stocks to see how much money I'd made.

It was great fun . . . until the competition in the solid rocket fuel industry caught up with Thiakol. I *think* that's what happened; I don't know for sure. But the price of my Thiakol stocks leveled off, burned out, and began tumbling slowly back to earth. I didn't know it right away, but my luck with the stock market had run out. I should have sold right then, but watching those shares of stock had been such a sensational experience, I couldn't bring myself to sell until almost a year later, when the price had splashed down at around $15 a share.

Like all gamblers, I kept waiting for my lucky streak to come back. Winning a little wasn't enough. I wanted my stocks to go back up again. I was disappointed.

Perhaps the worst upshot of my first stock market speculation was: I attempted to relive the Thiakol stock market experience several times in later years, and ended up losing *my own* money. I lost money even with what my stockbrokers and I considered to be good stocks that had been carefully researched.

In case you're wondering, the U.S. Steel stock just sat there and boringly paid me a few nickels in small quarterly dividends. I don't think the price of U.S. Steel moved more than a couple of points in either direction for the two years I held it.

That was about it for my early financial education. I don't remember being taught anything else about money until I went off to college.

Perhaps it's because middle-class people think they are pretty well off . . . at least compared to the huddled masses in, choose one: China, Bangladesh, or Appalachia; or maybe it's because they don't expect to ever have much money; or, most likely, it's because they don't know much about money themselves; but as parents and teachers they are allowing something essential to be left out of their young peoples' education. Don't allow the same fate to befall your kids! Give them each their own personal copy of this book, and see to it that this book becomes required reading material in your local schools!

My venture into the stock market was not the actual end of my financial education. I took a required beginning accounting class at Texas Lutheran College. Compared to the liberal arts classes like Art History and English Literature that I was accustomed to, accounting was a really hard, no-nonsense, practical course. It was actually the toughest class I took in college.

In this accounting class we were supposed to learn about the nature of, and how to account for: assets, liabilities, and net worth; income and expenses; profits and losses. In addition, we had to learn about paradoxical little buggers called debits and credits. We also had to do a lot of math, and unfortunately, the teacher had the only adding machine. The students had to do their math with only the aid of pencils and paper. The math presented a major problem for me. I never was any good at it!

I was so confused by the mathematics of accounting that practically everything else in the course escaped me. I quickly found myself in danger of failing my first college course. In desperation, I committed myself to a crash program of asking fellow students for help and apple polishing the teacher. I really earned my D for the semester.

Mathematics scared me away from the business school for the rest of my years at college. I avoided the place like it was a porcupine "in heat."

It was a full ten years later, after I'd come into receipt of what seemed, at first, like more than my share of money, that I decided I needed to know more about business, accounting, and money management. I settled down to the task of learning about finances on my own.

My problems with mathematics might have stopped my pursuit of financial knowledge again, but by this time the microchip revolution had made it possible for me to own a miracle—a little hand-held calculator with a tape printout. With it my math improved remarkably.

This little machine could add, subtract, multiply, divide, and even do percentages! All of a sudden I no longer had to be concerned with drawing funny shaped things, or carrying numbers from one place to another, or any of that confusing stuff. All I had to do was know how to push a few keys (in the right order!) on a calculator. The answer I was looking for would automatically appear . . . *every time!* I could forget about my math and concentrate on figuring out what debits and credits and all that other accounting stuff was all about. (As it turned out, none of it was all that tough to understand . . . once my math problem was solved!)

If these miraculous little gadgets had been around when I was in school, I might even have become a business major and started on my road to wealth much earlier. But that's another "what if," isn't it?

Enough about me. The important thing now is to get you started. By the way, do you have a calculator? If not, put the book down right now and go get one.

The Money Life-Style Truth-or-Consequences Quiz

All right now, I caught you—skimming ahead to the following chapters of the book, looking at the charts and graphs and pretty pictures, wondering if you can skip ahead, trying to weasel your way out of the lesson. Well, it's not going to work.

In the final chapters of *The Park Avenue Money Diet,* we are going to set up your own Ten Year Real Estate Investment Schedule, your Personal Accounting Process, and give you the guidelines for establishing your Prosperous Mental Attitude. *The Park Avenue Money Diet* is going to be your salvation from the middle class—so if you don't want out, well, that's another problem. Get your fingers out of the back pages of the book and take this project one step at a time. Okay?

You guessed it. Before we really get down to the nuts and bolts of your *Park Avenue Money Diet,* you have to take this little commitment quiz. It should be of value to you. It'll show you something about your personal commitment and your self-knowledge, or lack of it, regarding your present financial position and your potential for achieving future wealth. You'll see where your insides stand as compared to your outsides. It will point out your sense of purpose, or alert you to your lack of direction—and that may be something you're not conscious of right now.

As an average middle-class person, you probably think you know where you're headed when you point yourself toward your job each morning and when you walk toward the television room each evening and each Saturday and Sunday afternoon. The quiz you're about to take describes, in the form of questions, a few of the things you should be doing to achieve self-direction and financial independence. If you find that the following are not what you are doing or thinking now, get ready to consider making some changes.

Because you *think* you've been headed in some self-prescribed direction, you may be tempted to discount the importance of doing those thing that would really put you on a positive superhighway to self-direction and financial independence. You may feel that you'll have to dismiss your score for this quiz as being inaccurate. Your ego may demand it. Ignore the little guy. I want you to keep an open mind. To see yourself as you really are.

So here we go with the next quiz. Get rid of that pencil you've been twisting in your fingers and grab a big heavy pen. (Perhaps you could get a chisel and engrave your answers to this one on a slate of granite!)

1. As of this moment, do you participate in a regular program directed toward achieving your financial independence?

    a. Yes.
    b. Tell me more.
    c. No.

2. Given the choice of reading a book about money or a detective novel, do you:

    a. Read about money.
    b. Depends on the book.
    c. Read the detective novel.

3. If you have a chance to go to a first-run movie or a business or investment seminar, do you:

    a. Go to the seminar.
    b. Depends on the movie and the seminar.

     c. Go to the movie.

4. Do you make a list of the six most important things you have to do each day and concentrate on accomplishing those before doing anything else?

     a. Yes.

     b. Sometimes.

     c. No.

5. Do you take time each day to take account of yourself and think prosperous positive thoughts?

     a. Yes.

     b. Are you nuts?

     c. No.

6. When was the last time you took some time off to rejuvenate and rededicate yourself?

     a. Recently.

     b. My last vacation.

     c. A long time ago.

7. Have you written down your monetary and material goals for the next twelve months, the next two years, and the next five years?

     a. Yes.

     b. I plan to do that later.

     c. No.

8. Have you written down a list of successful people in your community and made plans to meet them?

     a. Yes.

     b. I'll do that later.

     c. No.

9. Are you willing to make a directed effort to achieve wealth, doing whatever is necesary to achieve it?

   a. Yes.

   b. What do you have in mind?

   c. No.

10. Are you prepared to form the specific habits necessary to achieve your financial goals?

   a. Yes.

   b. I'm not a creature of habit.

   c. No.

11. Do you have faith in yourself and your ability to deal with your future?

   a. Yes.

   b. Maybe.

   c. No.

How To Score:
All **(a)** answers are worth 5 points.
All **(b)** answers are worth 3 points.
All **(c)** answers are worth 1 point.

45–55 Points

You're off to a good start, and I predict great things for you. You are preparing for a bright future, and you're taking care to move in the right direction. You're willing to take risks. You have a prosperous and positive mental attitude, and you have faith in yourself and your ability to deal with whatever comes your way. You've got the confidence of a person with a plan. Keep reading; perhaps you'll pick up a few more ideas, good habits, and pointers for directing your efforts to help you achieve your financial independence.

15–44 Points

Your life seems to have a general direction to it, but that direction is not as clear as it needs to be to achieve financial independence. It's my guess that you work hard—probably too hard. It's amazing you have the strength to lift this book. You get tired in the afternoon, work too long without enough time off for yourself, and you're a little fuzzy about your goals. You need to believe in yourself and your abilities to deal with your future. You'll want to fine-tune your mental attitude and those goals of yours so that they acquire the hypnotic, warming qualities of diamond blue flames.

10–14 Points

If you're not already doing it, sit down. I want to break this to you gently, because I've got something to tell you that you probably don't want to hear. You're in a lot of trouble, and you're headed for a lot of detours and aimless circles in your life. You're somewhat spoiled, very lazy, and terribly unimaginative. Your idea of planning is leaving the covers pulled down on the bed when you get up in the morning so that you can get back in quicker that night. You'd better memorize this book and begin following my instructions if you ever want to do more than just dream about the day your ship will come in.

What's Your Excuse? ⎯⎯⎯⎯⎯⎯⎯⎯⎯⎯⎯

"I've thought about investing and setting monetary goals to achieve financial independence, but I haven't been able to stay interested in the idea. There are just too many distractions and more interesting things to do."
— *The Average Middle-Class Financial Survey*

A common feeling of people I've talked to, as well as people who returned my survey, is that financial matters are a real drag, not the least bit entertaining. Entertaining, isn't that great? What do they want, balloons and party hats? I can fully understand why many people look upon financial matters—accounting, investing, tax planning, etc.—as a grind. But I happen to think that working at a job I hate for years and years, simply to collect my retirement; being constantly over my credit limit; alcoholism; and being average and middle class are also a grind.

As for being boring—all things can be boring. Even being alone with yourself can be boring. And you know where being bored leads you—right to the shopping center, the TV, the bottle of bourbon. You'll do a lot better being bored in a goal-oriented financial and investment program than without it. And I guarantee you'll like it better after awhile.

"A friend of mine who first got me interested in planning my financial future told me that, in his opinion, I was not really bored with financial matters, that I was really afraid of being successful, and that's what keeps me from planning my future. I think he's probably right."

Not planning for your own future because of fear of success is probably an all too common and reasonably good apology for how you got yourself stuck in the middle class, but it's still just an apology.

If once you've given it a try, you find you still need reinforcement or encouragement, why not try to get some support from your average middle-class friends and neighbors?

Try Starting an Investment Group

Planning with other people is a way to overcome the fear, the boredom, and the imagined drudgery you may at first experience with planning your financial future. It's a means of sharing common experiences, problems, and new ideas. It's stimulating, motivating, challenging, fun, and an excellent way to get an investment club started.

"I called up a buddy once and asked him if he'd like to come over and look at an investment I'd come across. He called another friend, who called someone else, and that's how the group got started. Several times a week, the four of us meet after dinner and go over investment opportunities, new investment books, accounting problems, and investment strategies. We've bought a number of investments together. To tell the truth, financial planning has become such an important part of my life now, I miss it on the nights we don't meet."

"I'd love to do some financial planning and set some goals, but I can't. I'm just so busy."

This torn and tattered apology reappears every time you think about doing something you don't want to do. Have you ever met anyone too busy to take a half hour coffee break, to gossip about a fellow worker, or to watch a rerun of *The Graduate* on the afternoon movie? Of course not. No one is ever too busy to do what he wants to do. And because you don't want to plan for your financial future, well, you'll come up with almost any justification. Folks who use the "I'm too busy" excuse generally back up their excuse with reasons that are supposed to make everything all right. This method of rationalizing convinces them that they are doing an adequate job of planning and are getting the proper amount of goal orientation as part of their busy day.

"I spend all my waking hours thinking about my job."

"I have to spend several hours a day commuting, and I do my planning then."

"I have a car pool three days a week, and we're always talking about business."

"I cook, clean the house, and run everybody's errands. When am I going to have time to waste on a goal-oriented investment program?"

"It's a big enough job to take care of my company's business. I'll leave it to the company to take care of me."

Every one of those apologies is shortsighted. Unless you are a real estate broker, an accountant, or a lawyer who sees a lot of good investments, or unless you come across good investments or moneymaking opportunities on a regular basis, the work you do to make a living and the life you live are not giving you the preparation you need to be able to achieve financial independence. If you use the rationale that your everyday activities or the company you work for will make you rich—don't skip a word of this chapter.

What is important for you to realize is:

1. You have to schedule time for the important things in your life, and your own personal financial planning is one of those things.

2. Goal-oriented investing and self motivation can make your busy day even more productive.

It's all a matter of organization. If you plan your day properly, I'll bet you there's an hour each day that you could use to plan and motivate yourself to financial achievment. There may be more.

Make a schedule of your time so you can get a good look at how you're programming your activities each day. Write down your daily activities, obligations, or roles in this space.

Get up

Breakfast

Lunch

Dinner

Go to Bed

Now compare your list with the one I've made for you.

Sleep	8 hours
Eat (1/2 hour each for breakfast and lunch, and 1 hour for dinner)	2 hours
Shower, brush your teeth, and get dressed in the morning	1/2 hour
Work	8 hours
Commuting time	1 hour
Free time (TV, recreation, walk dogs, go to the doctor, etc.)	3 1/2 hours

That's a total of twenty-three hours. You still have an hour a day left in which to plan your financial future. Believe me, if you worked on your finances for only one hour a day, you'd be wealthy in no time! And you'd have done it all yourself.

If you lose that hour somehow, make it up by not watching one situation comedy on TV. Get up half an hour earlier, go to bed half an hour later. Work for yourself on your lunch break. Cut that thirty-minute telephone conversation fifteen minutes short. You can make time for the important things in your life, can't you? You know you can.

Are You Getting Your Share?

It's apparent that there are an infinite number of theories about how to make it rich in this world. Otherwise, there wouldn't be so many investment books available. There wouldn't be the enormous number of experts whose business it is to teach you their methods. Needless to say, I have my own theory. If you've been introduced to the majority of the investment programs we've discussed so far, and none of them has appealed to you, or made any money for you, or even returned your original investment, you're probably wondering how I'm going to offer you something sensible that works.

Well, here it is, *The Park Avenue Money Diet* that promises extraordinary wealth for ordinary people. It's a three-part program, with each part being important to the success of the others. The sum of all the parts equals your escape plan. You will now begin to make some real money by developing a vision of your future financial independence, finding out where you actually stand financially today, keeping track of your financial progress, and maintaining a mind-set that will guide you unerringly towards a more prosperous life.

What You Can Expect While On
The Park Avenue Money Diet _____

Each and every one of us who was brought up to be middle class and average was taught not to expect a great deal out of life. If you do something nice for somebody and you don't get a thank you or a reciprocal kindness, you're supposed to smile and feel good about having done a good deed. You are taught to believe your reward will come later . . . perhaps in another lifetime. If you don't "expect anything," you will avoid being disappointed, and anything that comes in your direction will be a nice surprise. In some cases, that way of thinking may be acceptable, but on *The Park Avenue Money Diet*, you should expect a lot . . . and you will be rewarded in your expectations if you follow the program correctly. I'm sure you're asking yourself all of the usual questions: "What can I expect if I follow this program, how quickly will I see results, and when will I be wealthy?"

The time periods projected for collecting the fruits of various investment programs vary. Some promise to double your money overnight, or suggest that you'll be able to retire in six to twelve months. On the other hand, the savings and loan industry guarantees to make you a token millionaire with a new IRA plan—if you and your spouse can afford to make deposits of $4,000 a year for thirty years, and wait thirty to thirty-five years to make a withdrawal.

But what about *The Park Avenue Money Diet*? If you follow my Ten Year Real Estate Investment Schedule, do your accounting, and train yourself to think rich, you will see results. Don't worry about how fast those results will take place. There are a number of variables that will affect your program. You've been treading the economic waters for a long time now. The longer you've gone without any real personal financial successes, the more quickly you will notice the changes. Still, don't become a clock or calendar watcher. Try to be patient.

The First Month: This is the most difficult time you will spend on *The Park Avenue Money Diet*. Much will be new and different, and you will be faced with a lot of study, some planning, a few mental attitude exercises, and several major decisions. You will begin to concentrate your efforts and form habits that will eventually lead to your achieving financial independence. You will begin keeping careful detailed records of your progress. At the end of the month, or soon after, you will sign a contract to purchase your first income-producing residential rental investment property. Once you get through this month, you will have created the basic material of your *Park Avenue Money Diet* for achieving wealth. You'll also experience a feeling of pride in the fact that you've made it so far. If all goes well, you will be on your way to making it to the end of the program. If it sounds complicated now, don't worry. I'm going to take you through it, step by step.

The Second Month: You will fight a number of battles with a very painful affliction called *decision maker's remorse*. It's a form of self-doubt that affects everybody who has just committed himself (or herself) to a major decision, especially a financial one. You'll ask yourself, "What have I done? Am I crazy?" Don't be surprised when it hits you, because it will hit you. After all, you will have made some major changes, and it may take a little while for you to get your bearings and feel secure again. You will have taken some risks. You'll probably be facing some negative cash flows common to the early years of owning most income-producing investments. At the very least, you'll literally be facing the unknown. Just remember, decision maker's remorse hits everybody who ever makes a major decision. You can handle it, because you're going to be prepared for it. Relax. Everything will be all right. You'll look back very soon and wonder what all the panic was about.

Your accounting of your personal finances will begin putting you in control of your financial situation. You'll experience a new feeling of self-control, which will help you overcome whatever obstacles might be placed before you, including your battles with decision maker's remorse. You will continue the process of forming habits and directing your efforts toward more profitable, moneymaking activities. You will be forming the mental attitudes which will guide you unerringly towards your financial independence.

The First Year: Equity will have built up in your first income-producing residential rental property, and you'll probably be preparing to buy another.

You'll have a clear picture of your present, past, and future finances; and you'll have developed the confidence that money and self-knowledge can give you. Because you have prepared your mind to see them, once-in-a-lifetime moneymaking opportunities, which you've been missing up to this point, will be popping up every week and a half or so. Your mental attitude will have changed. You'll be thinking about yourself and the world around you differently. It will be as though you were looking at your world from a higher, more knowledgeable plain. You will have acquired an air about you of someone who knows something others around him don't know. You'll quite literally be a new person.

The Tenth Year: Your present and your future are secure. The blueprint for continued success is laid out in front of you. You will feel very good about yourself and your ability to continue to chart your own course; and you'll be providing wonderful things for yourself and your family. As your wealth increases, you will notice that people treat you with deference and respect. You will be living the life you prepared yourself to live.

Unfortunately, you may also be experiencing a bit of jealousy, and maybe a cold shoulder or two, from (former?) friends. It's one of the ways members of the middle class have to accept and justify their own mediocre lives. They'll remind you of all the namby-pamby things you've been missing since you escaped, and remind you of where you came from. Your resolve will be strengthened never to go back.

C H A P T E R 6

WHAT IS WEALTH?

The only true measure of wealth or poverty, even today, remains the historical one . . . the ownership of real property. Recent published reports seem to infer that there is a new yardstick for measuring wealth and poverty: income. But income is an incomplete and inaccurate measure. From the dawn of recorded time to the most recent past, wealth has always been entered as the amount of real property a person owns.

It is true that societies have differed in their definitions of real property. Real property has been variously listed as a man's wives (the chauvinists!), one's cattle, one's gold, and one's real estate holdings. But the varying definitions notwithstanding, in all cultures, and at all times, the wealthiest people have always been the people with the most real property.

Being poor, on the other hand, has traditionally been defined as having little or no property. By that standard, average middle-class people are uncomfortably close to being poor.

Middle-class people sometimes own their own homes, but they usually own little else of lasting value. The income of average middle-class people does not normally come from the real property they own. Their primary source of money is the income they derive from personal labor. Income derived from personal labor is more susceptible to interruption or loss than is income from property. It can be lost overnight as a result of layoffs, incapacitation, or even a simple change of attitude on the part of the income producer.

If there is one thing that distinguishes money-class people from average middle-class people, it's the ownership of real property. Real property gives a person prestige. It creates wealth. It produces income. It provides tax shelter. It appreciates in value. Real property can be used as collateral for borrowing, or it can be sold to produce capital income. It can make a person financially independent all by itself, or it can be the financial springboard to accomplish almost anything else in life one wants.

Most present-day fortunes were either made in, or are presently being held in, the form of real property. Real property may be the only way people can easily acquire substantial wealth of any kind today. Ninety percent of all people who accumulate an estate of $50,000 or more, either in the form of cash or equity, do so by owning real property. And that real property is their homes.

Retirement

Many older people are able to retire today only because they own their homes free and clear. The amount of Social Security or pensions average middle-class people receive at retirement would not allow many of them to survive if they had to make large mortgage payments or pay rent.

Some older citizens must sell their homes and use the proceeds from the sale to subsidize whatever income they get from other sources. Even if this means they have to rent, they can at least be thankful they were provident enough to buy a home when they were younger. Imagine if these older citizens had had the providence to acquire additional investment properties.

Their retirement years would look much brighter, wouldn't they?

But that's the last we're going to be talking about retirement as part of *The Park Avenue Money Diet*. The insurance company's actuarial tables on people who retire are too depressing. Instead of retirement, we're going to talk about a program that could keep you busy and interested, and living, well past the time you would normally retire from your everyday employment. Instead of retirement, we're going to talk about a program to achieve "financial independence."

Before we start, be sure you have that handheld calculator you went out to get a while back, several sharp pencils, and a pad of paper. Go ahead. We won't start 'til you're ready.

The first thing you are going to do is plan to find, and sign a contract to purchase, a piece of income-producing residential rental investment real estate within thirty days from the day you finish reading this book. Let's define income-producing residential rental investment real estate as either a townhouse, condominium, single family house, duplex, triplex, fourplex, or a multi-unit apartment building.

Hold on now. Put down the phone. We don't want to get your real estate broker all excited just yet. There are a few things we should discuss before you buy your first building. We want to be sure you get the highest possible and the safest possible return on your investment.

Residential Rentals—The Basics

Why are we going to concentrate on residential rentals? A combination of six elements in the income-producing residential rental package make it the outstanding investment vehicle today.

Leverage

Leverage is the first key to making big profits in investing. Do you remember when you learned about leverage in your high school physics class? You learned that a lever is like a seesaw. If you put a big rock on one end of a seesaw and push on the other end, the seesaw will rotate around a point in the middle that it rests on, called the fulcrum. The lever lifts a rock that you might not be able to lift if you were to walk around the seesaw and try and lift the rock all by yourself. It at least makes the task easier. The lever multiplies your strength, allowing you to do much heavier work than you could do without it.

In buying real estate, the typical investor uses a financial lever which allows him to purchase much larger pieces of real estate. In real estate, the lever we use is borrowed funds, and the investor's strength is equal to the money the investor has to invest, plus the amount of money he can borrow to use as a lever. If an investor had $20,000 and were to attempt to buy, let's say a house, with only the strength of that $20,000, he could only buy a $20,000 house. (Lots of luck finding one!)

If, on the other hand, he could get a loan for $30,000, he could use that $30,000 as a lever which, in addition to his $20,000, would multiply his strength and let him buy a $50,000 house. In effect, his $20,000 is able to do two and one half times as much work with the $30,000 lever as it could do without it.

Another thing about levers is, the longer they are, the more weight they can lift. For instance, an $80,000 lever would let an investor's $20,000 lift a $100,000 investment.

The more borrowed funds an investor uses in proportion to the amount of his own money he invests, the more the property he buys is said to be leveraged. It is possible to leverage a property to the tune of 100 percent or more. If a property is leveraged 100 percent, the investor doesn't put any of his own money into the property and, if the property is leveraged more than 100 percent, the investor can take cash out of the deal when he purchases the property.

Purchasing an investment with nothing or less than nothing down requires creative financing techniques and is often tempting. But remember, investors have often gotten themselves into big trouble using levers this large. The major risk involved in using really big levers is that they often have a tendency to snap if the load they're attempting to lift is too large.

Appropriate sized levers differ from one investment to another and from one investor to another. I'm going to suggest some arbitrary sized levers for you. On average, the lever limit (the loan size) for a new investor should be no more than 80 percent of the investment's purchase price, with the investor investing no less than 20 percent of his own funds (the down payment).

Perhaps you've heard that the best way to buy investment real estate is with 10 percent down, or less. You may think 20 percent down payments will cramp your style, especially after you see the third chart in Chapter 9 of this book. Once you feel comfortable with the rules of the game, you might want to put less than 20 percent down, but in no case do I want to tell you to attempt to purchase a property with less than 10 percent down.

The reason for these arbitrary lever lengths is simply for your own safety. It is normally true, as you'll see in Chapter 9, that the more heavily a property is leveraged, the greater the potential return for the investor. However, properties that are heavily leveraged often become what is commonly referred to in investment circles as alligators (more recently as Pac Mans!). The mortgage payments on heavily mortgaged properties can eat you up alive.

If you find a property you can invest in for less than 20 percent down, a yellow caution flag should drop down in front of your eyes. Not a stop sign, mind you, just a caution flag. Investigate carefully to see that the property you're interested in is worth the price being asked. You will often find low downs on properties that are overpriced. You will also find opportunities for low down payment purchases on properties that have defects, or on properties which for some reason are hard to sell. You don't want to purchase someone else's headache, do you?

But, if you can determine that a property with a low down payment (or any sized down payment, for that matter!) is well priced—that is, priced at market value, or below—that it can be rented at reasonable rates, is not located downwind from a stockyard, does not have a leaky roof, corroded plumbing, or a rusty hot water heater, go ahead and buy it.

To summarize (and as a very general rule): you will normally find that the lower your leverage . . . that is, the more of your own money you put down . . .the less your potential profit will be, but at the same time, the safer your investment should be. If you put less money down, your potential profit will be greater, but (at least right at first!) your investment might be somewhat less secure.

Let's Try Some Math

It is normally possible to get at least 80 percent of a rental unit financed. In other words, you get a loan to cover 80 percent of the property's value, and you put up your own cash to cover the remaining 20 percent. This means that you only have to put down (or up) $10,000 on a $50,000 piece of property. Follow these calculations through on your calculator:

$$\$10,000 \text{ divided by } \$50,000 = .20 \text{ or } 20\%$$

$20,000 on a $100,000 piece of property,

$$\$20{,}000 \text{ divided by } \$100{,}000 = .20 \text{ or } 20\%$$

$30,000 on a $150,000 piece of property,

$$\$30{,}000 \text{ divided by } \$150{,}000 = .20 \text{ or } 20\%$$

and so on.

If you can arrange to only put down 10 percent, you can control a $50,000 piece of property with only $5,000,

$$\$5{,}000 \text{ divided by } \$50{,}000 = .10 \text{ or } 10\%$$

a $100,000 piece of property with only $10,000,

$$\$10{,}000 \text{ divided by } \$100{,}000 = .10 \text{ or } 10\%$$

and a $150,000 piece of property with only $15,000.

$$\$15{,}000 \text{ divided by } \$150{,}000 = .10 \text{ or } 10\%$$

As you will see, the more leverage you have, the greater your potential return—providing, of course, you use common sense and avoid leveraging yourself into bankruptcy and the property into foreclosure.

The Government Encourages Ownership of Income-Producing Residential Rental Properties —————

The present tax laws overwhelmingly favor income and profits derived from the ownership of real property, when compared to the way they treat income earned from personal labor.

Investors are given substantial government subsidies to own residential rental properties. These include tax write-offs for actual out-of-pocket expenses, including: interest on the mortgage payments, utilities, maintenance, management, property taxes, and insurance payments. With investment real estate, the government allows you tax benefits through ownership by allowing you to deduct your expenses from your ordinary income. Not only that, but if you know exactly what you're doing, and if you buy the right kind of property, you are not asked to pay any income tax on the cash flows from the property you invest in.

This is because the investor gets to write off an amount from his income taxes each year for depreciation or, as it's more recently been called, cost recovery. The cost recovery expense, or depreciation, costs you no money out of pocket, but it does allow you to pay less income tax. Cost recovery compensates the investor for the annual loss in value the property theoretically suffers. In reality, providing the property is well maintained, and to the extent the property doesn't actually depreciate, but rather appreciates, or remains constant in value, the cost recovery deduction is a freebee. It's simply a paper write-off. Cost recovery is a tax incentive for investors that compensates them for owning rental properties and suffering whatever risks, high interest rates, and negative cash flows they may experience in the early years of ownership.

Since it costs you nothing, cost recovery is the major and perhaps the only legitimate tax shelter element in most real estate investments. Cost recovery is what allows you to take positive cash flows from the property, if you do it right, without paying taxes on them. To the extent your cost recovery deduction is not used up by the property's positive cash flows, it can be used to offset taxes you would normally pay on your ordinary income. We will talk more about cost recovery later. If you use it correctly, it's wonderful stuff—the icing on the investment cake.

Note: If you own real property and have excess deductions from that property which you can carry over and apply against your ordinary income from salary, you may legally claim extra dependents to the extent of those excess deductions. When you claim extra dependents, you can have your employer reduce the withholding tax deducted from your paycheck each week. That way you can take advantage of your deductions immediately, rather than waiting 'til after April 15 to get the money in the form of an income tax refund.

The extra cash generated by the withholding tax reduction can be a source of extra funds to cover any negative cash flows you may be experiencing from the operation of the property.

Exchanging

If you want to dispose of your property sometime down the road, you can do so without paying any taxes at the time of transfer by using a maneuver in the tax law called an exchange. If you exchange for a like-kind property that is larger, one that has a bigger mortgage, and which accrues greater benefits to you, you will not have to pay any capital gains taxes on the transfer. Those taxes are deferred until some point in the future when you sell.

The exchange procedure is much simpler than it sounds. You don't have to trade your property directly to the person who has property you want to own. Most exchanges are three-way exchanges, which are as easily arranged as simply selling one property and buying another.

The first thing you do is find a property you want to own. Then you find a buyer for the property you already own. You arrange for the buyer of your property to momentarily take title to the new property you want to trade into, and then exchange it with you for your old property. The result is, the seller of the property you want to own ends up with the cash from the buyer of your first property. You get the new property you want. The fellow who originally started out with the cash ends up with your original property. The only rules are easy ones to follow. Your *intent* has to be to effect an exchange, and the closing transfer papers have to do some fancy acrobatics at the title company.

You benefit from a tax-free exchange because the tax on your profit is deferred. You can buy a much larger piece of property than you could if you had to use a part of your equity to pay the taxes on your profit. Thus you are able to accrue much larger benefits in the form of tax deductions, appreciation, and potential income from the new property.

Capital Gains

When you sell your investment property, you should be able to pay taxes on any profits at capital gains rates. To get capital gains treatment, an investor must hold his investment for at least a year and a day. Capital gains rates are a lot lower than ordinary income tax rates. Capital gains income is taxed on only 40 percent of the gain. The other 60 percent of the gain is tax-free.

If at any time you—the investor—want some of your equity in cash, either when you sell or at the time you exchange one of your properties, you pay capital gains taxes only on the profit portion of the equity you withdraw.

A SIMPLE EXCHANGE

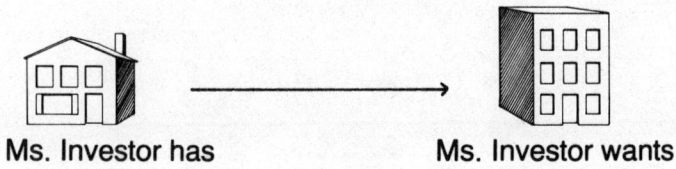

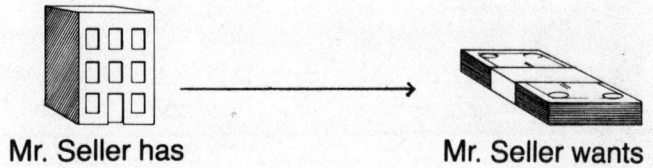

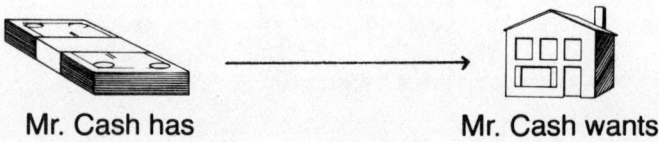

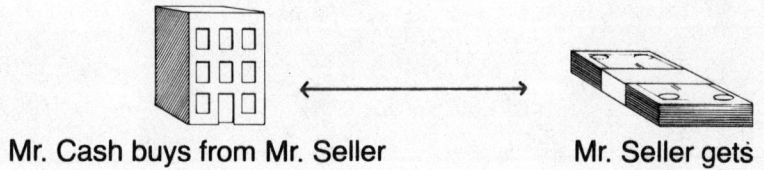

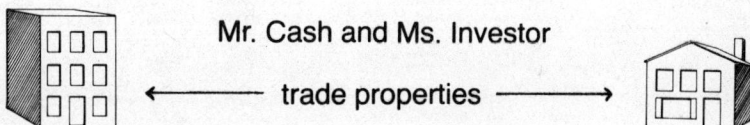

Ms. Investor has → Ms. Investor wants

Mr. Seller has → Mr. Seller wants

Mr. Cash has → Mr. Cash wants

Mr. Cash buys from Mr. Seller ↔ Mr. Seller gets

Mr. Cash and Ms. Investor
← trade properties →

Note: If you never sell, your heirs inherit the property, and all of the back capital gains taxes on the appreciated value of the property are wiped out.

For the sake of comparing the capital gains tax with ordinary income tax, if you earn $20,000 of ordinary income at your regular job, and if you have no offsetting deductions, you have the privilege of paying income taxes at approximately an average rate of 30 percent, which amounts to $6,000 on an income of $20,000.

$$\$20,000 \times .30 = \$6,000$$

Taking the $6,000 away from the $20,000 leaves you $14,000 after taxes.

If, on the other hand, you made $20,000 profit by selling a rental house or a corporate stock which you'd held for at least six months and a day, you would only have to pay income taxes on 40 percent of the profit, or on $8,000.

$$\$20,000 \times .40 = \$8,000$$

The tax on the $8,000, if the taxpayer paid taxes at an average rate of 30 percent, is only $2,400.

$$\$8,000 \times .30 = \$2,400$$

Twelve thousand dollars, or 60 percent of the $20,000, is tax-free.

$$\$20,000 \times .60 = \$12,000$$

This $12,000 added to the $5,600 remaining after capital gains taxes on the $8,000 leaves you $17,600 after taxes.

So, if you pay taxes on your ordinary income at the average rate of 30 percent, and if you paid ordinary income tax on the $20,000, you'd have only $14,000 left after taxes. However, if you had a capital gain and paid capital gains tax on $20,000, you'd have $17,600 remaining after taxes. You can see why rich people like you and me will always attempt to collect as much of our income as we can in the form of capital gains.

(That's as hard as the math is going to get in this book. It's not too hard if you use your calculator, is it?)

Collateral

You can sometimes borrow against the equity in your property, have your property make the loan payments for you, and pay no taxes on the loan proceeds until sometime in the future, if or when you decide to sell.

Income

Since its name implies it, income-producing residential rental property should produce income. Ideally, a property produces enough income to cover mortgage payments, utilities, maintenance, management fees, property taxes, and insurance payments. Realistically, you probably won't have a break-even situation in most properties right away. It's not uncommon to have a negative cash flow situation during the early years of your ownership of a property. After a time, the rents should be able to be raised to the point where the property begins to break even.

When, as eventually will happen, your property starts to make more income than is needed to cover its expenses and mortgage payments, some of the tax shelter benefits of cost recovery will have to be used to protect the positive cash flows from income taxes. Less tax shelter will then be available from the property to protect other personal income.

Perhaps you're thinking that that doesn't sound like a major problem, since money you get from your investment property looks, feels, works, and needs shelter, just as much as the money you take home from your job. You may be right. But sometimes investors don't want additional cash flow from their investments, because it pushes them into higher tax brackets. The point where the property starts throwing off positive cash flow is the point where they start looking for that tax-deferred exchange in order to start accruing larger tax shelter and appreciation benefits.

Appreciation

Appreciation should really be one of the subtitles of *The Park Avenue Money Diet*. Appreciation is the ultimate benefit we will be looking for in the Ten Year Real Estate Investment Program. Appreciation is the rose which will bloom, radiate, and create your wealth.

Note: We ought to take a moment at this point to differentiate between inflation and appreciation. We hear a lot about inflation on the radio, on television, and in the newspapers. It's on everybody's mind. Inflation or the threat of inflation affects many things, from the price of gasoline to the cost of food.

Inflation is totally beyond our personal control. Fortunately, inflation is only one factor affecting appreciation, especially when we're talking about income producing residential rental properties.

Things can appreciate even if there is only slight general economic inflation. The overall inflation rate might be 5 percent, but a particular piece of real estate might appreciate at the rate of 10 percent, 15 percent, or more, due to such things as supply and demand; finding and purchasing a property below market value; a change in management, which could affect occupancy rates and/or stimulate rent increases; location; a zoning change; interest rates; or any number of factors.

A whole lot of things other than inflation can, and usually do, affect a property's appreciation rate. Some of these you can control, such as finding and purchasing a property below market value; cosmetic changes; or changing a property's use to a higher and better one, such as converting an apartment building to a condominium. Some, like the effect of higher or lower interest rates, you have no control over.

Safety

If you are conservative in your purchases; buy market value; select location, location, location; and are reasonable in your demands for leverage, thereby lessening your potential for large negative cash flows, income-producing residential rentals are comparatively safe investments.

Pride of Ownership

Real estate has the pride of ownership market cornered. If you don't believe me, ask yourself this question: would you rather show your friends and neighbors a picture of your four-unit apartment building, or a picture of your investment in pork bellies? If you're not sure, have your commodities broker send you a Polaroid snapshot of one of those pork belly beauties.

Note: A word of caution is in order at this point. Don't get too carried away with the pride of ownership benefit. As you'll see in a couple of pages, the Ten Year Real Estate Investment Schedule is predicated on your ability and willingness to move your equity, from time to time, out of a smaller property and into another one which is larger and which has greater benefits accruing for you as an investor.

I've seen several investors start out on my program for financial independence, fall madly in love with their first residential rental, and forget that their original intent was to become wealthy. That situation calls for a variation on an old joke. When you find yourself up to your neck in waterlilies, it's sometimes hard to remember that your original objective was to drain the pond.

Mid-Chapter Summation

There is no other investment, business opportunity, or what-have-you, which offers you as sweet a packaged deal as the one you can get by owning residential rental real estate. You can't get a prepackaged deal like this by opening a liquor store, a frozen yogurt shop, or a video game arcade. This complete combination of advantages is not available in the stock market, or in an oil and gas limited partnership tax shelter. And nothing similar can be had by putting your money in a savings account.

Let's Try to Compare the Incomparable _____

Are you still skeptical?

Okay, take a moment with me to compare the many advantages of income-producing residential rental real estate with a few of these other investments. I'm pretty sure you'll find the others lacking.

Savings Accounts

Take an ordinary savings account at a bank or savings and loan. First, what you put into your savings account is what the bank pays you interest on. You get no leverage when you invest in a savings account.

Second, a savings account offers you no tax shelter. The interest you receive is taxed at your ordinary income tax rate. This means that if you pay taxes at a marginal rate of 30 percent, and you earn 12 percent on your savings, you really only earn 8.4 percent after paying the taxes on the interest you earn.

Check the math.

.12 (or 12%) × .30 (or 30%) tax rate = .036 (or 3.6%) for taxes.
Then, 12% - 3.6% = 8.4% remaining.

Next, you have to consider the effect of inflation. Inflation works against a savings account, because the money you invest depreciates in value with inflation rather than appreciates. A dollar today is worth more than a dollar tomorrow.

Let's continue to work with the above example. If the inflation rate is 7 percent per year, you must subtract 7 percent from the 8.4 percent you make after taxes, leaving you only 1.4 percent per year on your invested dollars on a 12 percent savings account.

$$8.4\% - 7\% = 1.4\%$$

Taking into consideration inflation and taxes, in the above example, if you made much less than 12 percent on your savings you would end up in a negative position at the end of the year.

And finally, there's not much pride of ownership in a savings account, unless, of course, you're really kinky.

Raw Land

A savings account is probably too obviously an inferior investment. But how about an investment in land? Land has the potential for having all of the benefits that you find in residential rental properties, except for two major differences. The first difference is income. In most instances, raw land produces no income at all. When income is derived from land, it is usually limited to agricultural activities, which are seldom profitable on a small scale. Therefore, any expenses incurred, such as interest and property taxes, are generally paid for out of pocket.

Secondly, the tax law does not allow you to depreciate, or recover, the cost of land. Land is indestructible; hence, non-depreciable. And what is the only true tax-shelter benefit of owning real estate? Right! The cost recovery expense, because it costs you nothing out of pocket. Therefore, residential rental property is better to own than land, at least from that tax standpoint.

Don't misunderstand me. You can make a lot of money by owning land. But your largest profits usually derive from effecting a change in the use of the land. Such changes may come either by subdividing a property, getting it rezoned, or making it available for a more profitable use in some other way.

Once you've effected a change and increased the land's value, your challenge often is to get the land sold before property taxes are increased and gobble up your profits. You might be lucky enough, however, to own a piece of land and have a developer want to move a major shopping center in on top of you. The appreciation in land can be considerable, but it's a bigger gamble than income-producing residential rental property.

Commercial Property

Shopping centers, office buildings, medical buildings, etc., are less beneficial than residential rental properties for three reasons. First, in commercial property you're usually dealing with longer term tenant leases, making it somewhat harder to raise the rents to reflect current economic conditions.

Secondly, although you can depreciate, or recover the cost of, a commercial property exactly the same way as you do residential rental property, there is a provision in the tax law that treats the recapture of depreciation on commercial and residential rental properties differently. On commercial property, if you use the most beneficial method of cost recovery when you sell the property, all the depreciation you've taken over the years must be recaptured at ordinary income tax rates instead of at capital gains rates. When you use the same beneficial method of depreciation on residential rental properties, only a portion of the depreciation must be recaptured at the higher rates. Most of the recapture on residential rentals is treated at capital gains rates.

Finally, during periods of economic downturn the rate of business failures increases. Businessmen tend to abandon marginal businesses that are losing money during a recession. This means that commercial properties often lose their weaker tenants. In comparison, people always need a place to live. The last thing most people give up in a recession is their homes. And since residential rental construction is generally weak in a recession (contributing to a tight market!) the demand for residential rentals usually remains strong!

Stock

How about the stock market? Theoretically, an investor can make a profit in the stock market. He can make money in stocks in two ways. The stock can provide dividend income, which is treated the same as interest income for tax purposes. The stock can also go up in value and make him a profit. If the investor buys a stock that increases in value, and if he holds the stock for at least six months and a day before he sells it, he would get long term capital gains tax treatment on that gain.

If the stock goes down in price, and if it's held for six months and a day, the investor has a long term capital loss. He can deduct half the amount of that loss from his income tax.

In either case, if the stock were held for less than a year and a day, the investor would have a short term capital gain or loss. Short term capital gains are taxed as ordinary income, and short term capital losses cannot be used as deductions!

Note: The rules for long and short term capital gains apply in exactly the same way to real estate. The only difference is that the chance for a long term loss is considerably less likely for a sensible investment in real estate than in the stock market.

Stocks do not have any of the other tax benefits or tax shelter aspects of income producing residential real estate; and you cannot defer the tax on stock profits by exchanging them. You can get leverage in stocks by buying on margin, but you can't get anywhere near the leverage that you can in real estate.

Oil and Gas

Practically every dollar invested in an oil and gas limited partnership or joint venture can be written off as intangible drilling costs. After the tax write-offs, you either lose everything, or you strike oil and take your percentage share of the profits. But your odds are variously estimated at 9 to 1 and 13 to 1 against hitting a well with commercial potential.

Starting a Business

If you are knowledgeable about a given business; if you think you have a different way of filling a particular need; if you've invented that better mouse-trap, you might do better in that business than in income-producing residential rental properties. In most cases, it's probably a bigger gamble than you'd be taking with residential rental real estate!

Tax benefits for starting a new business come in the form of deductions for expenses incurred. You also get investment tax credits, and depreciation write-offs for equipment, which are to compensate you for the actual depreciation of the equipment you will experience. You get no real tax shelter like that afforded by the cost recovery expense in *appreciating* real estate, unless, of course, your business somehow involves the purchase of real estate.

Overall, your chances for achieving financial independence are probably better with income-producing residential rental properties than in starting a new business. If your ultimate dream is to launch some new business venture, you might want to consider establishing some capital in a real estate investment program before launching that business. This strategy might keep you from the fate of so many small businesses which are started and run on shoestrings, most of which fail within two years.

When you compare, I believe you will always find that income-producing residential rental properties are incomparable.

CHAPTER 7

INVESTING IN RESIDENTIAL RENTAL PROPERTIES IS A BUSINESS

How to Select the Right Property

I want to touch briefly on how to locate the best residential properties for investment. Finding the best buy for your investment dollar is a lot like hunting for pearls in a pile of oysters. You'll have to pry open a lot of shells before you'll find a treasure.

It has been my experience that properties which have proven to be poor investments in the past have in common one or more of the following characteristics: (1) poor location, (2) overpriced, (3) overfinanced, (4) excessive deferred maintenance (with inadequate funds set aside to cover it), (5) underestimated operating expenses, and (6) overestimated income.

In seeking out a prospective residential rental property, it is helpful to have a check list of requirements which must be met by the property. You must be in a position to turn down any and all properties which do not meet your criteria. There are five critical elements which you must consider if you expect to locate the pearls: (1) location, (2) condition of the property, (3) price, (4) terms, and (5) physical design.

Location

The location of your property must be desirable. Location will determine the quality of the tenants your property will attract. Location will also be the determining factor assuring you that there will be a demand for your property when you're ready to sell or exchange it.

How do you decide which location is best?

Look at the neighborhood. Does it appear to be in a state of deterioration, or is it prospering? Is the street free from debris? Are the surrounding buildings suffering from deferred maintenance? Are the lawns manicured? Are cars jacked up or sitting on blocks in the street? Bear in mind, you're buying a neighborhood along with your building; so take a good look around.

Most tenants and prospective buyers will be drawn to properties which are in close proximity to such attractions as shopping centers, freeways, schools, and colleges. Is your property situated in or near a growth area? Is it in an area of declining population? How close is the subject property to sources of employment and entertainment?

As a paramount rule, it is a good idea to search out the worst property in a good neighborhood rather than buying the best property in a poor one. You can always upgrade a poor property to the standards of the neighborhood and thereby increase its value. The value of the best property in a poor neighborhood will always be adversely affected by its neighbors and lose value.

You should make a rental survey of the area as well as a comparable market analysis of the subject property. It is important to know what similar properties are rented for and what comparable properties are listed and selling for. Drive through the neighborhood. Make a list of any properties which may have "For Rent" or "For Sale" signs.

Check with local realtors. Ask them to get the information you need. Much of the information you're looking for can be pulled up in minutes on your realtors' MLS computer. Call a local property management company and ask if they manage any properties in the area. Ask if they know of any other properties in the area which might be rented, and if so, could they direct you to the owners. Ask what a comparable two- or three-bedroom house might rent for. Ask them about rental rates and market values. Ask for their most forthright professional opinion of the neighborhood.

Don't overlook the opinions of the neighbors. Knock on ten or twenty doors around the subject property. Stop at "For Sale" signs. Tell the owners or tenants who come to the door that you're considering buying in the neighborhood and ask if they'd mind if you asked them a few questions. I've found that most people are glad to offer their opinions when asked. You must recognize that much of the information gained from homeowners, especially those in the process of selling their homes, and from tenants, while sincere, may be less than objective. Nevertheless, some good insights into the pros and cons of neighborhoods can be gleaned this way. Finally, go to the city planning department and ask what is planned for the area.

If after careful study you sense that your property is in a good location, go on to the next step.

Condition of the Property

If you've set your sights on a used building, spare no amount of effort and expense to inspect everything in and about the property. Unaccounted for and unplanned for deferred maintenance can throw your investment profitability projection way out of whack. In order to bring objectivity to the matter, you might want to seek out the services of a licensed building contractor or a certified property manager. Ask them to inspect the building and report their findings to you. Have them estimate the cost of correcting any problems. Their inspection services will likely be rendered on a fee basis. Whatever the cost, it will be money well spent.

Never underestimate the cost of recarpeting; repairing or replacing a roof; repainting; rejuvenating the landscaping; repairing the plumbing, heating, and cooling; replacing broken windows and screens; and so on. It is important that your property be in good shape if you're to command top rental rates. The price negotiated for the property must provide for the costs of implementing any of the above repairs and improvements, and the cash required must be considered. An $80,000 building requiring $8,000 down but suffering from $5,000 in deferred maintenance becomes an $85,000 building requiring $13,000 down unless negotiated otherwise.

Price ————————————————————————

It might seem like I'm waxing a never-wax floor to stress the need for negotiating the purchase of an investment property at the right price; however, the long term consequences of paying too much for an investment are so great, and the problem is so common, that I'd be remiss in not emphasizing such an obvious requirement.

You must establish a price in conformity with a comparable market analysis, comparable rental rates, and an objective investment analysis. Don't accept the seller's estimate of value without your objective appraisal. Never accept the seller's past income and expense figures or his estimate of future income and expenses without evidence that those figures are correct. Always ask to see utility bills, tax bills, insurance bills, and maintenance records. If you still have questions, hire an appraiser and get a professional opinion. Compare the appraiser's estimate of value with the information you've gathered independently.

Once you've determined the price you're willing to pay for a property, stick to your guns, irrespective of the demands of, or perks offered by, the seller. The desirability of the property, its location, or even the attractive financing being offered can seldom make up for paying too high a purchase price. Many buyers have paid too much for a property because of attractive terms which seemed too good to be true.

Paying too much for an investment is usually the result of inexperience. Be extracautious in this area, especially if this is your first investment. It is always more prudent to walk away from a negotiation which is not going your way than to get stuck with a deal you can't live with.

Remember ... when you're out there looking ... once-in-a-lifetime opportunities seem to come along every two weeks or so. If you miss this one, catch the next one.

Financing

The lure of purchasing a residential rental property with a low down payment with its resultant high leverage has proven to be the downfall of many investors. As was mentioned in our discussion about leverage, it is true that a well priced, heavily financed building carries a high profit potential. But heavy debt service also carries with it a higher risk that the property might fall into receivership. High payments along with unexpected or unplanned for expenses have often spelled foreclosure for imprudent investors. A slush fund savings account may be the hedge you need.

Physical Design

Look for properties which will make sense to prospective tenants and to future buyers. Most families with children will require three or four bedrooms, and one and three-quarters to two baths. It is best to stay away from two- and five-bedroom homes or homes with only one bath or a one-car garage. The market for those oddball homes is limited.

Energy efficiency is an important consideration. Check the quality and quantity of the insulation. Check out the number and size of the windows. Inquire about the efficiency and location of heaters and hot water tanks. All of these considerations can add to or detract from the attractiveness of your property as an investment. If you are interested in multiple units from duplexes on up, find out which of the utilities are master metered (example: one gas meter for all the units). The owner can count on paying for any master-metered utilities. With individual metering, utility expenses may be payed for by the individual tenant.

There Will Be Exceptions

The aforementioned criteria are generally accepted norms throughout the real estate investment community. Everyone of them should be considered before buying any real estate investment.

I want to point out, however, that if all there was to making a good investment was following a check list, a computer could do it. Other criteria which are very important and which should be considered are your instinct for value, your willingness to act, and your sense of timing.

A fair number of good residential properties will fall into the outer limits, and even outside, of the aforementioned criteria. It may not always be necessary to look only at first-class properties or even only in first-class neighborhoods. You can even profit from oddball properties.

To illustrate, let me share with you the unvarnished, real world details of my first multi-unit apartment complex.

As was mentioned in Chapter 1, I managed to accumulate enough equity to purchase my first large apartment complex several years after launching my real estate investment program. It was a twelve-year-old, twenty-nine-unit building consisting of mostly one-bedroom units in Oklahoma City. It was purchased for $290,000. I put $29,000 down. The seller carried the remaining $261,000 on a note. Like a beginner, I jumped in with both feet. I didn't make the thorough investigation or the sort I've just recommended. The price and terms on the property seemed just too good to turn down. I was afraid I'd lose the deal if I waited.

As a result, I found myself making some adjustments in my thinking along with some adjustments in my budget. I had planned to repaint and recarpet the units, which I did. I didn't plan to have to make two major roof repairs, rewire most of the units, or make several major plumbing repairs. Neither did I expect to find out that the project was on the Oklahoma City Police Department's list of places to keep under close surveillance. This apartment complex seemed to attract a rough class of tenants, making it difficult to collect rents and keep the units leased.

The property maintained a healthy negative cash flow the entire time I held it. Once the reserve I'd set up to cover contingencies was gone, I found myself supporting the property monthly out of my pocket. Billie and I found that we had to put off a number of other goals we'd planned in order to support our investment. Nevertheless, I was eventually able to sell the building for $450,000 . . . a substantial profit after two and a half years, even counting the negative cash flows. Looking back now we both agree that this was probably one of the best investments we ever made.

I simply want to point out with this story that the generally accepted rules which I outlined above may be overly cautious in some situations. Investing, like life, is a dynamic process. You may create your greatest rewards by breaking the rules occasionally. You're seldom going to find the perfect property which will meet all of your requirements. Problems will come up even in the best of situations. Sometimes one or more of the positive factors about a property, along with your faith and ability to deal with whatever problems arise, will outweigh many negatives—even unexpected ones.

Management Can Be a Problem

I love real estate. I take a great deal of pride in the properties I own. I get very excited about what real estate has done in creating my family's estate. But purchasing real estate investments has meant committing myself to a lot of work and worry. It's a lot like raising kids. It may not be the easiest investment in the world, but it's one of the most rewarding.

Not anticipating the management aspects of owning residential rentals is the most common reason investors lose interest in real estate. Investing in residential rental properties is a business. It must be treated like a business. Day-to-day problems must be solved. Your manager (if you have one) must be kept happy. Your good tenants must be kept satisfied. Your problem tenants must be dealt with. Accurate records must be kept. Budgets must be made and followed. Income and expenses must be carefully monitored. The property must be maintained and should be continually upgraded. Attention must be paid to every detail of the business, and care must be taken to see that the business runs at a profit.

Professional Solutions

Some people have a knack for managing properties. They're good at making repairs. They can handle the paperwork. They're able to deal with tenants and resident managers on an effective person-to-person basis. You may be one of those people. You'll never know until you try. I tried, and I can tell you . . . I'm not one of those people!

The way I solve most of my management problems is to avoid them. I turn the day-to-day operation of my properties over to professional management companies. I've used management companies almost from the day I started. I've always figured that the 5 to 10 percent of gross income which these companies charge is money well spent. The use of professional management leaves me free to use my time more profitability in the areas where my talents lie.

Of course, management companies are not necessarily a panacea. Standards and practices of managers vary widely. Some companies will only deal with large properties. Others will take both large and small properties (i.e., single-family homes, condominiums, duplexes, etc.), but they charge quite a bit more for the smaller properties—usually in the range of 8 to 10 percent.

I learned long ago that even with professional management, it is important to inspect my properties on a regular basis. I question my managers carefully concerning every aspect of the operation. I try to make suggestions for improvement when necessary. On occasion, when major problems have arisen, I have found it necessary to change management companies.

Hang in There _____

It's been my observation that when investors focus on only the short term details and problems encountered in searching for and managing real estate investments, they sometimes forget the long range benefits. Eventually they may decide they'd rather not be bothered. Whenever this happens I consider it a tragedy. Investing in real estate is the last great hope of the average man to share the American Dream and accumulate a fortune. That is, unless or until someone invents the microchip mousetrap!

There are a lot of details to consider in buying and managing residential rental properties. Investing in residential rental properties is not without its problems. I don't want you to get into your own residential rental program and be disillusioned. I don't ever want to hear you say, "Hey, Baumgartner, this looking for good real estate investments is a lot of work." Or, "You didn't mention I'd be getting calls from tenants in the middle of the night demanding that I come over and unplug a commode. Why not?"

Now you're aware that there will be problems and worries with real estate investments as with most everything else in life. You're prepared. You've got some ideas on how to proceed. So, let's get on with our Ten Year Real Estate Investment Schedule, okay?

CHAPTER 8

THE TEN YEAR REAL ESTATE INVESTMENT SCHEDULE

The Ten Year Real Estate Investment Schedule is structured for any level of investor: one with a lot of starting-up funds, or one with a smaller nest of money eggs. Everyone, no matter how much he or she has to invest, begins at the beginning. Everyone follows exactly the same steps. Naturally, the more funds you start with, the larger the properties, and the more cash, equity, tax shelter, and pride of ownership you're going to accumulate.

The strategy behind the Ten Year Real Estate Investment Program is simple. *Sell, exchange, or refinance your property and reinvest your profits in larger properties whenever and as often as it is profitable to do so.* By doing this, you use the proceeds from the smaller properties as the down payments on larger, more expensive, and more profitable properties. With little or no out-of-pocket expense, you are able to dramatically increase the combined benefits of leverage, tax shelter, income, appreciation, safety, and pride of ownership.

That's all there is to it. The plan is simple. It's so simple that only the wealthy and the soon-to-be wealthy use it. This is both an aggressive and a conservative strategy. It contrasts sharply with the passive role played by the traditional real estate investor.

We are going to get into a little more math (groan!) now. You'll get more out of these next two chapters if you'll continue to follow me through with your calculator. I guarantee, once we're finished, you'll be glad you made the effort. All of the formulas are designed in a step-by-step format, and there will be quite a bit of repetition. If you're using your calculator, the way I suggest, it should be easy.

You'll learn how to estimate and project the appreciating values of the properties you buy, how to estimate the value of your equities in those properties, how to estimate the costs of selling (trading up!) each of your properties; and in Chapter 8, you'll see what the effect of withdrawing cash at each sale is, and how to figure and estimate the tax shelter value of the cost recovery deductions you'll be taking on each property. By the time we're through with Chapters 7 and 8 you should have a clear picture of how the Ten Year Real Estate Investment Schedule works. Then you'll be able to set up one for yourself.

What's more, I'll even let you skip the last few calculations in Chapter 8 if you'll stay with me up 'til then.

First, let me tell you that all of the calculations we're going to do involve only the simplest of addition, subtraction, multiplication, and division. Okay, maybe there'll be a few percentages thrown in for good measure. (Don't worry. You and your calculator can handle them!)

The Equity-to-Debt Ratio

From the moment the investor first signs a contract to purchase a piece of property, he establishes his equity position in it. Equity is the value of the investor's interest in the property.

The equity position is not a static position. As the property increases in value, the investor's equity increases. The investor must constantly remain aware of the changing ratio of his equity position in his property to the remaining balance of the loan on the property. This is called his equity-to-debt ratio.

Let's consider a "for instance." (The next few paragraphs may seem just a little bit confusing. If they do, just keep reading. When we get into the following discussion of Casa de Walter, it should all become clear!)

In order to purchase a property, an investor puts some money down and gets a loan to cover the balance of the purchase price. Let's say the investor puts 20 percent down and gets an 80 percent loan for the balance.

$$20\% \text{ equity} + 80\% \text{ loan balance} = 100\%$$

Now let's assume the investor holds the property for one year, during which time it appreciates in value by 10 percent. As the property appreciates, the total appreciation amount is added to the investor's equity side of the ratio. If the property appreciates 10 percent in the first year, the ratio between the investor's equity and the remaining loan balance at the beginning of the second year would be 27 percent to 73 percent.

$$27\% \text{ equity} + 73\% \text{ loan balance} = 100\%$$

Note: Again, if the numbers confuse you at this point, don't worry about them. They'll become clearer as we go along. Just pay attention to the way the investor's equity percentage keeps increasing while the loan balance percentage decreases.

You'll notice that after the first year, the investor has slightly more equity in the appreciated property's value, and as a result, the remaining loan balance percentage decreases. This is because even though we know the value of the property is increasing, the property value can only be expressed as being 100 percent. The ever changing equity-to-debt ratio, then, is simply a division of that 100 percent.

Continuing with our 10 percent annual appreciation rate, after the second year the equity-to-debt ratio becomes 34 percent to 66 percent.

$$34\% \text{ equity} + 66\% \text{ loan balance} = 100\%$$

Now, let's look at an actual case history which uses exactly the same percentages, but with specific numbers. We're going to watch as an investor named Walter projects his equity buildup in an investment property. Then we'll watch him project the effects of a tax-free exchange, which will dramatically increase the value of his property holdings and the benefits which will accrue to him from owning a larger residential rental property.

A $100,000 Apartment Building————————————

Walter, our investor, purchases a $100,000 triplex which he (modestly!) decides to call Casa de Walter. He puts up $20,000 of his own money and obtains a loan from the bank for $80,000.

$$\$20{,}000 \text{ equity} + \$80{,}000 \text{ loan balance} = \$100{,}000$$

or

$$20\% \text{ equity} + 80\% \text{ loan balance} = 100\%$$

Walter holds the property for several years, during which time the property appreciates at an average rate of 10 percent per year.

Note: This doesn't mean Casa de Walter appreciates exactly 10 percent each year. That would be an unrealistic assumption. The appreciation rate will probably vary each year. But just to keep things simple, we'll use the average rate of 10 percent for Walter's calculations.

As we go through this description of the appreciation analysis of Walter's Casa de Walter, it's important to remember that while the value of the *entire* property appreciates at an average rate of 10 percent per year, the total appreciation amount is added only to *Walter's side* of the equity-to-debt ratio. The lender, who loans Walter 80 percent of the property's value at the time it's purchased, receives no benefit from the appreciation (other than more security for the loan!).

The lender's profits come from the interest he charges. The investor's profits come from the property's appreciation.

For simplicity, we will assume that the rental income from the property is sufficient to cover all of the loan payments and all of the expenses. Also, because very little principal is paid off in the first few years of a new fully amortized loan, we'll assume that the loan balance remains constant. (Imagination makes things so much easier! It makes our calculations much simpler, and they'll be almost as accurate!)

When Walter purchases Casa de Walter, his equity-to-debt ratio starts at 20 percent equity to 80 percent debt. (Look familiar?) During this year, the Consumer Price Index is projected to show an inflation rate of approximately 5 percent. But Walter doesn't plan to sit on his buns, just waiting for inflation alone to make him rich. Walter plans to change management, replace some carpet, trim up the landscaping, and raise his rents. Since Walter will improve his property and raise his rents, he feels safe in assuming a 10 percent annual appreciation rate on this property for the first year.

By Walter's estimate, at the end of the first year Casa de Walter would have increased in value $10,000, giving it a second-year estimated value of $110,000. Since all of the appreciation goes to Walter's side of the equity-to-

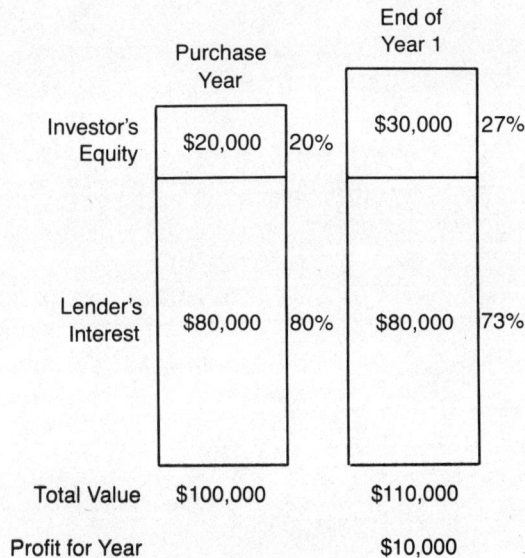

	Purchase Year		End of Year 1	
Investor's Equity	$20,000	20%	$30,000	27%
Lender's Interest	$80,000	80%	$80,000	73%
Total Value	$100,000		$110,000	
Profit for Year			$10,000	

debt ratio, Walter, after the first year, expects to have an equity position in this property of $30,000. Walter's equity-to-debt ratio at the end of the first year becomes 27 percent equity to 73 percent debt. (Notice, these are exactly the percentages in our earlier discussion of the equity-to-debt ratio!)

$$\$30,000 \text{ equity} \div \$110,000 \text{ property value} = .27, \text{ or } 27\%$$

$$100\% \text{ property value} - 27\% \text{ equity} = 73\% \text{ debt}$$

Walter intends to continue to improve his property and raise his rents. During the second year, Walter assumes his property appreciates another 10 percent . . . a total of $11,000 the second year.

$$\$110,000 \times .10 = \$11,000$$

At the end of the second year, Casa de Walter should be worth approximately $121,000. Walter's equity position is $41,000. The equity-to-debt ratio in Casa de Walter, at this point, is estimated to be 34 percent for Walter's equity and 66 percent for debt.

$$\$41,000 \text{ equity} \div \$121,000 \text{ property value} = .34, \text{ or } 34\%$$

$$100\% \text{ property value} - 34\% \text{ equity} = 66\% \text{ debt}$$

At the end of the third year, Casa de Walter is worth $133,100. Walter's equity in the property is $53,100. The equity-to-debt ratio is approximately 40 percent for equity, 60 percent for debt.

$$\$53,100 \text{ equity} \div \$133,100 \text{ property value} = .40, \text{ or } 40\%$$

$$100\% \text{ property value} - 40\% \text{ equity} = 60\% \text{ debt}$$

Here's a complete picture of what Walter expects his first three years of equity buildup in Casa de Walter to look like.

	Purchase Year		End of Year 1		End of Year 2		End of Year 3	
Investor's Equity	$20,000	20%	$30,000	27%	$41,000	34%	$53,100	40%
Lender's Interest	$80,000	80%	$80,000	73%	$80,000	66%	$80,000	60%
Total Value	$100,000		$110,000		$121,000		$133,100	
Profit for Year			$10,000		$11,000		$12,100	

Total Profits for the Three Year Period = $33,100

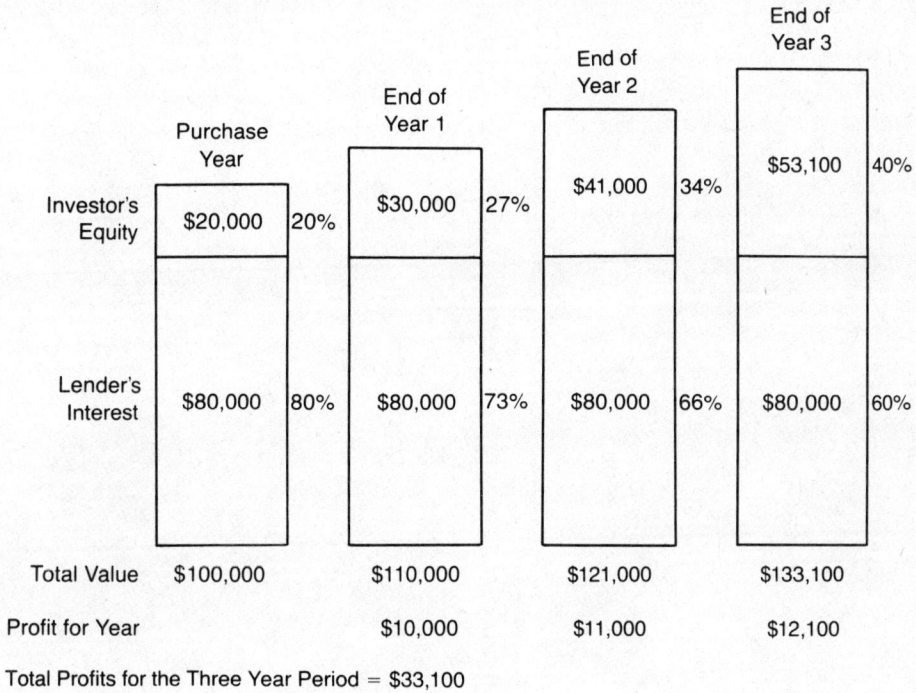

Now Walter has a decision to make. He projects that at the end of the fourth year of ownership, Casa de Walter will be worth $146,410. Walter's equity in the property would then be $66,410. His equity-to-debt ratio will be 45 percent for equity and 55 percent for debt—only 5 percent short of being equal to the bank's percentage in the investment.

$66,410 equity ÷ $146,410 property value = .45, or 45%

100% property value - 45% equity = 55% debt

If all goes as planned, Walter will have made a lot of improvements to Casa de Walter. He will have raised the rents to the point where the apartments will be throwing off considerable positive cash flow. This presents a problem for Walter. His salary income from his job will also have increased, and Walter expects to be in need of more tax shelter . . . not more cash flow!

End of
Year 4

Investor's Equity	$66,410	45%
Lender's Interest	$80,000	55%

Total Value $146,410

Profit for Year $13,310

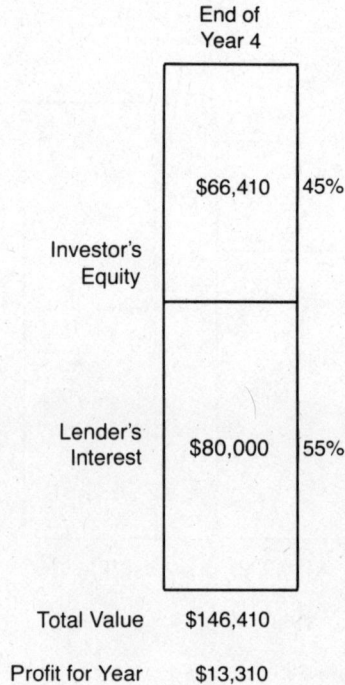

And that's only half the problem. You see, Walter is a tad on the greedy side. He knows that he could remain passive at this point and simply assume Casa de Walter will appreciate at the average rate of 10 percent for another year. He would be making a profit if he did this, but he knows he could be making a larger profit if he owned a more valuable piece of real estate. He also knows he'll probably acquire a certain amount of negative cash flow right at first if he buys a bigger piece of property. (Decisions, decisions!)

Walter figures out a way to own a more valuable piece of property without taking any more cash out of his pocket. He decides to institute one of the more profitable elements of his own Ten Year Real Estate Investment Schedule, a tax-free exchange. This, along with the other appreciation and tax benefits he will receive from owning a larger property, he figures will more than compensate him for any negative cash flows he may sustain from the newer, larger property right at first.

Even though Walter feels a certain fondness for Casa de Walter, he plans to trade his equity in those older units for a gorgeous, newer, six-unit apartment complex called Foxfire Glen. An apartment building like Foxfire Glen, he projects, would sell for around $220,000 at the time he was ready to trade up. After estimating the costs to arrange a sale on Casa de Walter to be approximately 7 percent of its present value, or $9,300,

$$\$133,100 \times .07 = \$9,300$$

and subtracting the $9,300 from his equity of $53,100 in Casa de Walter at the end of year three, Walter finds that he'd have $43,800 to put down on Foxfire Glen.

$$\$53,100 - \$9,300 = \$43,800$$

Almost $44,000. As luck would have it, this would be 20 percent of a sales price of $220,000.

$$\$44,000 \div \$220,000 = .20, \text{ or } 20\%$$

Since Walter expects to be putting 20 percent down on Foxfire Glen, his equity-to-debt ratio in the new property would start at 20 percent for equity and 80 percent for debt, just as it had been in the first year he owned Casa de Walter.

Walter knows that a 20 percent equity to 80 percent loan position in Foxfire Glen is better than the 45 percent equity to 55 percent loan ratio he would have in old Casa de Walter!

Next, Walter projects what would happen to his equity position at the end of the fourth year (the first year he holds Foxfire Glen) if he goes ahead and trades for the new property. He again assumes that his improvements, in addition to the inflation rate, will allow the property to appreciate at 10 percent per year. At the end of year four, Walter's equity-to-debt ratio in Foxfire Glen is estimated to be 27 percent to equity and 73 percent to debt, just as it had been in year two in Casa de Walter. In cash, Walter's equity buildup in Foxfire Glen would be in the neighborhood of $22,000.

$$\$220,000 \times .10 = \$22,000$$

	Purchase Year 4		End of Year 4	
Investor's Equity	$44,000	20%	$66,000	27%
Lender's Interest	$176,000	80%	$176,000	73%
Total Value	$220,000		$242,000	
Profit for Year			$22,000	

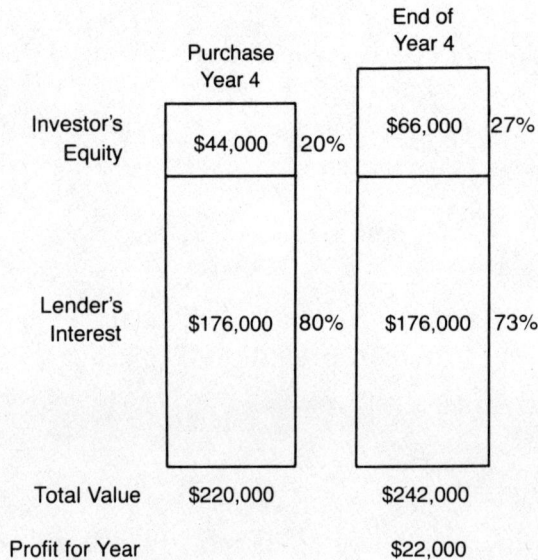

Compare this to the smaller $13,310 equity buildup he would get in year four if he decided to simply hold on to Casa de Walter (refer to chart on page 132).

An additional benefit from trading up, which is not shown on the graphs above, is the fact that Walter will get much larger write-offs on his income tax for cost recovery by trading up into Foxfire Glen. As we'll see in the next example, Walter will get the larger write-offs because he would be recovering the cost of a much larger property.

Now let's take a look at what happens to another investor, Simon Richards, as he follows a similar strategy of planning to trade up a series of Texas properties over a ten-year period.

CHAPTER 9

SIMON RICHARDS' TEN YEAR REAL ESTATE INVESTMENT SCHEDULE AND ODYSSEY THROUGH THE STATE OF TEXAS

In this example, we will follow the investment adventures of Simon Richards. Simon is an industrious and creative fellow. From a variety of activities, Simon has accumulated $10,000 in spare change, which he plans to invest in residential rental real estate. Simon has a goal: to make enough money with the $10,000 to be financially independent at the end of ten years.

To accomplish this, Simon plans to buy residential rental properties, let them appreciate for approximately three years each, and then, in each case, arrange for a tax-deferred exchange and trade up. Not only that, but Simon intends to withdraw 10 percent of the equity he realizes from each property transfer, thereby establishing a slush fund to cover unexpected expenses. He also expects the slush fund will help to support a life-style which he expects to become progressively more grandiose during this ten-year period. Since there are transaction costs in any investment, Simon's computations include a 7 percent deduction from his equity for transaction costs each time he exchanges his properties.

To crystallize his plan in his mind, Simon has done some calculations and used his vivid imagination to picture the actual properties he expects to buy. He has developed a chart to help him visualize his Ten Year Real Estate Investment Plan.

The math that follows is the math that was used to develop the chart on pages 156 and 157. Again, be sure to follow Simon's progress through with calculations on your calculator. Don't skip ahead just yet.

At the beginning of year one, Simon plans to use his $10,000 as a 20 percent down payment on a $50,000 condominium unit in Brownsville, Texas.

$$\$10,000 \div .20 = \$50,000$$

Simon has recently heard some phenomenal growth statistics about Texas, and knows that Brownsville is a fast-developing vacation and retirement area on the Texas Gulf Coast. He thinks the appreciation rate there might exceed the average national inflation rate. Besides, once he owned the property he could take tax-deductible trips to the area to check on his investment. He might even be able to use the condo occasionally, if it wasn't rented to a tenant, for his personal use.

Simon's computations, detailing his annual progress through his ten-year real estate investment program, follow. First, we'll start with year one. Simon buys a $50,000 condominium which he expects to appreciate at 10 percent per annum.

Simon's math at the end of year one:

$50,000 × .10 = $5,000 of appreciation.

$50,000 + $5,000 = $55,000 condo's value at the end of year one.

$10,000 + $5,000 = $15,000 Simon's equity position in the condo at the end of year one.

Now Simon makes a graphic display to help him visualize what his math tells him has happened to the value of his condominium·investment and his equity position after holding it for one year.

BROWNSVILLE CONDOMINIUM

	Beginning of Year 1	End of Year 1
20% Down Payment		
Property Value	$50,000	$55,000
Owner's Equity	Start $10,000	$15,000

That's pretty clear, isn't it? Did you notice that Simon's equity position at the end of year one reflects a 50 percent increase on his original investment? That's after only one year. He doesn't have to pay any taxes on the appreciation until he actually sells this property (or one of the properties down the line that he expects to trade up for)!

Simon's computations to detail his investment position at the end of year two start with the first year appreciated value of his condominium of $55,000.

Simon's math at the end of year two:

$55,000 × .10 = $5,500 of appreciation.

$55,000 + $5,500 = $60,500 condo's value at the end of year two.

$15,000 + $5,500 = $20,500 Simon's equity position in the condo at the end of year two.

Simon's math for year three follows the pattern of year one and year two. The only change is that he starts with the second year's appreciated condominium value of $60,500. (And you thought you hated math. This isn't so hard, is it?)
Simon's math at the end of year three:

$60,500 × .10 = $6,050 of appreciation.

$60,500 + $6,050 = $66,550 condo's value at the end of year three.

$20,500 + $6,050 = $26,550 Simon's equity position in the condo at the end of year three.

Simon doesn't want to get too far ahead of himself; therefore, he stops at this point to extend his graph. He wants to incorporate the new figures he's developed covering his projections for the first three years of ownership.

BROWNSVILLE CONDOMINIUM

20% Down Payment	Beginning of Year 1	End of Year 1	End of Year 2	End of Year 3
Property Value	$50,000	$55,000	$60,500	$66,550
Owner's Equity	Start $10,000	$15,000	$20,500	$26,550

At the end of three years, Simon has a condominium worth $66,550 and an equity position in this property of $26,550. This represents a profit of

$16,550 over his original investment of $10,000. And, he hasn't paid a penny of taxes on the property's appreciated value. Does Simon feel guilty? Does he feel like he's cheating the government out of its fair share of his appreciation? No, I don't think so. Would you feel guilty? Simon's a law abiding citizen. He's following the government's rules, and they say it's okay. Believe me, if the government wanted taxes on the appreciation at this point, they'd be bold enough to ask for them.

Speaking of taxes, let's go back now and add projections for an important consideration in Simon's purchase of this property ... . tax shelter. What kind of cost recovery has he been accumulating over this three-year period?

Cost Recovery, the Paper Write-Off for Depreciation

The tax laws provide for cost recovery under what is called the Accelerated Cost Recovery System, or ACRS. Under this system you can recover the cost of residential rental property over eighteen, thirty-five, or forty years. (Of course, those people who choose thirty-five or forty years do so because they're middle class, and they feel guilty about taking the additional benefit of the shorter time period!) In addition, we are allowed to use the 175 percent declining balance method.

Note: When you go to figure your depreciation amounts for your income taxes under the ACRS system, you won't actually do the math the way we're doing it here. The IRS has provided charts and tables like the one on the following page, which they require you to use. These charts help you to find the precise amount of cost recovery or depreciation that you may claim on your income tax return.

For the purposes of this book, however, so we can better understand the system, we're going to actually do the math. The results work out approximately the same.

What does cost recovery mean to you in real dollars saved? Let's take the example of Simon's condominium.

Accelerated Cost Recovery System (ACRS)

ACRS Cost Recovery Tables for Real Estate
1. All Real Estate (Except Low-Income Housing)

(Use the Column for the Month in the First Year the Property Is Placed in Service)

If the Recovery Year Is	Month of Year											
	1	2	3	4	5	6	7	8	9	10	11	12
1	12	11	10	9	8	7	6	5	4	3	2	1
2	10	10	11	11	11	11	11	11	11	11	11	12
3	9	9	9	9	10	10	10	10	10	10	10	10
4	8	8	8	8	8	8	9	9	9	9	9	9
5	7	7	7	7	7	7	8	8	8	8	8	8
6	6	6	6	6	7	7	7	7	7	7	7	7
7	6	6	6	6	6	6	6	6	6	6	6	6
8	6	6	6	6	6	6	5	6	6	6	6	6
9	6	6	6	6	5	6	5	5	5	6	6	6
10	5	6	5	5	5	5	5	5	5	5	6	5
11	5	5	5	5	5	5	5	5	5	5	5	5
12	5	5	5	5	5	5	5	5	5	5	5	5
13	5	5	5	5	5	5	5	5	5	5	5	5
14	5	5	5	5	5	5	5	5	5	5	5	5
15	5	5	5	5	5	5	5	5	5	5	5	5
16	—	—	1	1	2	2	3	3	4	4	4	5

In the year that Simon buys his condominium, it is valued at $50,000. The tax law, however, will not let Simon recover the cost of the entire $50,000. This is because the land the condominium is sitting on, which is part of the value of the property, is a nondepreciating commodity. Therefore, he must first deduct the cost of the land to find out how much of this property's value can be written off in tax deductions.

The $64 question is: How do you find out how much of the property's value is attributable to the land? There are three ways.

Condominiums are a little different than other real estate. Simon should first check with his condominium association to see if they have determined a value for the land. He would then use his pro rata share of their estimate (the amount of land attributable directly to his condo). If this were not a condo, Simon might check to see what raw land in the immediate area is selling for per lot (or per square foot) and then apply that comparable figure to the lot the building is sitting on. Or, Simon could see what value the property tax assessor used for the land. (The IRS likes this method. The only problem is, the tax assessor's estimate is seldom more than just a guess, and his guess is usually wrong!)

After checking comparable sales, Simon estimates that the land is worth 10 percent of the condominium complex's total value. Since his unit is worth $50,000, Simon takes 10 percent, or $5,000, off the condominium's value, leaving $45,000 worth of building to depreciate. The value of the property after the cost of the land has been removed is called the *depreciable basis.* (Remember that term!)

His next step is to divide the $45,000 by eighteen years. Since Simon in no way considers himself to be an average middle-class person, he's not in the least embarrassed about taking the additional benefit of the shortest cost recovery period. He uses eighteen years. Forty-five thousand dollars divided by eighteen equals $2,500 of write-off in the first year, using straight line depreciation or cost recovery.

Although Simon could choose to use the simple straight line cost recovery method and just write off the $2,500, Simon chooses to use the more beneficial 175 percent declining balance method. He multiplies the $2,500 by 175 percent, which equals $4,375. Four thousand, three hundred seventy-five dollars is the amount of Simon's first-year income tax write-off for cost recovery.

It will save Simon a lot of time later if he does one more calculation now. This calculation simplifies finding the amount of depreciation he can take in succeeding years.

What percent is the $4,375 of $45,000? Divide the $4,375 by $45,000 and memorize the number you get.

$$\$4,375 \div \$45,000 = .09722, \text{ or } 9.7 \text{ percent}$$

That *.09722* is a factor—a magic number. You can use it and multiply it times the depreciable basis or the remaining depreciable basis of any property. It will always tell you know much cost recovery, you are allowed to take on that property, that year, using the eighteen-year, 175 percent method. So remember the number:

$$.09722$$

Okay, let's continue with the cost recovery calculations for Simon's chart. We said that Simon is using a *declining balance* cost recovery method. This means that the amount of cost recovery that Simon takes in one year must be subtracted from the depreciable basis of the property for that year to see how much cost he can recover in the succeeding year. The method is called declining balance because the property's value for tax purposes keeps declining by the amount of cost recovery taken the previous year.

In the second year, Simon must subtract the amount of cost recovery he took off the property's depreciable basis the previous year.

$$\$45,000 - \$4,375 = \$40,625$$

This $40,625 is the condominium's depreciable basis for the second year. All we have to do now is multiply that number by our memorized number,

$$.09722$$

to find out how much cost recovery Simon can take out of his condominium the second year.

$$\$40,625 \times .09722 = 3.950$$

In the third year, Simon again subtracts the amount of cost recovery he took in the second year from that year's depreciable basis. With these calculations, he arrives at a depreciable basis for the third year of $36,675.

$$\$40,625 - \$3,950 = \$36,675$$

By multiplying

$$\$36,675 \times .09722 = \$3.566$$

he gets the cost recovery amount of $3,566 for year three.

Here is a summary of the three years' depreciation. Simon gets $4,375 the first year, $3,950 the second year, and $3,566 the third year. Notice that the amount of depreciation declines each year. That's because the depreciation is being figured, for tax purposes, on a declining property value.

Simon adds these cost recovery figures to his chart.

1. BROWNSVILLE CONDOMINIUM

20% Down Payment	Beginning of Year 1	End of Year 1	End of Year 2	End of Year 3
Property Value	$50,000	$55,000	$60,500	$66,550
Owner's Equity	Start $10,000	$15,000	$20,500	$26,550
Cost Recovery (175%, 15 years)		$4,375	$3,950	$3,566

Simon Sells

At the end of the third year of ownership, Simon decides he has too much equity in his condominium in Brownsville. He elects to trade for a larger property. (Remember, this projection is in Simon's imagination. He's really just in the planning stages of his Ten Year Real Estate Investment Schedule.) After careful study and research, Simon decides to buy an older duplex in San Antonio, Texas. He considers one that can be bought for $98,500.

Simon does some figuring to see how much equity he has in his Brownsville condominium at the beginning of year four, after subtracting 7 percent for the cost of selling the condo and an additional 10 percent to use as a slush fund. His calculations are as follows.

First, Simon needs to know what his sales costs on the condominium are going to be. He multiplies the condominium's present value, $66,550, by the 7 percent estimated sales cost:

$66,550 × .07 = $4,658 in sales costs.

Second, Simon needs to subtract the sales costs, $4,658, from his present equity in the condominium, $26,550:

$26,550 − $4,658 = $21,892 Simon's equity minus the sales costs.

Third, Simon wants to take 10 percent of his remaining equity out of the investment to set up a slush fund to cover closing costs on his next investment or in case his new property has some negative cash flows. He calculates 10 percent of $21,892:

$21,892 × .10 = $2,189 cash Simon withdraws to set up a slush fund.

Then he subtracts the $2,189 from his equity of $21,892 to find out how much equity he has remaining for his down payment on the San Antonio duplex:

$21,892 − $2,189 = $19,703 Simon's equity remaining for reinvestment in
the San Antonio duplex.

Finally, Simon takes his remaining equity of $19,703 and divides it by 20 percent, because he wants to use the $19,703 as a 20 percent down payment on the San Antonio duplex. He finds out that he can afford to pay $98,515 for the duplex:

$19,703 ÷ .20 = $98,515 purchase price of the San Antonio duplex.

It appears that Simon will have enough equity left, after paying approximately 7 percent sales costs and deducting 10 percent from his equity for his personal use, to put 20 percent down on the San Antonio duplex. Simon's graph now looks as follows:

BROWNSVILLE CONDOMINIUM

SAN ANTONIO DUPLEX

20% Down Payment	Beginning of Year 1	End of Year 1	End of Year 2	End of Year 3	Beginning of Year 4
Property Value	$50,000	$55,000	$60,500	$66,550	$98,515
Owner's Equity	Start $10,000	$15,000	$20,500	$26,550	$19,703
Withdrawal of 10% of Owner's Cash Equity					$2,189
Cost Recovery (175%, 15 years)		$4,357	$3,950	$3,566	

Sale End of Year 3

Property #1 is sold. The equity is reinvested in property #2 ($2,189 withdrawal)

Did you notice that Simon put the amount that he withdrew from his equity for the slush fund on his chart in the space between the owner's equity and the cost recovery figures? He'll do that on his chart every time he sells a property and exchanges up.

Simon's San Antonio Duplex

The San Antonio duplex is well located in an established neighborhood several blocks from the Alamo and the San Antonio River Walk. The property is well maintained, and gets good rents. As we know, it's valued at $98,515.

Simon holds the property for three years, during which time it appreciates, on average, approximately 10 percent per year.

Simon's math at the end of investment year four:

$98,515 × .10 = $9,852 of appreciation.

$98,515 + $9,852 = $108,367 duplex's value at the end of year four of the investment program (year one of Simon's ownership of the duplex).

$19,703 + $9,852 = $29,555 Simon's equity position in the duplex at the end of year four of the investment program.

Simon's math at the end of year five:

$108, 367 × .10 = $10,837 of appreciation.

$108,367 + $10,837 = $119,204 duplex's value at the end of year five of the investment program (year two of Simon's ownership of the duplex).

$29,555 + $10,837 = $40,392 Simon's equity position in the duplex at the end of year five of the investment program.

Simon's math at the end of year six:

$119,204 × .10 = $11,920 of appreciation.

$119,204 + $11,920 = $131,124 duplex's value at the end of year six of the investment program (year three of Simon's ownership of the duplex).

$40,392 + $11,920 = $52,312 Simon's equity position in the duplex at the end of year six of the investment program.

Simon Sells Again

At the end of the sixth year on his Ten Year Real Estate Investment Program, Simon realizes he has too much equity in his San Antonio Duplex. He hears from fellow investors that there are some real bargains to be had in west Texas. After thoroughly investigating the markets in various west Texas cities, he decides to trade his duplex for a six-unit apartment building in Lubbock. It can be purchased for around $194,000.

Simon does some figuring to see how much equity he has in his San Antonio duplex after 7 percent cost of sale and a 10 percent personal deduction from equity. His calculations are as follows.

Simon's math at the beginning of year 7:

$131,124 × .07 = $9,180 in transfer costs.

$52,312 − $9,180 = $43,132 Simon's equity minus the transfer costs.

$43,132 × .10 = $4,313 cash Simon withdraws for his own personal use.

$43,132 − $4,313 = $38,819 Simon's equity remaining for reinvestment in the Lubbock six-unit.

$38,819 ÷ .20 = $194,095 purchase price of the Lubbock six-unit.

It appears that Simon will have enough equity left after paying sales costs, and deducting 10 percent from his equity, to put 20 percent down on the six-unit in Lubbock.

Simon's Lubbock Six-Unit

The Lubbock six-unit is valued at $194,095. Simon holds the property for three years, during which time it appreciates, on average, approximately 10 percent per year.

Simon's math at the end of year seven:

$194,095 × .10 = $19,410 of appreciation.

$194,095 + $19,410 = $213,505 six-unit's value at the end of year seven of the investment program (year one of Simon's ownership of the six-unit).

$38,819 + $19,410 = $58,229 Simon's equity position in the six-unit at the end of year seven of the investment program.

Simon's math at the end of year eight:

$213,505 × .10 = $21,351 of appreciation.

$213,505 + $21,351 = $234,856 six-unit's value at the end of year eight of the investment program (year two of Simon's ownership of the six-unit).

$58,299 + $21,351 = $79,650 Simon's equity position in the six-unit at the end of year eight of the investment program.

Simon's math at the end of year nine:

$234,856 × .10 = $23,486 of appreciation.

$234,856 + $23,486 = $258,342 six-unit's value at the end of year nine of the investment program (year three of Simon's ownership of the six-unit).

$79,650 + $23,486 = $103,136 Simon's equity position in the six-unit at the end of year nine of the investment program.

Simon Sells a Third Time

At the end of the ninth year on his Ten Year Real Estate Investment Program, Simon realizes he has too much equity in his Lubbock six-unit, so he again goes off to look for another larger investment. This time he decides to trade for a sixteen-unit apartment building that he finds in Amarillo, Texas. It is priced at $383,000.

Simon does some figuring to see how much equity he has in his Lubbuck six-unit after the 7 percent cost of sale and a 10 percent personal deduction from equity. His calculations are as follows.

Simon's math at the beginning of year ten:

$258,342 × .07 = $18,084 in transfer costs.

$103,136 − $18,084 = $85,052 Simon's equity minus the transfer costs.

$85,052 × .10 = $8,505 cash Simon withdraws for his own personal use.

$85,052 − $8,505 = $76,547 Simon's equity remaining for investment in the Amarillo sixteen-unit apartment building.

$76,547 ÷ .20 = $382,735 value of the Amarillo sixteen-unit.

It again appears that Simon will have enough equity left after paying 7 percent sales costs, and deducting 10 percent from his equity, to put 20 percent down on the sixteen-unit complex in Amarillo.

Simon's math at the end of year ten:

$382,735 × .10 = $38,274 of appreciation.

$382,735 + $38,274 = $421,009 sixteen-unit's value at the end of year ten of the investment program (year one of Simon's ownership of the sixteen-unit).

$76,547 + $38,274 = $114,821 Simon's equity position in the sixteen-unit at the end of year ten of the investment program.

The end of year ten is as far as we follow Simon on his imaginary investment program through the state of Texas. The complete chart of his Ten Year Real Estate Investment Program is found on pages 156 and 157.

Although Simon's plan is to be financially independent at the end of ten years, once he actually completes the ten-year program, he probably will be so enthralled with his net worth, especially in the later years, that he will decide to continue with the program for another ten years. There is no reason for the strategy to stop at the end of ten, fifteen, or even twenty years. It can be continued with progressively multiplying wealth accumulations for as long as the investor finds it profitable.

The Last of Simon's Calculations

Earlier, we discussed how the depreciation was figured for the first three years of the program when Simon owned his Brownsville condominium. Simon could have simply sold that property and his succeeding properties outright, paid his capital gains taxes, and then reinvested what remained. If he had done that, the procedure for figuring his depreciation for the San Antonio duplex, for the Lubbock six-unit, and for the Amarillo sixteen-unit would have been the same as it was for the Brownsville condominium. (See pages 139-143.) However, Simon elected to exchange his properties and thereby defer his capital gains taxes. To figure the cost recovery amounts allowed for tax write-offs on the succeeding properties, we have to make some additional calculations.

After deducting the cost of the land from the value of each property at the time of its purchase, we must deduct the total depreciation taken over the three-year period on the previous property or properties. The amount that we arrive at is then divided by eighteen years to get the depreciation amount for the first year of the new property. Sound complicated? That's because I'm trying to explain it with words. Numbers are much clearer. Just follow me through Simon's calculations on his second property, the San Antonio duplex.

The San Antonio duplex was valued at $98,515 when Simon purchased it. We'll guess that the land is worth 10 percent of the property's value, or $9,852.

$$\$98,515 \times .10 = \$9,852$$

Subtracting,

$$\$98,515 - \$9,852 = \$88,663$$

gives us $88,663, the number we'd use as the depreciable basis for the San Antonio duplex if Simon had simply bought the duplex outright instead of exchanging for it. However, since Simon did exchange into it, we have to subtract the total cost recovery taken on the Brownsville condominium to find Simon's actual depreciable basis in the San Antonio duplex.

We need to go back and total up the cost recovery amounts that Simon deducted on the Brownsville condominium for the three years that he owned it. We get a total of $11,891.

$$\$4,375 + 3,950 + \$3,566 = \$11,891$$

Subtracting,

$$\$88,663 - \$11,891 = \$76,772$$

gives us a depreciable basis in the San Antonio duplex of $76,772.

Simon, of course, uses the eighteen-year cost recovery period and the 175 percent cost recovery method. He remembers that the easy way to figure his depreciation, using the eighteen-year cost recovery schedule and the 175 percent method, is to multiply the depreciable basis of the property by the number he'd memorized:

.09772

Therefore,

$$\$76,772 \times .09722 = \$7,464$$

This $7,464 is Simon's cost recovery amount for his first year ownership of the San Antonio Duplex.

In the second year, Simon must subtract the amount of cost recovery he had deducted from the depreciable basis of the San Antonio duplex the previous year.

$$\$76,772 - \$7,464 = \$69,308$$

The $69,308 is the duplex's depreciable basis for the second year. All we have to do now is multiply that number by our memorized number, .09722, to find out how much cost recovery Simon can take out of his duplex the second year.

$$\$69,308 \times .09722 = \$6,738$$

In the third year, Simon again subtracts the amount of cost recovery he took in the second year from that year's depreciable basis.

$$\$69,308 - \$6,738 = \$62,570$$

By multiplying,

$$\$62,570 \times .09722 = \$6,083$$

Simon finds that $6,083 is the cost recovery amount for year three.

For owning the duplex for three years, Simon got depreciation deductions of $7,464 the first year, $6,738 the second year, and $6,083 the third year, or a total of $20,285.

Figuring the Depreciation on the Lubbock Six-Unit —

Note: I told you earlier that I'd let you skip some of the math. Well, here's your chance. Feel free to skip over the rest of these calculations and go right to the chart on pages 156 and 157. The chart should be easy to understand now that you've studied this far. If you have any questions about how a number on the chart is arrived at, come back and read through these numbers until you find the answer you're looking for.

The Lubbock six-unit was valued at $194,095 when Simon purchased it. We'll guess that the land is worth 10 percent of the property's value, or $19,210.

$$\$194,095 \times .10 = \$19,410$$

Subtracting,

$$\$194,095 - \$19,410 = \$174,685$$

So $174,685 is the depreciable basis of the Lubbock six-unit.

Again, since Simon is dealing with a tax-deferred exchange and he has to reduce the new property's basis by the amount of cost recovery he took on the previous property(s), we have to go back and total up the cost recovery amounts he'd taken on the Brownsville condominium, $11,891, plus the total amount of cost recovery he'd taken on the San Antonio duplex for three years of $20,285.

$$\$7,464 + \$6,738 + \$6,083 = \$20,285$$

to give us a grand total of previous depreciation taken of $37,192.

$$\$11,891 + \$20,285 = \$32,176$$

Subtracting,

$$\$174,685 - \$32,176 = \$142,509$$

gives us $142,509 as the depreciable basis in the Lubbock six-unit.

Again, using the eighteen-year cost recovery period and the 175 percent recovery method, Simon multiplies,

$$\$142,509 \times .09722 = \$13,855$$

which gives us $13,855 as Simon's cost recovery amount for his first year of owning the Lubbock six-unit.

In the second year, Simon must subtract the amount of cost recovery he had taken off the property's depreciable basis the previous year.

$$\$142,509 - \$13,855 = \$128,654$$

The Lubbock six-unit's depreciable basis is $128,654 for the second year. We multiply

$$\$128,654 \times .09722 = \$12,508$$

to get $12,508 as Simon's cost recovery amount for his second year of owning the Lubbock six-unit.

In the third year, Simon again subtracts the amount of cost recovery he had taken in the second year from that year's depreciable basis.

$$\$128,654 - \$12,508 = \$116,146$$

By multiplying

$$\$116,146 \times .09722 = \$11,292$$

we get $11,292 as the cost recovery amount for year three of Simon's ownership of the Lubbock six-unit.

Note: If you're a real glutton for punishment; if you enjoy working with the numbers; or if you just want to, go ahead and read the section that follows about how to figure the cost recovery on the Amarillo sixteen-unit apartment. Otherwise, skip ahead and study the chart on pages 156 and 157. You'll find all of the cost recovery figures there. Then if you want to practice figuring them out, come back and read this section. I promise you, the method used on the Amarillo sixteen-unit is exactly the same as we've used on the San Antonio duplex and the Lubbock six-unit.

Figuring the Depreciation on the Amarillo Sixteen-Unit

The Amarillo sixteen-unit apartment building was valued at $382,735 when Simon purchased it. We'll follow our established pattern and assume the land is worth 10 percent of the property's value, or $38,274.

$$\$382,735 \times .10 = \$38,274$$

Subtracting

$$\$382,735 - \$38,274 = \$344,461$$

leaves $344,461 as the depreciable basis of the Amarillo sixteen-unit before subtracting all previous cost recovery amounts taken on the three previous properties.

Simon has to reduce the sixteen-unit's basis by the amount of cost recovery he took on the previous properties. We have to go back and total up the cost recovery amounts he'd taken on the Brownsville condominium, $13,985; plus total amount of cost recovery he'd taken on the San Antonio duplex for three years, $23,207; and the total cost recovery taken on the Lubbock six-unit:

$$\$13,855 + \$12,508 + \$11,292 = \$37,655$$

to give us a grand total of previous depreciation taken of $69,831.

$$\$11,891 + \$20,285 + \$37,655 = \$69,831$$

Subtracting

$$\$344,461 - \$69,831 = \$274,630$$

gives us $274,630 as the actual depreciable basis in the Amarillo sixteen-unit.

Finally, we multiply

$$\$274,630 \times .09722 = \$26,700$$

to arrive at $26,700 for Simon's cost recovery amount for his first year of owning the Amarillo sixteen-unit.

That's all there is to it. Those are all the numbers you need to make the chart on the following pages; or more importantly, the method you can use to make one like it using your own numbers, projections, and assumptions.

Simon's Ten Year Real Estate Investment Program —

1. BROWNSVILLE CONDOMINIUM

	Beginning of Year 1	End of Year 1	End of Year 2	End of Year 3
20% Down Payment				
Property Value	$50,000	$55,000	$60,500	$66,550
Owner's Equity	Start $10,000	$15,000	$20,500	$26,550
Withdrawal of 10% of Owner's Cash Equity				
Cost Recovery (175%, 18 years)		$4,375	$3,950	$3,566

Sale End of Year 3

Property #1 is sold. The equity is reinvested in property #2 ($2,189 withdrawal)

3. LUBBOCK SIX-UNIT

	Beginning of Year 7	End of Year 7	End of Year 8	End of Year 9
	$194,095	$213,505	$234,856	$258,342
	$38,819	58,229	$79,650	$103,136
	$4,313			
		$13,855	$12,508	$11,292

Sale End of Year 9

Property #3 is sold. The equity is reinvested in property #4 ($8,505 withdrawal)

2. SAN ANTONIO DUPLEX

Beginning of Year 4	End of Year 4	End of Year 5	End of Year 6
$98,515	$108,367	$119,204	$131,124
$19,703	$29,555	$40,392	$52,312
$2,189			
	$7,464	$6,738	$6,083

Sale End of Year 6

Property #2 is sold. The equity is reinvested in property #3 ($4,313 withdrawal)

4. AMARILLO SIXTEEN-UNIT

Beginning of Year 10	End of Year 10	At End of Ten Years
$382,735	$421,009	You have a property worth $421,009
$76,546	$114,821	You have equity in this property of $114,821
$8,505		Over the ten year period you've withdrawn $15,007
	$26,700	You've taken income tax deductions over ten years of $96,531

Perhaps you're saying to yourself, I wonder what would have happened if Simon had simply held on to the Brownsville condominium instead of trading up every three years. He would have saved all those costs of sale and saved himself a lot of hassles. The chart on the next page depicts that "what if" situation.

What If Simon Simply Held On to his Brownsville Condominium for Ten Years?_____

BROWNSVILLE TOWNHOUSE

20% Down Payment	Beginning of Year 1	End of Year 1	End of Year 2	End of Year 3	End of Year 4	End of Year 5
Property Value	$50,000	$55,000	$60,500	$66,550	$73,205	$80,526
Owner's Equity	Start $10,000	$15,000	$20,500	$26,550	$33,205	$40,526
Cash Withdrawal Percentage of Owners Equity						
Depreciation (18 years, 175%)		$4,375	$3,950	$3,566	$3,219	$2,906

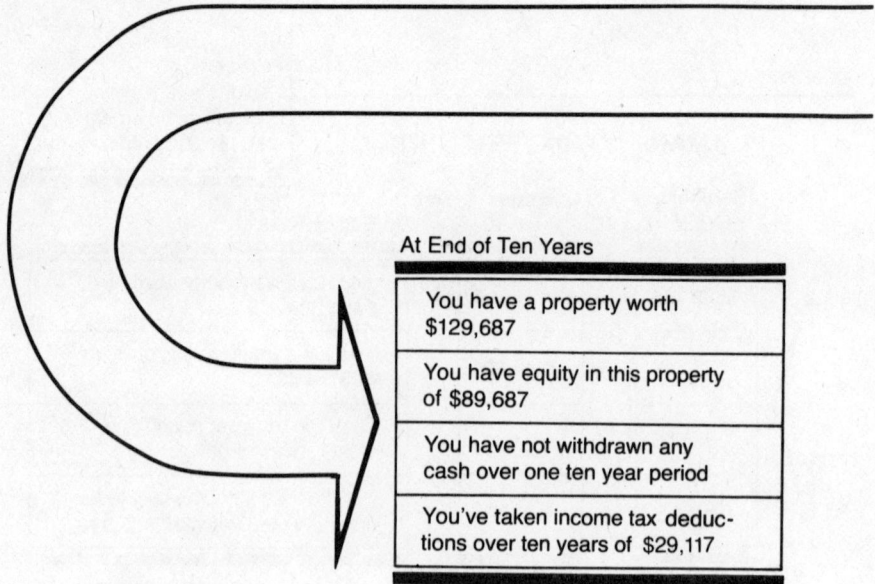

At End of Ten Years

You have a property worth $129,687
You have equity in this property of $89,687
You have not withdrawn any cash over one ten year period
You've taken income tax deductions over ten years of $29,117

End of Year 6	End of Year 7	End of Year 8	End of Year 9	End of
$88,578	$97,436	$107,179	$117,897	$129,687
$48,578	$57,436	$67,179	$77,897	$89,687
$2,623	$2,368	$2,138	$1,986	$1,986

Switch to straight line depreciation

Of course, Simon would not have taken any equity out of his condominium over the ten-year period unless he'd borrowed against the equity.

This discussion of a Ten Year Real Estate Investment Program would not be complete without the chart on the next two pages. This chart was prepared in exactly the same way as the chart on pages 156 and 157, with one exception. Instead of buying property with 20 percent down payments as Simon had done, this investor puts only 10 percent down on each of his investments. It is immediately apparent that the less you invest in a property, the larger the property you'll be able to buy; the more you'll benefit from appreciation; the more tax shelter you'll get; and the faster your money will grow.

Caution! As we discussed in Chapter 6, what is not apparent on the following chart is the fact that the less money you put down, the more chance you take of getting into a troublesome property that the seller is trying to unload, or one that the seller has overpriced. As a rule of thumb, it is also reasonable to expect that you will experience higher negative cash flows because you will be paying more interest on the bigger loan.

I don't mean to tell you that you should never purchase a property with a low down payment. Just be very careful.

Ten Percent Down Ten Year Real Estate Investment Program

1. BROWNSVILLE CONDOMINIUM

10% Downpayment	Beginning of Year 1	End of Year 1	End of Year 2	End of Year 3
Property Value	$100,000	$110,000	$121,000	$133,000
Owner's Equity	Start $10,000	$20,000	$31,000	$43,100
Withdrawal of 10% of Owner's Cash Equity				
Depreciation (175%, 15 years)		$8,750	$7,899	$7,131

Sale End of Year 3

Property #1 is sold. The equity is reinvested in property #2 ($3,378 withdrawal)

3. LUBBOCK SIX-UNIT

	Beginning of Year 7	End of Year 7	End of Year 8	End of Year 9
	$924,422	$1,061,865	$1,118,551	$1,230,406
	$92,442	$184,884	$286,571	$398,426
	$10,271			
		$72,157	$65,140	$58,807

Sale End of Year 9

Property #3 is sold. The equity is reinvested in property #4 ($31,230 withdrawal)

2. SAN ANTONIO DUPLEX

Beginning of Year 4	End of Year 4	End of Year 5	End of Year 6
$304,040	$334,444	$367,888	$404,677
$30,400	$60,808	$94,252	$131,041
$3,378			
	$24,292	$21,929	$19,797

Sale End of Year 6

Property #2 is sold. The equity is reinvested in property #3 ($10,271 withdrawal)

4. AMARILLO SIXTEEN-UNIT

Beginning of Year 10	End of Year 10	At End of Ten Years
$1,405,340	$1,545,874	You have a property worth $1,545,874
$281,068	$421,602	You have equity in this property of $421,602
$31,230		You've withdrawn over the ten-year period $44,879
	$95,171	You've taken income tax deductions over ten years of $381,073

Just for fun, let's do some quick figuring to see what your own Ten Year Real Estate Investment Program might look like at its completion, ten years down the road. Each of the worksheets on the following three pages corresponds to one of the preceding charts.

For the purpose of this exercise, you're going to have to accept the assumptions I used to make up the charts:

1. Twenty percent down payments on each property for worksheets 1 and 2

2. Ten percent down payments on each property for worksheet 3

3. Seven percent sales costs

4. Ten percent cash withdrawals from your equity at the close of each sale

5. Cost recovery figured at eighteen years, 175 percent.

Other than that, all you need to know before we get started is how much money you have to invest today. Once you've got that figured out, grab hold of your calculator, sharpen your pencil, and start filling in the blanks.

Worksheet No. 1 ———————————

Assumption:

1. TEN YEAR REAL ESTATE INVESTMENT PROGRAM

2. THREE TAX DEFERRED EXCHANGES AT THREE YEAR INTERVALS

3. TWENTY PERCENT DOWN PAYMENTS ON EACH INVESTMENT

4. TEN PERCENT PROPERTY APPRECIATION PER YEAR

5. SEVEN PERCENT SALES COST AT EACH SALE

6. TEN PERCENT WITHDRAWALS FROM EQUITY AT EACH SALE

——————————— $\div$ .0870920 = ———————————

Amount of money you have to invest today.

Equity dollars you'll have in ten years using the Ten Year Real Estate Investment Program.

——————————— $\div$ .0237525 = ———————————

Amount of money you invest today.

Value of the investment you'll have in ten years using the Ten Year Real Estate Investment Program.

——————————— $\div$ .6663557 = ———————————

Amount of money you have to invest today.

Amount of cash you could withdraw over the ten years.

——————————— $\div$ .1035937 = ———————————

Amount of money you invest today.

Amount of tax write-off you would have been able to take over the ten years.

Worksheet No. 2 (Investor simply holds on to property number 1)

Assumptions:

1. TEN YEAR REAL ESTATE INVESTMENT PROGRAM

2. INVESTOR SIMPLY HOLDS ON TO THE INVESTMENT FOR TEN YEARS

3. TWENTY PERCENT DOWN PAYMENT ON THE INVESTMENT

4. TEN PERCENT PROPERTY APPRECIATION PER YEAR

_____ ÷ .1114988 = _____

Amount of money you have to invest today.

Equity dollars you'll have in ten years using the Ten Year Real Estate Investment Program.

_____ ÷ .0771087 = _____

Amount of money you invest today.

Value of the investment you'll have in ten years using the Ten Year Real Estate Investment Program.

_____Not Applicable_____ ÷ .0000000 = _____Not Applicable_____

Amount of money you have to invest today.

Amount of cash you could withdraw over the ten years.

_____ ÷ .343442 = _____

Amount of money you invest today.

Amount of tax write-off you would have been able to take over the ten years.

Worksheet No. 3 (10 percent down payments) _____

Assumptions:

1. TEN YEAR REAL ESTATE INVESTMENT PROGRAM

2. THREE TAX DEFERRED EXCHANGES AT THREE YEAR INTERVALS

3. TEN PERCENT DOWN PAYMENTS ON EACH INVESTMENT

4. TEN PERCENT PROPERTY APPRECIATION PER YEAR

5. SEVEN PERCENT SALES COST AT EACH SALE

6. TEN PERCENT WITHDRAWALS FROM EQUITY AT EACH SALE

_____ ÷ .0237190 = _____
Amount of money you have to invest today. / Equity dollars you'll have in ten years using the Ten Year Real Estate Investment Program.

_____ ÷ .0064688 = _____
Amount of money you invest today. / Value of the investment you'll have in ten years using the Ten Year Real Estate Investment Program.

_____ ÷ .2228214 = _____
Amount of money you have to invest today. / Amount of cash you could withdraw over the ten years.

_____ ÷ .0262417 = _____
Amount of money you invest today. / Amount of tax write-off you would have been able to take over the ten years.

Those are some pretty fascinating numbers, don't you think? Of course, they're only meant to be approximations. To be more accurate, you should take the time to work out several charts of your own like the ones on pages 156 through 161. Use your own assumptions, including what you think you might expect in terms of the average rate of appreciation for the next ten years. You might want to take more than 10 percent of your equity out at each sale. You might not want to take any out. Tailor your charts to your own situation. Apply your numbers to the mathematical formulas I used on pages 135 through 155.

There are a lot of variables that can change the results you anticipate in any investment program. These include the availability of good properties that you can get into for 10 to 20 percent down, the availability of financing, and average rates of appreciation. Another is . . . you might change your mind about what your goals are!

Variations on the Ten Year Real Estate Investment Theme _____

Sell Every Five Years, Every Two Years, Every Six Months

It may be that some years 10 percent annual appreciation might be overly optimistic. You might find that your property only experiences 7 percent appreciation and you will have to wait five years to get the desired appreciation on your property before you will want to trade up. You might experience appreciation higher than 10 percent per year. It would follow, then, that it might be profitable to sell every two years, one year, or possibly even every six months. Try working out some charts with varying appreciation rates.

Invest in One New Property Every Year

Make plans to buy a new investment every year and start a new Ten Year Real Estate Investment Schedule to run concurrently with the first one you started. Working the numbers, and projecting your wealth at the end of the ten-year period for a multiple Ten Year Real Estate Investment Schedule, should get that sluggish old middle-class dream machine (heart!) of yours working again.

Carry Notes on the Properties You Sell

If you take part of your profits on paper (which in some markets you will have to do in order to sell your property) you can begin creating present income along with the long-term appreciation on the properties themselves.

There are advantages to carrying paper. One is, you'll probably be able to sell your property more quickly (or at least in a reasonable period of time!), because you can offer better terms for the buyer than he can get with bank financing. A second advantage is that you will probably be able to get a better sales price, because buyers will often pay more to get better terms. Third, your cash flow situation, looking at the investment program as a whole, will improve.

There are two disadvantages to carrying paper. First, your equity available for successive investments will not be as great; and second, you'll get interest income (not always a disadvantage!) and may suffer additional tax consequences.

The ideal way for a seller to finance a sale is to carry a note at an attractive interest rate, with monthly payments accruing. It's often a good idea to include *an all-due clause* . . . say in five to seven years. That way you'll get some equity up front, and income for as long as you carry the note. The rest of your equity will then come to you in a lump sum, which you can reinvest several years down the road.

Cash Flow

At some point in your investment program you may wish to redirect the emphasis away from pyramiding growth and toward creating income. In that case, you could do a couple of things.

You could simply hold on to the property or properties you have; wait a couple of years for your rents to rise to the point where the property's income exceeds the expenses and debt service; and then sit back and collect the excess cash flow as it's delivered to your mail box each month. If you want cash flow sooner, it's possible, at times, to refinance your property, make your debt service payments lower, and therby create immediate cash flow.

A rule of thumb, which may vary, is that a property should throw off cash flow of approximately 10 percent of its value. A $1,000,000 property ideally should produce $100,000 annually for the investor. The excess cash flow amount should increase each year with the property's increased value, acting as an income inflation hedge. It will take time for most properties to reach this 10 percent ideal, but it is achievable, even in a high interest rate market.

Conversion to a "Higher and Better" Use

You might be able to convert your investment property to something other than what it's primarily been used for, and thereby increase its income potential and/or its value when you sell. For instance, many apartment buildings have been renovated and converted to condominiums and even office complexes. Major changes like these generally require approval from local governing bodies, but once approved, the profit potential can be enormous.

Do Something Entirely Different

Dare to dream! Is there something else you'd like to do with your life? If so, once you've established enough money in your real estate investments and you feel secure, forget about the Ten Year Real Estate Investment Schedule. Live your dreams.

Real Estate: An Imperfect Market

In contrast to perfect markets like the stock market, where buyers and sellers are dealing with identical products and basically the same information, the real estate market is an imperfect market.

All real estate can have several different values. No two pieces of real estate are ever exactly alike. Every piece of real estate has multiple uses. Real estate markets are limited in size. The information available to buyers and sellers in the real estate market is not always equal. For these reasons, buyers and sellers can and do have differing opinions over a particular property's worth, and all of them can be right; hence, the real estate market is an imperfect market.

For instance, picture a neighborhood in which there are three homes for sale. Each home is identical . . . the floor plans, the age of the homes, the financing available, the care the previous owner has taken of it, the landscaping, etc. But one home is on a corner lot. Another backs up to a busy street. The third is on a quiet cul-de-sac. Each of these properties may command a premium price; or they each may have to be sold below market, because the sellers and potential buyers might have differing opinions about the benefits of or drawbacks to the various locations.

One buyer might be willing to pay more for the quiet house on the cul-de-sac because reduced traffic makes it safer for the kids to play outside. Another buyer might discount the house on the cul-de-sac, but pay extra for the house that backs up to the busy street, because it's closer to the bus stop. The seller of the home on the corner lot might promote the privacy aspects of his location, while a prospective buyer might worry about the possibility of increased traffic noise at that location.

Or consider comparable tracts of land in two towns of equal size. One is located in a town on a major interstate highway. The other is located in a town off the beaten path. If sold as agricultural land, both would command an equal price.

Now imagine for a moment that you are a developer looking for a site for a regional shopping mall. You might be willing to pay twenty times the land's agricultural value for the tract in the town located on the interstate highway, and still feel you'd paid a fair price, wouldn't you? The obvious reason is because the tract of land near the freeway will attract more business than the tract in the town off the beaten path.

The farmer who owns that land will become an overnight millionaire, because you believe his land is the ideal site on which to locate the shopping mall. On the other hand, you stand to become a multi-millionaire because you'll have an ideal location for your project.

Can you see what I mean when I tell you all real estate has multiple values?

Finally, real estate markets do not have instant communication networks reporting every sale to the entire world. Real estate markets tend to be small and localized, seldom larger than the size of a specific neighborhood, city, or region. Often a real estate market comprises no more than a few blocks within a town.

An imperfect market like a real estate market works in favor of the interests of the studious investor, because it is governed by documented facts, knowledge, and research about specific individual properties. In any particular imperfect market like the real estate market, if you do the things necessary to become knowledgeable about property and property values, your chances for success are more certain than in a perfect market like the stock market.

Even an unknowledgeable investor has a better chance to avoid losses and make profits in the imperfect real estate market, because the imperfect market tends to be considerably more stable and less volatile than a perfect market. It is less prone to be influenced by emotions of the moment.

Concluding the Ten Year Real Estate Investment Schedule

The process we've just been through in this chapter and the previous one is simply a way to visualize a particular goal. Prophecy, fortune-telling, and forecasting the future can be risky and disappointing businesses; just ask Tom Dewey. But not making plans and projections for your future can be equally as dangerous. Even considering the uncertain world we live in, the Ten Year Investment Schedule outlined in these last two chapters will give you a foundation upon which to build your future.

You will always be ahead if you make plans and set goals. If you set off on your investment program with the charts you've just drawn, even if you have to adjust them to take into account obstacles and opportunities found along your way, it is certain that you will travel a farther, faster, and truer course than you would if you simply take off without them, or worse yet, if you don't take off at all.

The charts you make are a guide to the basic direction you want to go in. Your program won't work out exactly as you plan, so don't be so rigid in your projections that you insist on buying and selling right on schedule, no matter whether it's the most profitable time or not. Stay alert for opportunities to increase your return. Investing, like life, is a dynamic process, not a static one.

CHAPTER 10

A GUIDE FOR THE INVESTOR WHO'S SHORT ON CAPITAL

Okay, I know what you're thinking. You're thinking: *"The Park Avenue Money Diet* is a plan to make somebody fat in the pocketbook all right, but it's not me. It's you, Dan—and people like you who already have some money."

You're saying to yourself, "Wonderful! I want to go out and sign a contract to purchase a residential rental property within thirty days of the day I finish this book. I'd love to buy a bunch of apartment buildings and trade up and get a lot of tax shelter and appreciation and pride of ownership and all that. But I don't have $10,000. I don't have $5,000. I may not have the money to pay the utility bill. Where am *I* going to get the money to get started?"

If you don't have the start-up capital, and if you have no idea where you're going to get it, this chapter is for you. Not having a lot of money sitting around is not unusual. It's the normal state of affairs for most people. And it's not an insurmountable problem. Believe me, finding money is as easy as walking on water—if you know where the rocks are!

If you don't already have the money, there are basically three ways you're going to get it. You can: (1) borrow it, (2) save it, or (3) earn it.

Borrow the Funds You Need to Get Started _____

Before we begin this discussion, let me remind you that inflation works for the borrower. A dollar today is worth more than a dollar tomorrow. A dollar borrowed today can be paid back in cheaper dollars tomorrow. In an inflationary economy, the prudent borrower is the prudent man.

Banks and Savings and Loans—The Retail Outlet ___

Money, when you borrow it, is a commodity; and your bank or savings and loan is the retail outlet. Banks and savings and loans will be your most expensive source of money (with the possible exception of the consumer finance companies—the Philistines of the lending industry!). Banks and savings and loans will also be your most conservative source of borrowed money.

Loan officers will be unimpressed with your plans to borrow money to invest in real estate and make a fortune—even though your bank invests in real estate all the time! Loan officers are only impressed by whatever security or collateral you can provide them with. They will normally lend you money if you have what they call "compensating balances" on deposit with them. That means that they'll lend you any amount of money, providing you keep a like amount in your checking or savings account. These institutions will probably be the last place you'll look for your starting out funds. That is, unless you already have a relationship established with your banker.

While banks may not prove useful to you in your starting-out stage, they can be helpful to you once you've established yourself. When you're starting out, however, is the ideal time to begin building a relationship with one or more banks within your operating area. Open an account with one as soon as you are able to. Pledge the balance in that account as collateral and take out a small loan ($500 to $1,000). Make payments on it for a while and then repay it. Then take out another. Do this several times and you'll have established a trade record as a credit-worthy customer. Be sure that you don't miss a payment or you'll defeat your purpose.

After establishing credit with your bank, you should begin efforts toward establishing a line of credit. Individual lines of credit can be for amounts as small as a thousand dollars or as large as several hundred thousand, or more. It is great to have money available when you need it, whatever the interest rates. Even if rates are high, when you've got to have it, the cost of money is seldom as important as the availability of money. So long as you make a net profit with the money you borrow, interest rates are cheap.

Friends, Relatives, and Associates—
The Wholesale Outlet

Is there somebody you know who might be willing, or anxious, to loan you money? I'll bet there is . . . for the right incentive, and if you could just get up your courage to ask. Try searching out three nonexclusive categories: friends, relatives, and associates. Mom and Dad might be a good place to start. Do you have a well-to-do aunt or uncle? How about a local merchant or your family doctor. They don't have to be all that rich. You just need to find someone who has $5,000 or $10,000 who would like their money to earn the excellent rate of return you're going to offer them.

I'm always amazed at what people will do for me if I offer them a good deal . . . and if I ask! One reason this abundant personal source of funds is not tapped by more people is because most of us think friends and relatives should be willing to help us out for just "love and affection." Some of us have tried to float loans like that in the past and we've been disappointed. Others of us are afraid to test those waters, so they don't ask. Sometimes it's a matter of ego. Often it's a fear of rejection. Well, let me suggest how you can deal with either or both of those problems.

If you're going to borrow from people you know, do it right. Friends, relatives, and associates deserve no less a fair shake than your local finance company. If they lend you money, they are doing you a favor. Show them you appreciate their help and insure that their help will be there if you need it again. Put everything in writing. Sign a note, pay market interest rates, set a due date, and offer collateral—a trust deed against your home or the investment you are buying, or the pink slip(s) to your car and/or boat will work just fine. Don't even allow people you know to offer you their help for free. It's not fair to them. If they realize that, or if they change their minds down the road, you may have problems.

You might want to offer an ownership interest in the investment in addition to, or in lieu of, interest. (See the subchapter on partnerships coming up.)

Here is an assignment for you. Set the *Park Avenue Money Diet* aside and take several minutes to make up a list of people you know who might be willing and able to lend you money. Arrange your list in order of most likely to least likely. Put the list at the end of the book so you'll have it when you're ready to get started. When you've finished the book, the list will be there. Contact the people on your list and ask for money! Start with the person at the top of the list and work your way down.

Borrow Against the Cash Value of Your Life Insurance

If you own whole life (cash value) insurance and if you're committed to starting your own investment program, you can take a big step toward financial independence if you trade in your whole life policy and take out a term insurance policy for the same amount. Of course you'll want to be certain that you are physically insurable before cancelling your old policy. Have the new term insurance in place before cancelling your old policy. Unless you're at an advanced age and your policy has been in effect for a long time, the premiums for the term insurance will be less. The difference of the cost of the premium for whole life and the premium for term insurance can be used in your investment program.

If your whole life policy has been in effect for a long time and you're an older person, the money you're paying into your whole life policy is not buying much insurance. It's just adding to your savings account with the insurance company. I'll bet the face value of your policy doesn't look like it has as much purchasing power as it did when you took the policy out. You, more than most of us, know what years of inflation has done to the value of cash value insurance.

If the above is true in your case and if a savings account is all that remains of your insurance, you, too, would profit from cashing in your policy and investing the cash value in more profitable investments. You may find an additional term insurance policy too expensive to consider at your age, but also consider: do you really need insurance anymore? After all, all you have is a savings account with an insurance company earning minimal interest. Wouldn't a good conservative real estate investment program accomplish the goal of providing for your family after you're gone, better than a deflating savings account?

When you cash in your whole life policy, the cash value you have built up in it will be returned to you, and you can use it as your starting-out funds. You'll accomplish more in a real estate investment program of your own, using your own money, than the insurance company will do for you.

As a second alternative, if you don't feel comfortable trading in the whole life policy you've been paying on all these years, your insurance company will loan you your money back. In other words, borrow against the cash value of your policy. The money is yours for the asking. The interest on the loan will be low, and there will be no great pressure for you to pay it back.

At the same time you might want to look into the cost of taking out a small term insurance policy with a face value equal to the amount of cash value you borrow.

Credit Unions

Many professional organizations, employee organizations, and trade unions have set up credit unions for their membership. Are you a member in good standing with a credit union? Could you become one? You may be able to borrow from that source and take advantage of what are normally low-interest, low-cost loans.

Borrow the Dead Equity from Your Home

If you've owned your own home for several years, you probably have more equity built up in this property than in all your other assets combined. That dead equity can be a source of start-up funds. Naturally, it's a personal decision as to whether or not you should pull the equity out of your home.

If you want to free the equity in your home there are two ways to get money from your home: (1) sell it or (2) refinance it. Either way you must consider, among other things, the stability of your income and your emotional readiness to dispose of, or further encumber, the family's castle.

Sell the Castle _____

If you sell your property, you must decide whether to use some of the sale proceeds to make a new down payment on another home, or to rent. While I'm a firm believer in home ownership for family stability, pride of ownership, and long term economic benefit, I must admit that when the total cost of home ownership is added up (i.e., down payments, mortgage payments, insurance payments, maintenance costs, property taxes, time and worry, etc.), a reasonably good case might be made for renting your residence and using the money saved to invest in residential rental properties.

While both homeowners and investors benefit from appreciation in real estate values and income tax write-offs for interest and property taxes, there are tax benefits like depreciation and additional expense write-offs that real estate investors are allowed, which homeowners don't get.

By the way, at least one state, the state of Texas, has a Homestead Law which makes it difficult for a person to refinance his personal residence. In Texas and any other state with a similar law, the only way for a homeowner to take his equity out of his home is to sell it.

Refinance the Castle _____

Should your state government allow you to refinance your home, and should you decide to do so, your decision should be based on the following: (1) the amount and the stability of your income, (2) the purpose to which the money will be put, and (3) the cost of borrowing the funds.

Ask yourself the following questions in light of these three criteria:

1. If the increased monthly payment brought about by refinancing is $_____ (use actual figures); and the negative cash flow from the investment, plus the increased monthly payment brought about by the refinance, is $_____ per month; and this negative cash flow is expected to last for _____ years; will I be able to carry the burden?

2. What would happen if the investment were to sit vacant for several months?

3. Should I borrow enough to buy the investment and set up a contingency fund to put in the bank for just such eventualities?

4. Does the total cost of the refinance and the investment make economic sense?

Examples of Creative Borrowing _____

A friend of mine, let's call her Marilyn, has been looking for the ideal real estate investment on and off for the last several years. She has come close to buying several times but could never bring herself to finally close a deal. As an unmarried mother of three, she has been concerned with her family's security. She hasn't wanted to do anything which would put her family's finances in jeopardy.

Marilyn likes her job as a school administrator and would never consider changing careers. Still, she knows her salary is not keeping her ahead of taxes or inflation. She astutely recognizes that to be a serious threat to her financial well-being.

Several months ago she started looking for a residential rental property investment, again. This time, she found a single- family home which was priced well. It was on the market for $80,000 and required a down payment of $8,000. With current rents the property would have a negative cash flow of about $100 per month after paying all expenses and mortgage payments. She conservatively estimated that it would take three years for the cash flow from the property to equal mortgage payments and expenses. Closing cost on the property would be $2,500. The down payment, closing costs, and the $100 a month negative cash flow for three years totaled $14,100.

Investment Down Payment	$ 8,000.00
Closing Costs	2,500.00
Slush Fund @ $100 for 36 Months	3,600.00
Total	$14,100.00

It was the perfect investment for Marilyn, except for one thing. She didn't want to part with $14,100 of her savings. Determined to do something this time, she and I sat down with a yellow tablet, a calculator, and a pencil to look for a solution which would fit her situation. Here's what we came up with.

Marilyn had a house which she'd lived in for five years. The house was presently worth close to $85,000, and it had a mortgage against it of $25,000. This left $60,000 of equity which was just sitting there doing nothing. The $25,000 mortgage was at 9 percent on a fully amortized pay-back schedule. The monthly payments totaled $292.19.

Marilyn had recently bought a new car, financing $11,500 at 15 percent for three years. The payment on the car was $401.47.

The combined payment on the house and the car totaled $693.66.

House Mortgage Payment	$292.19
New Car Payment @ 15.5% (3 years)	401.47
Total	$693.66

We came up with a plan which lowered her total monthly payment for mortgages and finance charges, paid off her car, put a down payment on the investment she'd found, and created a $3,600 contingency slush fund to cover any negative cash flow she anticipated from the investment property for three years.

"What would happen if I were to refinance my house with a new loan," she asked? "Could I get enough money to pay off the old loan, pay off the car, and purchase the new investment?" We determined that she could take out a new loan for $51,600 and accomplish all that.

Payoff Original House Loan	$25,000.00
Payoff New Car Loan	11,500.00
Investment Funds Required	14,100.00
Cost of New Loan	1,000.00
Total	$51,600.00

Market interest rates were 13 percent for a fixed rate thirty-year loan, which meant she would have a payment of $570.80.

Payment on New Loan
($51,600 @ 13% for 30 years) $570.80

That was $122.86 less than the total she was used to paying for her house and her car. Isn't this exciting!

I suggested that the $122.86 monthly windfall she'd gain by refinancing would eliminate her need for a slush fund. But Marilyn wanted to know that she had plenty of reserve to handle any unexpected eventuality. She decided to go ahead and take the extra money for the slush fund. She is a really cautious lady.

But wait! I haven't told you the best part.

In addition to the $122.86 a month Marilyn was saving with her new loan payment, she was legally allowed to go to her employer and claim seven to nine additional dependents against her withholding tax. Why? That was the extent that the estimated expenses from her new investment property exceeded the rents. In figuring those expenses, she was allowed to include a first-year annual deduction of $7,000 for cost recovery (depreciation) in addition to the $100 per month negative cash flow that she anticipated. Cost recovery, remember, is a paper write-off which cost her nothing out of pocket. She was in a 37 percent marginal tax bracket, which allowed her to take home an additional $244 in withholding tax savings per month. Marilyn had a total of $378 additional to spend each month because she owned this investment.

Savings in Monthly Payments	$122.86
Withholding Tax Savings	244.00
Total	$366.86

Marilyn now owns two appreciating assets—her home and the rental property. Both of them will increase in value in the coming years. She owns a new car free and clear. She is getting substantial tax shelter benefits. And she has more money to spend every month.

Isn't it interesting to see what a little creative borrowing can do?

Partnerships—Creative Negotiating _____

Do you consider yourself a creative person? Do you get along well with other people? Can you be persuasive? If so, partnerships may be the perfect vehicle for you to use to get started in real estate investing. Remember, the cardinal rule for making big profits in real estate is the use of leverage, OPM—Other People's Money. Partnerships are the perfect vehicle to do just that.

The most obvious source of partners—the ones you'll want to explore first—are the ones we have already talked about as sources of borrowed funds: friends, relatives, and associates. But don't limit yourself to just these sources. Every person you know, and every person you meet, is potentially your partner. Partners are easy to find if you've got control of the best real estate investment in town.

If you're like most people, I'll bet you don't have control of the best real estate investment in town, do you? Well, finding or creating the best real estate deal in town will be your job if your goal is to attract money partners. Don't worry. The competition is not all that keen. If the best real estate investment in town is what you decide to look for, you'll probably be the only person in your market actively looking for it.

Of course, when we're talking about the best real estate investment in town, we're talking about a really good deal . . . the kind that has to be searched out and negotiated for. If you're willing to do the work necessary to find it and if you're creative, you're going to find that the biggest problem in real estate is not that there are not enough good properties to go around. Your problem will be running out of time to deal with the partners who are attracted to your partnerships.

Most people don't have the time or inclination to do the research and negotiating necessary to structure outstanding real estate transactions, but many people will pay a premium to buy into such deals. The premium they pay is splitting the profits with the person who finds the deals and who puts the partnership together.

As the one who structures, negotiates, and puts a partnership together, you should not have to contribute cash to the venture. Instead, your contribution will be talent and hard work. Arranging profitable partnerships may sound easy, but it will probably take quite a bit of effort on your part. You will learn to appreciate the meaning of what, in partnership jargon, is called "sweat equity."

Here's how to get started:

1. Look through the classified advertising section of your local paper for ads which look like the seller would be negotiable. Phrases like "low down," "owner anxious," "take over payments," "below market," and "help" are usually good clues to a negotiable seller.

2. Look in the public notice section of your local paper for notices of default, sheriff sales, trustee sales, lawsuits, and divorces, etc. Civil proceedings and sudden changes in peoples' lives often are tip-offs to anxious or negotiable sellers.

3. Go down to the courthouse and ask for a list of properties which are in various stages of receivership.

4. Let local realtors know that you are a buyer of properties within certain parameters.

5. Call on "For Sale By Owners." Be prepared to look at lots of properties, turn down lots of properties, and make lots of offers which won't be accepted.

6. Find and/or structure the best deals in town.

A Classic Partnership

Bob was a first-year college student at the junior college. I met him at a seminar I'd given. After that he was always hanging around my office asking questions.

Bob was committed to a goal. He wanted to be a millionaire by the time he was twenty-five. He realized after my seminar that the way to do that would be to invest in real estate. He'd established criteria which seemed modest enough; however, he had to make a lot of offers before he got the first one accepted. Bob's principal criterion was simply that he wasn't going to buy a property unless he could buy it at least 10 percent below market.

One of the things Bob did on a regular basis was to stop by the courthouse on his way home from school to look through the county records for foreclosure notices which might have been filed that day. Foreclosure notices are a matter of public record and are recorded at the county courthouse. One day he came across a property that had a $58,500 loan on it which was being foreclosed on. The owner was three months behind on his mortgage payments, and the bank had just filed a notice of default.

Bob copied down the address and went over to talk to the owner. The first thing he saw when he arrived was a "For Sale By Owner" sign in the yard. The house was on the market. The home was priced comparably to other homes in the area. The owner was asking $87,000, which, Bob figured, left $28,500 of equity.

$87,000	market value
− 58,500	loan
$28,500	equity

On first consideration Bob didn't think this looked like the best deal in town. Still, Bob figured it would be worth talking to the homeowner.

Bob was very good and very direct with people. He handed the man a card which had his home phone number on it and stated that he was in the business of buying houses (something of an exaggeration at that point!). He explained that he only bought houses that were priced at least 10 percent under the market, or which had very attractive terms. He told the man that he understood the mortgage on the house was in foreclosure and wondered if the man would be interested in a fair deal for cash.

The homeowner denied there was a problem. This, Bob found, was a typical reaction when talking to people whose property was in foreclosure. Most people don't want their personal problems aired publicly—especially not with a stranger. It had taken a certain amount of courage for Bob to bring up the subject, but he knew facing the foreclosure issue was the key to his making a good deal for both of them. The homeowner told Bob that he already had several tentative full-price offers on his property and expected it to be gone by end of week. Bob thanked the man for his time and left.

The following day Bob received a call from the homeowner. He wanted to talk to Bob. Bob went back over to the house, but this time he mostly listened. He wanted to understand the full extent of the problem so he might be able to structure a solution which would be both fair to the homeowner and profitable to himself.

Like most people who get into financial problems, this man was not a dead-beat. He had been a bit liberal in his use of credit, and it had come back to haunt him when he'd lost his job several months previous. He'd just received another job offer which was acceptable but which meant he'd have to move out of the area.

The man was very concerned about his credit rating. He was far behind on all his payments. He owed $1,800 in back payments on his mortgage. He also owed $15,500 to other creditors, which included $5,000 on a new car loan, and $3,000 on his two credit cards. He wanted to get his debts cleared up as quickly as possible before he left for his new job.

Bob decided to offer the man $250 for an option to purchase the property in two weeks according to the following terms: Bob would assume the man's car loan, as well as the rest of his consumer indebtedness, make up the back payments on the loan, and take over the loan and the house. As per the terms of the option agreement, if Bob exercised the option, the $250 would be returned to him; if Bob didn't exercise his option, the homeowner could keep the $250. In effect it was an offer of $75,800 ($11,200 less than the man was asking) to be executed two weeks from that day.

$87,000	market value
− 75,800	offer
$11,200	discount

The man agreed to give Bob the option, and he agreed to Bob's terms except that he wanted an extra $5,000. He indicated that the $5,000 did not have to be in cash and that he would carry it on a 2nd TD and note at 12 percent interest. They compromised on a note of $3,000 at 10 percent. The transaction, if the option was exercised, was going to look like this:

$ 1,800	back payments plus interest
15,500	consumer debt to be assumed
3,000	2nd TD to be executed in favor of the seller
+ 58,500	1st TD loan to be assumed, subject to bank approval
$78,800	negotiated purchase price (approximately $8,200 or 9% below market. That was below Bob's requirement of 10% below market.)

Next, Bob and the homeowner called the bank to see what the bank would require of Bob were he to assume the loan. It turned out that the bank would not be cooperative. The loan could not be assumed without renegotiating the interest rate. The bank would charge a 1 percent fee up front to allow the assumption, and they would require a loan application and a credit check. In effect, they wanted all the requirements of a new loan. They said they would be willing to lend up to 80 percent of the property's value, $69,600, if Bob wanted new financing.

So those were the parameters within which Bob had to work. Oh, one more thing! I don't think I mentioned that Bob only had $500 cash, did I? And he'd given $250 of that for option money. If he were going to exercise his option, Bob had to find a partner who would put up the rest of the cash and/or qualify for a new loan.

As the transaction stood, it didn't meet Bob's criteria of buying 10 percent below the market value. But Bob had some ideas to change that.

As soon as Bob left the house, he started looking for ways to make the investment even more attractive and profitable. Bob called on each of the homeowner's creditors and offered to pay off what the homeowner owed at 50 cents on the dollar. Every one of the creditors, except the bank which held the car loan and the major credit cards, accepted the offer. This meant that the $15,500 debt could be paid off for $11,750. A built-in profit of $3,750.

$15,500	Consumer Debt to be assumed
− 11,750	debt remaining after discounts
$ 3,750	Profit

In effect Bob would be buying the house for $75,050, which was 14% below its $87,000 market value.

The next problem was finding a partner. Being new to the town, Bob didn't know many people. He knew that doctors were generally interested in real estate and tax shelters. So Bob went looking for a hospital.

Bob knew that if he called a local doctor cold and offered him a business deal, he'd never get through the receptionist. He decided to call and make an appointment to take a physical exam. As a matter of record Bob told me that he was prepared to take physicals until one of the doctors bought his deal, or until he ran out of doctors.

Fortunately, somewhere between Bob's third or fourth blood pressure test and his second eye exam, an optometrist agreed to become Bob's partner.

The partnership agreement was handled by a simple informal written agreement which Bob drew up. It stated that it was the intent of both parties to hold the property for no more than five years. The profits from a sale would be divided 50/50. The doctor put up cash to close the deal and then would use his personal financial statement to get a new loan in an amount large enough to make up the back payments, pay off the present loan, and pay off the $11,750 of consumer debt.

He would provide the $2,450 difference between the purchase price and the new loan. He'd also pick up the costs involved in closing the transaction including the points on the new loan. Closing costs amounted to $1,869.

As an added incentive, Bob agreed that the property would be put solely in the doctor's name so that the doctor would get all the tax benefits. In return, the doctor agreed to pay any negative cash flows generated from the operation of the property as a rental unit, which were anticipated to be $1,500 per year. Bob agreed to handle all the paperwork and manage the property for 6 percent of the gross rents.

These up-front costs and carrying costs, plus 8 percent annual interest, would be paid back to the doctor when the house was sold before any profits were distributed 50/50. The transaction at closing looked as follows:

$ 1,800	back payments plus interest
11,750	discounted consumer debt to be assumed
3,000	2nd TD to be executed in favor of the seller
− 58,500	1st TD Loan to be assumed, subject to bank approval
$75,050	negotiated purchase price

Once the new financing was in place the transaction looked like this:

$69,600	new first loan
3,000	2nd TD
$72,600	total financing

The doctor was required to leave $4,319 cash in the transaction after the refinance.

$75,050	negotiated purchase price
− 72,600	total financing
$ 2,450	cash down payment

$ 2,450	cash down payament
+ 1,869	loan points and closing costs
$ 4,319	total cash required to close

Twenty-four months later Bob and the doctor sold the property for $92,000. After costs and compensating the doctor for his up-front cash and negative cash flow expense, the partners split a $10,000 profit, a net to Bob of $5,000 less the cost of four or five physical exams. He also had a happy partner who referred Bob to his associates and who offered to participate in the same sort of deal any time Bob came up with something.

Other Partnerships Forms

Partnerships come in all sizes, shapes, and textures. Most are much simpler arrangements than Bob's. Our first single family home was bought with another couple. It was a very simple arrangement. Everything was 50/50. We each contributed half of the capital and half of the labor, and we split the profits equally. The property was put in all of our names as tenants in common.

Sometimes partners don't share equally in the partnership. If you are sure you've got the best deal in town, you might offer your money partner a guarantee of 15 to 20 percent on his money. Then you would take whatever profit remains. This can be a very satisfactory arrangement for both partners, since most investors are very satisfied with a 15 to 20 percent yield on their investments.

Many creative financing techniques involve seller carry-back financing. This in effect makes the seller a partner with the buyer, at least insofar as the seller retains an equity position in the property and thereby facilitates the transfer. Normally the seller will just receive interest on his note. However, some seller carry-back arrangements have called for the seller to participate in future appreciation of the property in lieu of interest. In the later case, the seller is truly a partner of the buyer.

Limited Partnerships

Limited Partnerships are the Cadillac of partnerships. As was discussed in Chapter 4, limited partnerships are made up of at least one general partner who takes the responsibility and liability for the formation and operation of the partnership, and at least one limited partner. The limited partner(s) supplies the capital for the formation of the partnership. The limited partner(s) takes no responsibility or liability for the creation or operation of the partnership. His liability is limited to the funds he contributes to the partnership. He can lose those and no more.

A limited partnership in its most basic form is just a means of taking title. Once you've established a track record, you may want to investigate the use of limited partnerships in putting together your transactions. As general partner you would have total control over the formation, management, and disposition of the investment.

As a general rule, limited partners look to the track record and financial strength of the general partner when investing. It probably is not something that a person would use when just starting out.

The Partnership Agreement

In most small partnerships a simple agreement drawn up by the parties which spells out the terms of the partnership is commonly used. The agreement might also be drafted by an attorney. It is often advisable to at least have the agreement gone over by an attorney.

Limited partnership agreements should always be drafted by an attorney.

Save the Money

What can you do if you don't already have the money, or if you can't, or don't want to, borrow your starting-up funds? You could save the money!

The profitable world of real estate investing is still open to you. It's just going to take you a little bit longer to get started. You're going to have to learn to squeeze the money out of what's going through your hands right now. And let me remind you, there's thousands, even tens of thousands of dollars going through your hands every year.

You're just going to have to start living without some of those things you've felt you just had to have—like "Fou Fou Toilet Paper." Save that money and open a special "First Step To Financial Independence" savings account. It will be your first step toward achieving your goal.

Did you know that if you were to save $193 a month at 8 percent interest for two years you'd have $5,000—enough to get started. Don't think of it as $193 a month but, rather, as the amortized down payment on your million-dollar estate.

On the following pages I've written out nine tables depicting various savings plans. These tables are simple modified compound interest tables.

In my opinion, compound interest tables are fascinating. Take the time now to analyze them. Don't yield to the temptation of thinking, "Oh, I probably won't understand them," and flip past them. You don't need a lot of information from these tables. As a matter of fact, you're just looking for one number. There is just one number in all nine of these charts which applies directly to you.

Tables 1 and 2 allow you to determine the monthly savings amount required to equal $10,000 or $5,000, respectively, at various interest rates, over a specific number of years; Tables 3 and 4 allow you to determine the lump sum investment you'd need to make today at various interest rates to equal $10,000 or $5,000, respectively, in a specific number of years.

Tables 5 through 9 are especially interesting. They will allow you to determine the monthly savings amount required to equal $10,000 or $5,000, respectively, at various interest rates over a specific number of years assuming that you can afford to begin your savings plan with a lump sum investment of $1,000, $2,500, or $5,000.

Compare Tables 5 through 9 with Tables 1 and 2. Notice how much the monthly payments can be reduced and how quickly you can reach your goal if you can afford to start a savings plan with a lump sum and then add to it monthly.

We're going to take the various tables one at a time. Study them carefully. Remember, you're only going to be looking for one number in all of these charts—your number! The one number which applies to your present financial situation. Determine if you can afford to start with a lump sum investment and add to it monthly, or if you can just make a lump sum investment, or if you can just make monthly payments.

When you find your number, write it down in the blank space after Table 9 so you'll have it for reference when you go to open up your "First Step to Financial Independence" account.

Monthly Installments Only _____

Let's assume that you'd like to have $10,000 in four years. Let's further assume that the best rate your savings institution is paying on their savings plans is 8 percent. Look across the top of Table 1 until you come to the four-year column. Look down that column until you come to a number directly across the page from 8 percent. That number is $177, and it means that if you were to save $177 every month for four years (forty-eight months) you'd have $10,000 in the bank at the end of that period of time.

Now you do it. Choose a number of years and the best interest rate you can get from your savings institution. See how much you'd have to save monthly to accumulate $10,000 in your time frame.

If you'd like to save until you accumulate $5,000, use Table 2 the same way you used Table 1.

Table 1.   The approximate monthly investment required to equal $10,000 at the end of a specific number of months at varying savings rates.

Interest rate (%)	1 year (12 months)	2 years (24 months)	3 years (36 months)	4 years (48 months)	5 years (60 months)
5.5	$813	$395	$256	$187	$145
8.0	$803	$385	$247	$177	$136
10.0	$796	$378	$239	$170	$129
12.0	$788	$371	$232	$163	$122

Table 2.   The approximate monthly investment required to equal $5,000 at the end of a specific number of months at varying savings rates.

Interest rate (%)	1 year (12 months)	2 years (24 months)	3 years (36 months)	4 years (48 months)	5 years (60 months)
5.5	$406	$198	$128	$93	$73
8.0	$402	$193	$123	$89	$68
10.0	$398	$189	$120	$85	$65
12.0	$394	$185	$116	$81	$61

A Lump Sum Investment Only

Now look at Tables 3 and 4. Table 3 will tell you what lump sum you'd have to invest in a savings account at various interest rates to accumulate $10,000 over a specific number of years.

Let's assume your savings institution will pay you 10 percent on your savings and you'd like $10,000 in five years. Look across the top of Table 3 until you come to the five-year column. Then look down that column until you come to a number horizontally across the page from 10 percent. That number is $6,078. A lump sum investment $6,078 invested at 10 percent will equal $10,000 in five years.

Now you do it. Choose a number of years and an interest rate and see what lump sum you'd have to invest today to accumulate $10,000 in your chosen time frame.

If you only need to accumulate $5,000, use Table 4 the same way we used Table 3.

Table 3.   A lump sum invested at varying savings rates compounded monthly to equal $10,000 at the end of a specified number of months.

Interest rate (%)	1 year (12 months)	2 years (24 months)	3 years (36 months)	4 years (48 months)	5 years (60 months)
5.5	$9,466	$8,961	$8,482	$8,029	$7,600
8.0	$9,234	$8,526	$7,873	$7,269	$6,712
10.0	$9,052	$8,194	$7,417	$6,714	$6,078
12.0	$8,874	$7,876	$6,989	$6,203	$5,505

Table 4.   A lump sum invested at varying savings rates compounded monthly to equal $5,000 at the end of a specified number of months.

Interest rate (%)	1 year (12 months)	2 years (24 months)	3 years (36 months)	4 years (48 months)	5 years (60 months)
5.5	$4,733	$4,480	$4,241	$4,015	$3,800
8.0	$4,617	$4,263	$3,936	$3,635	$3,356
10.0	$4,526	$4,097	$3,709	$3,357	$3,039
12.0	$4,437	$3,938	$3,495	$3,101	$2,752

One Lump Sum Investment Plus Monthly Installments

If you're fortunate enough to have either $1,000, $2,500, or $5,000 which you can invest in a lump sum today you can drastically cut the size of the monthly installments needed or speed up the time required to accumulate $5,000 or $10,000. Tables 5 through 9 depict various situations. Find the chart which most closely parallels your present financial situation.

For example, let's assume you have $2,500 you can invest today and you'd like to accumulate $10,000 in two years. Go to Table 7. Assume your savings institution will pay you only 5.5% on your investment. Look across the top of Table 7 until you come to the two-year column. Look down that column until you come to a number horizontally across from 5.5%. That number is $285. A lump sum investment of $2,500 along with monthly payments of $285 per month, invested at 5.5%, will equal $10,000 in two years. That's not too bad, is it?

Now you do it. Decide what lump sum you can invest today to get things rolling. Choose a number of years and a realistic interest rate and see how much you'd have to invest in a lump sum today to accumulate $10,000 within your chosen time frame.

If you want to accumulate $10,000, use Table 5, 7, or 9. If you only need to accumulate $5,000, use Table 6 or 8.

Table 5.   Assuming an initial investment of $1,000—the approximate monthly investment required to equal $10,000 at the end of a specified number of months at varying savings rates.

Interest rate (%)	1 year (12 months)	2 years (24 months)	3 years (36 months)	4 years (48 months)	5 years (60 months)
5.5	$727	$351	$226	$163	$126
8.0	$716	$340	$215	$153	$116
10.0	$708	$332	$207	$145	$107
12.0	$700	$324	$199	$137	$100

Table 6.   Assuming an initial investment of $1,000—the approximate monthly investment required to equal $5,000 at the end of a specified number of months at varying savings rates.

Interest rate (%)	1 year (12 months)	2 years (24 months)	3 years (36 months)	4 years (48 months)	5 years (60 months)
5.5	$320	$153	$98	$70	$53
8.0	$315	$148	$92	$64	$48
10.0	$310	$143	$87	$60	$43
12.0	$305	$138	$83	$55	$39

Table 7.   Assuming an initial investment of $2,500—the approximate monthly investment required to equal $10,000 at the end of a specified number of months at varying savings rates.

Interest rate (%)	1 year (12 months)	2 years (24 months)	3 years (36 months)	4 years (48 months)	5 years (60 months)
5.5	$598	$285	$181	$129	$97
8.0	$586	$273	$168	$116	$85
10.0	$576	$263	$159	$107	$76
12.0	$566	$253	$149	$ 97	$67

Table 8.   Assuming an initial investment of $2,500—the approximate monthly investment required to equal $5,000 at the end of a specified number of months at varying savings rates.

Interest rate (%)	1 year (12 months)	2 years (24 months)	3 years (36 months)	4 years (48 months)	5 years (60 months)
5.5	$192	$87	$53	$35	$25
8.0	$184	$80	$45	$28	$17
10.0	$178	$74	$39	$22	$11
12.0	$172	$69	$33	$16	$ 6

Table 9.   Assuming an initial investment of $5,000—the approximate monthly investment required to equal $10,000 at the end of a specified number of months at varying savings rates.

Interest rate (%)	1 year (12 months)	2 years (24 months)	3 years (36 months)	4 years (48 months)	5 years (60 months)
5.5	$598	$285	$181	$129	$97
8.0	$586	$273	$168	$116	$85
10.0	$576	$263	$159	$107	$76
12.0	$566	$253	$149	$ 97	$67

Once you've found your number, write it down _____.

There are many ways to modify this savings plan to speed things up. For example, it might be possible to make additional lump sum investments at varying intervals. You might be able to gradually increase the amount of your monthly payment.

You might find the best deal in town and a partner with half the cash. You might decide to take a cash position in the deal yourself, withdraw your money early, and become a real estate investor ahead of time.

Most financial planners, including myself, will tell you that savings accounts are not good investments (see Chapters 5 and 6). However, if you need a place to store your money and earn a little interest while you're waiting to get started, or if you need a place to keep your money between investments, an insured savings account is somewhat better than burying your money in the backyard.

If you decide to save up the money to get started, don't waste the time while you're waiting for your nest egg to build up. Time is a valuable asset; use it profitably! Continue getting your mind in shape. Study about money. Read about taxes, tax shelters, accounting, self-made wealthy people, the stock market, life insurance, and real estate. Read books, take a college class or attend a seminar, listen to audio tapes, subscribe to newsletters. Then, when your savings account is finished cooking, your mind will be ready, too.

Make More Money

If you don't already have the money to get started and if you've rejected borrowing or saving the capital you need to get started, you and I are down to the wire. We're just going to have to find some way for you to earn some extra money.

Demand a Raise

Good luck!

Find a Second Income Source

Take an evening job at a store or shop in town. This won't be a lifetime occupation. You'll be there just long enough to establish your nest egg. Don't spend

the money you earn. Put it away in a "First Step to Financial Independence" savings account. When you've accumulated your nest egg, quit.

How about working toward earning your real estate license. Most schools
have night courses to help people prepare for their licensing exams. I know a
number of people who have created nice second incomes by obtaining their
real estate licenses and selling real estate part time.

Or how about being a "bird dog." Bow wow! A "bird dog" is a term used
by realtors to describe those friends and past clients who refer new clients to
them. "Bird dogs" collect a referral fee whenever the realtor closes an escrow
with the referred client. This is not a kickback, and it's perfectly legal, so long
as the "bird dog" only sells the realtor to the client, not the property itself.

Direct Sales

There are a number of direct sales programs such as Amway Products and Mary
Kay Cosmetics which have provided substantial second incomes for families
who have been able and willing to get with their programs.

Don't assume you can't do direct sales or that you wouldn't enjoy it. Both
of these companies specialize in taking totally untrained people and making su-
perstar salesmen out of them. And it's an experience to talk to some of these
super salesmen. It's almost like they have found a new reason for living.

Don't Do What I Did

Perhaps you've noticed I've thus far carefully avoided suggesting that you
should quit your present job and change careers. I haven't suggested that you
go into real estate investing full time, for instance. I don't think it's necessary. I
have seen enough people become very successful real estate investors in their
spare time while continuing in their chosen occupation.

Changing careers for me meant conquering a mountain of fear and uncertainty. While the fear and uncertainty acted as powerful motivators helping
to insure my success, I have also seen them act as tremendous inhibitors for
other people. While changing careers was very important in my life, it would
be presumptuous of me to recommend any such course of action to you. The
rewards of many careers outweigh the fact that they may not be financially re-

munerative. Should you decide to leave your present job for one which is more rewarding, don't say I told you to do it.

In the following chapters, you're going to add the other two essential elements of *Park Avenue Money Diet* to your Ten Year Real Estate Investment Schedule. You're going to learn how to set up your Personal Accounting Process and how to create a Prosperous Mental Attitude which will predispose your mind to achieving wealth. These two essential elements will complete your *Park Avenue Money Diet*.

CHAPTER 11

ACCOUNTING FOR YOURSELF

This book is called *The Park Avenue Money Diet* for a reason. But it may not be the reason you thought it was when you bought the book. Diets normally have something to do with food and losing weight. On a food diet, you try to take in fewer calories and learn to eat proper foods.

The goal of this diet is not to lose anything (except perhaps some bad habits!). This is a money diet. On this diet, you're learning how to properly spend, keep track of, and think about money. The goal of this diet is to make more money. *The Park Avenue Money Diet,* compared to the way middle-class people spend, keep track of, and think about money, is like the difference between eating healthy food and eating junk food.

As an average middle-class person, you've been on a junk money diet for most of your life. It's the reason why your present budget (if you have one!) is over its limits. It's the reason why you plunked down your hard-earned money to buy this book. Your financial life is going nowhere and chances are you need my help.

Just one more reminder. *The Park Avenue Money Diet* has three parts to it. This is part number two, The Personal Accounting Process, that will go along with your Ten Year Real Estate Investment Schedule and your Prosperous Mental Attitude Program. The three parts must work together. If you skip the accounting, forget it. If you don't learn to control the things you think about, which eventually lead you to the money you want, this money diet and the time you've already invested in reading this book are wasted.

The Personal Accounting Process isn't one of those impossible to maintain plans that insist you subsist on the meager pittance of a menial. In fact, it's just the opposite. It's a self-indulgent system with a heart. It will permit you to sustain and keep an accounting of a life of affluence and gratification.

I have tested *The Park Avenue Money Diet.* I didn't test it on hamsters, guinea pigs, or any other laboratory animals. I tested it on myself and other real middle-class people. And since it worked for me and for them, it's going to work for you, too. (Unless possibly, if you're a chimpanzee, or a white mouse!) Satisfied clients have sent me other clients who were dissatisfied with their economic state of affairs.

Why did I have so many people sent to me? Because I had freed myself from exactly the same predicament these clients found themselves in. I had experienced all the second rate, demeaning, and boring circumstances all middle-class people have to deal with. I've stayed free, and I know that I'll never have to go back again. Now it's your turn.

Before we get started on phase two of *The Park Avenue Money Diet,* there's one thing I'm going to insist on again. Use a calculator! You're going to be involving yourself with some more math, and the calculator will help keep it a simple and painless experience.

This won't take long; it won't be hard; so hang on, here we go!

The Personal Accounting Process

The Personal Accounting Process is a simplified accounting system. It has three parts.

1. *The Balance Sheet.* Most ordinary folks seldom know what they are worth. If and when they find out, they are usually amazed (sometimes pleasantly, sometimes unpleasantly!). Normally, so long as their financial lives stay uncomplicated, their ignorance doesn't really matter.

    The Balance Sheet is an accounting of your Assets, your Liabilities, and your Net Worth. Assets (your possessions) and Liabilities (your debts) are related. The difference between them is your Net Worth.

2. *The Income and Expense Statement.* Most middle-class people usually know what their monthly take-home income is, but they have only a very vague idea of what it actually costs them to live from day to day. At best, they approximate their living expenses so as to try and come out even at the end of each month. Income and expenses are related. You will want to account for them on a monthly income and expense statement.

3. *The Personal Accounting Process Budget.* Instead of attempting to simply survive financially from month to month, we're going to lay out a yearly earning and spending plan for you.

You're no longer going to have the luxury of an uncomplicated financial life. You'll need to keep accurate records for property loan applications, for income tax verification purposes, and for your own information.

The first thing we're going to do is get you a set of books. Go down to your local stationery store and get a hard binder and some simple accounting forms to fit it. Don't get a commercially prepared budget form. We're going to make up a budget that is you. Those prepackaged accounting systems aren't you.

Get some accounting paper that looks something like the accounting form on the next page.

Notice that there is a column at the left for the date, a large column in the middle to write the name of your accounts, and then two columns on the right for your figures (Debits and Credits). That's all you need.

BALANCE SHEET

ASSETS _____

Now fill in the top of the form just as I have in the example below.

Date 19___	Description of Entry	Debit	Credit
Jan 31	:	:	
	:	:	
	:	:	
	:	:	

Okay now, make a list of all of your assets. Naturally, by assets, I'm not referring to your appearance, personality, or exemplary work habits. Think of an asset as something material that you own and that has a value. It's your cash, and those things which can be sold to bring in cash—your money, your house, your car, your furniture, your stereo, your TV, your clothing, your real estate investments, your stocks and bonds, the cash value of your whole life insurance investment, farm or domestic animals, jewelry, silverware, china, glassware, motor boats, airplanes, snowmobiles, musical instruments, etc. Write them down in the middle column of your accounting sheet as in the example below.

BALANCE SHEET

Date 19___	Description of Entry	Debit	Credit
Jan 31	: Cash	:	
	: Stocks & Bonds	:	
	: Notes Receivable	:	
	: Townhouse Investment	:	
	: Home	:	
	: Auto #1	:	
	: Auto #2	:	
	: Household Goods	:	
	: Clothing	:	
	:	:	

Next, go down the list and put down a value for all the assets in the column immediately to the right of the description column.

For example, next to cash, put down the total amount of all the money you have. Next to your stocks and bonds, put today's value. Be careful with the rest of your assets. Put in the present value of each item. Some items will have increased in value since you bought them; some will have decreased. For instance: your car. Your car is probably worth less today than it was when you bought it. Call up your local car dealer and get its true "Bluebook" value.

On the other hand, your home and any investment real estate you have is probably worth more today than it was when you bought it. Find out its true value.

Note: It's easy to be overly optimistic when we're talking about the value of our homes and investments. For your real estate, call up a local real estate broker and get his opinion of value. Likewise, get an expert's opinion of the value of any antiques, art work, or collectibles you might own.

You'll probably have to guess at the true market value of your furniture and clothing. You might get an idea of their value by perusing your neighborhood furniture store, or by dropping in on some garage sales this weekend.

In valuing all of your assets . . . again, limit your guessing. There's no point in fooling yourself.

BALANCE SHEET

Date 19___	Description of Entry		Debit	Credit
Jan 31	: Cash	:	7,500	
	: Stocks & Bonds	:	2,500	
	: Notes Receivable	:	8,761	
	: Townhouse Investment	:	68,000	
	: Home	:	107,000	
	: Auto #1	:	11,500	
	: Auto #2	:	8,950	
	: Household Goods	:	20,000	
	: Clothing	:	4,500	
	:	:		

Liabilities

A liability is a debt. It means you owe somebody for something. The balance on your charge account or bank credit card statement is a liability. So is the mortgage on your home, the mortgage on your investment properties, and the loan on your car. If you owe a friend $20, that's a liability. (If you owe your mom a phone call, that's also a liability, but don't put that one down!) We're looking for liabilities payable in dollars—liabilities in the economic sense.

Just as you did with your assets, I want you to make a complete list of all your liabilities. Simply continue the list of liabilities under your list of assets. Put the present balances—the exact amount you still owe—in the second column to the right. Check the example below.

BALANCE SHEET

Date 19___	Description of Entry		Debit	Credit
Jan 31	:	Cash	:	7,500	
	:	Stocks & Bonds	:	2,500	
	:	Notes Receivable	:	8,761	
	:	Townhouse Investment	:	68,000	
	:	Home	:	107,000	
	:	Auto #1	:	11,500	
	:	Auto #2	:	8,950	
	:	Household Goods	:	20,000	
	:	Clothing	:	4,500	
	:		:		
	:	Accounts Payable/MasterCard	:		650
	:	Accounts Payable/Visa	:		325
	:	Accounts Payable/Am Express	:		835
	:	Townhouse Investment Loan 14%	:		57,000
	:	Home Loan 12%	:		66,000
	:	Auto Loan #1 13.5%	:		8,733
	:	Auto Loan #2 16%	:		7,750
	:		:		
		TOTALS		238,711	141,293

When you're sure you've got all of your assets and liabilities recorded correctly, total both columns. Your assets should total more than your liabilities.

Net Worth

Finally, subtract your liabilities from your assets. The figure you get is your present net worth. This is the classic accounting formula:

ASSETS − LIABILITIES = NET WORTH

BALANCE SHEET

Date 19___		Description of Entry		Debit	Credit
Jan 31	:	Cash	:	7,500	
	:	Stocks & Bonds	:	2,500	
	:	Notes Receivable	:	8,761	
	:	Townhouse Investment	:	68,000	
	:	Home	:	107,000	
	:	Auto #1	:	11,500	
	:	Auto #2	:	8,950	
	:	Household Goods	:	20,000	
	:	Clothing	:	4,500	
	:		:		
	:	Accounts Payable/MasterCard	:		650
	:	Accounts Payable/Visa	:		325
	:	Accounts Payable/Am Express	:		835
	:	Townhouse Investment Loan 14%	:		57,000
	:	Home Loan 12%	:		66,000
	:	Auto Loan #1 13.5%	:		8,733
	:	Auto Loan #2 16%	:		7,750
	:		:		
		TOTALS		238,711	141,293
		NET WORTH			97,418
				238,711	238,711

Put this balance sheet away in the binder. It's an important paper. Part of the Personal Accounting Process will be to update this balance sheet at regular intervals. How frequently is up to you. Some people like to update it only once a year; others do a new one every six months; some do one every three months (every quarter year). I like to update my balance sheet every month.

Your balance sheet is a reliable indicator of your financial situation and a good record of your progress. Every item on the sheet is important, but there are several things you'll especially want to check.

Number one is the amount of cash you have in the bank. You want to be sure to keep enough cash on hand to cover unexpected expenses and to be prepared for unexpected opportunities. By the way, in sharp contrast to what many anxious salesmen would lead you to believe, once-in-a-lifetime bargains come around considerably more often than Halley's Comet.

The next thing you want to be conscious of is your short term debt. Short term debt is any liability which is due or will be due in the near future. Short term debt means you don't have as much cash as you think you have, as calculated to the dollar amount of that short term debt.

Thirdly, you want to check your net worth. You want to see a continual improvement in your net worth.

The Income and Expense Statement

The next part of the Personal Accounting Process is to keep careful records of all of your income and expenses. You'll want to do an Income and Expense Summary monthly.

The same accounting sheets you used for your balance sheet can be used to keep track of your income and expenses.

First, fill in the top of the form just as I have in the example below.

INCOME & EXPENSE SUMMARY

Date 19__	Description of Entry	Debit	Credit
Jan 31	:	:	
	:	:	
	:	:	
	:	:	

Income

In the middle column, make a list of all your income from whatever source. List your salary, your husband's or wife's salary, interest income, rents, royalties, and your allowance from Mom and Dad, if you get one.

Put down the amount of income you took in from each source. The numbers should be placed in the second column to the right of the description of the entry. See the example below:

INCOME & EXPENSE SUMMARY

Date 19___	Description of Entry		Debit	Credit
Jan 31	: Salary Husband	:		$ 2,200
	: Salary Wife	:		1,950
	: Interest Income	:		87
	:		:	

That was the fun part. Now let's see how much of that income actually goes out each month.

Expenses

Keep a Written Record of Every Nickel You Spend. Every time you or any member of your family spends money, you and they want to have some sort of a written and dated record of the fact. Ideally, you should begin making all your payments by check or credit card. Certainly all your major purchases and tax deductible expenses should be handled this way. A written and dated record could also be in the form of a bill marked paid, a cash register total, a commercial receipt, etc., or, if nothing else is available, a note written to yourself (be sure to date it!). As each day progresses, you and the members of your family should collect these records. Stuff them in your pockets, or put them neatly into your wallets.

At the end of the day, empty the records you have collected into a receptacle like the large envelope at the top of page 180. Keep this collection dated envelopes like the ones on page 180. The number and titles of your ator is usually good!) Keep these records in this envelope until you're ready to start organizing them to record them in your Income and Expense Statement at the end of the month.

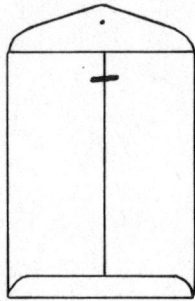

Monthly Collection Envelope

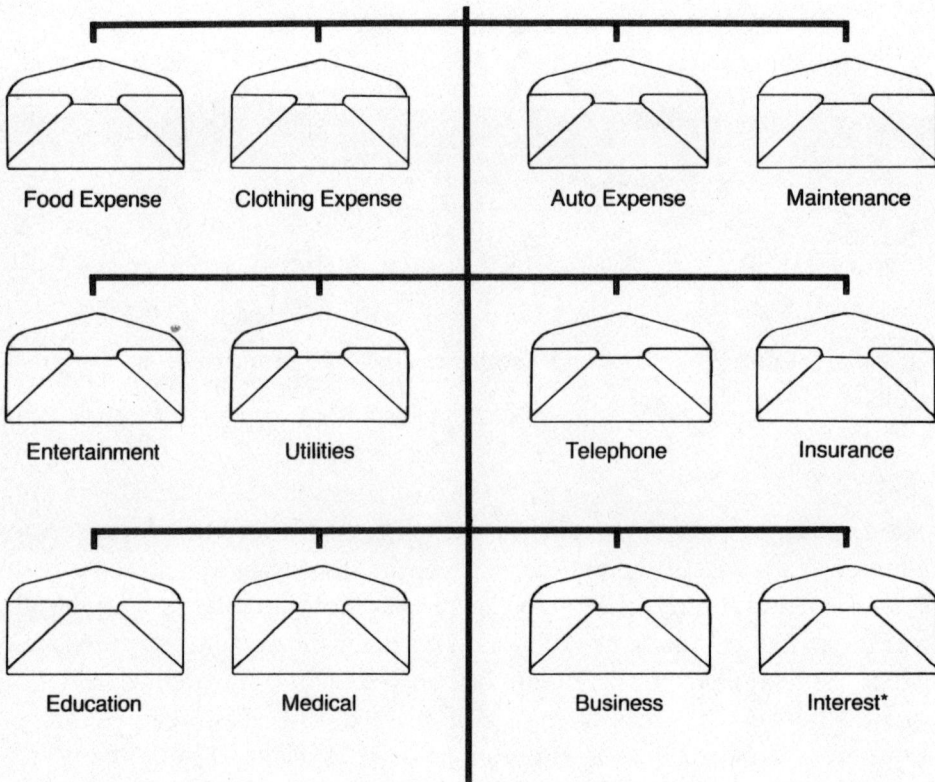

Food Expense   Clothing Expense   Auto Expense   Maintenance

Entertainment   Utilities   Telephone   Insurance

Education   Medical   Business   Interest*

*Most installment payments are made up of interest and principal. Only include a notation of the interest portion of your monthly payments (home mortgage, car payments, installment payments, etc.) in this envelope, along with whatever straight interest payments you might make on other loans.

The amount remaining from the total payment, after the interest from each payment has been subtracted and stored in the collection envelope, is the principal portion of each payment. Save that figure representing the principal amount and deduct it from the balance of the loan in question under the Liability section of your next Balance Sheet.

At the end of the month (or as you find time throughout the month) the collection envelope should be emptied and organized, according to date, into the various types of accounts for which you have titles.

This can be done by sorting them and putting them into labeled and dated envelopes like the ones on page 000. The number and titles of your expense accounts can be deteremined by you. Try to combine as many accounts under one title as you can so that your list of accounts won't become excessive. But be sure you have enough accounts to give you a clear picture of your expenses.

Note: Expenses should include *only* the interest portion of the installment payments you make. But do keep track of the principal payments. The principal amount will be subtracted from the loan balance on the *balance sheet* the next time (and each time) you revise it.

Finally, total all of the receipts in each envelope and put the total on the front of the envelope.

Next, record these totals on your Income and Expense Statement. List them right underneath the income. Once you finish recording these totals in the Income and Expense Statement, file the envelopes and keep them with your important papers. They're an important part of your Personal Accounting Process.

Like most people, your expenses will change from month to month. Don't let that bother you. Just make up some new envelopes and keep adding the new expenses to the bottom of your list of expenses.

Put the amounts of each expense in the first column next to the description of the entry. See below.

Jan. 31	:	Food	:	350
	:	Clothing	:	97
	:	Auto	:	125
	:	Maintenance	:	60
	:	Entertainment	:	285
	:	Utilities	:	280
	:	Telephone	:	49
	:	Insurance	:	185
	:	Education	:	0
	:	Medical	:	25
	:	Business	:	250
	:	Interest Expense	:	1,645

Profit or Loss

Now simply total your expenses and your income, subtract the smaller from the larger, and determine whether you had a profit or loss for the month. You had a profit if you took in more income than you spent, and you had a loss if you spent more for expenses than you took in in income.

INCOME & EXPENSE SUMMARY

Date 19___		Description of Entry		Debit	Credit
Jan 31	:	Salary Husband	:		$ 2,200
	:	Salary Wife	:		1,950
	:	Interest Income	:		87
	:		:		
	:	Food	:	350	
	:	Clothing	:	97	
	:	Auto	:	125	
	:	Maintenance	:	60	
	:	Entertainment	:	285	
	:	Utilities	:	280	
	:	Telephone	:	49	
	:	Insurance	:	185	
	:	Education	:	0	
	:	Medical	:	25	
	:	Business	:	250	
	:	Interest Expense	:	1,645	
		TOTALS		$ 3,351	$ 4,237
		PROFIT		886	
				$ 4,237	$ 4,237

Put your Income and Expense Summary away in the binder.

The Personal Accounting Process Budget ——————

One of the most common problems I've isolated and tried to solve while working with average middle-class people is their firm belief that they can get ahead simply by cutting back on expenses (staying on a starvation budget!). Convincing them that they're limiting their horizons and making themselves miserable is a monumental task. It goes against everything they've ever been taught. But it's a fact, nevertheless.

Putting yourself on a budget, the primary goal of which is simply to restrict your spending, is a defeatist concept . . . typically middle class. By cutting out movies, weekend trips, frozen yogurt after dinner, or whatever it is you decide to deprive yourself of, you will end up taking much of the fun out of your life. It's just like the person who decides to diet by eating only celery and carrots. It's boring! At best, that person is going to be miserable. At worst, his diet is going to fail. The Personal Accounting Process Budget is different than most of the budgets you've put yourself on in the past. It does not advocate severe reduction of expenses. It will help you to spend more wisely and constructively, and you may actually decide to cut back on your spending in some areas. However, *the goal of the Personal Accounting Process Budget is not to give you guidelines for cutting back, but rather to help you set your spending goals and adjust your earnings to meet those goals.*

Since you are going to attempt to structure your income to meet your spending goals, the first thing we want to do is find out how much money you'd like to spend. We are going to set up your Personal Accounting Process Budget on an annual basis. In other words, we're going to decide right now, in detail, how much money you're going to spend the rest of this year.

The first step is to lay out our format. For this budget, you're going to need a sheet of accounting paper with an entry description column on the left, and thirteen columns from left to right. Fill in the top of the form as shown below.

PERSONAL ACCOUNTING PROCESS BUDGET

Description	1 Jan	2 Feb	3 Mar	4 Apr	5 May	6 Jun	7 Jul	8 Aug	9 Sep	10 Oct	11 Nov	12 Dec	13 Annual

The Initial Layout
of the Personal Accounting Budget ————————————

Before we get started, I'm going to suggest that you be neat and careful, but I also want you to relax and stay loose. Treat this chart as a worksheet. Don't approach it as though you were writing anything down in concrete. Use a pencil and write lightly. Allow yourself the luxury of dreaming a little bit. This is the first draft of your personal financial plan for the year. Try to make it exciting and rewarding.

Starting at line three, fill in spaces for all of the income you have on your Income and Expense Statement, in that same order. Don't fill in any of the dollar amounts just yet. Leave several spaces in which to put any additional income sources that you might come up with while laying out the budget, or that develop during the year. Now draw a line underneath all of your income (be sure to skip down below the spaces for additional income). Draw it all the way across the page from left to right.

Skip a space and draw a double line below the single line across the page.

Next, put down all of your expenses exactly the way you have them on your Income and Expense Statement.

There will be one major difference. One of your entries will be an entry called Principal Payments. Principal payments aren't actually expenses (they're classified as debt reduction, or equity buildup), but they are an out-going cash flow item, and since this is a cash flow projection, we need to include them here.

As an example of what your worksheet should look like at this point, take a look at the one on the next page.

PERSONAL ACCOUNTING PROCESS BUDGET

Description	1 Jan	2 Feb	3 Mar	4 Apr	5 May	6 Jun	7 Jul	8 Aug	9 Sep	10 Oct	11 Nov	12 Dec	13 Annual
Salary 1													
Salary 2													
Interest Incm													
Other Income													
TOTAL													
Food Expense													
Clothing Exp.													
Auto Exp.													
Maint. Exp.													
Entertainment													
Utilities Exp.													
Telephone Exp.													
Insurance Exp.													
Education Exp.													
Medical Exp.													
Business Exp.													
Interest Exp.													
Property Tax													
Income Tax													
(Princ. Pmts.)													
TOTAL EXPENSE													
NET INCOME													

Just as we did with your list of incomes, skip some spaces at the bottom of your list of expenses. You will probably come up with a few more later. Don't draw any lines.

The idea now is to look at the list of expenses you have on your Income and Expense Statement and attempt to project monthly dollar amounts for them over the course of an entire year. Analyze and project each of your expenses individually.

To help you get started, let's you and I do your Utilities Expense together. What do you think your utility expense for the first month will be? Put it down in the first column to the right of the words Utilities Expense. Do you think that you will spend the same amount for utilities as you put down for the first month, every month next year? Do you think you'll spend less? More? Or will it vary from month to month? Is your Public Utilities Commission planning a rate increase? Would a uniform across-the-page percentage increase say of 5 percent or 10 percent apply, or should you put in a specific estimate of a figure on a month-to-month basis?

Put your estimate of your monthly utilities expense on your chart for every month of the year. Total up the numbers from left to right, and enter the total in the thirteenth column on your chart. That figure is your projection of your annual utilities expense.

PERSONAL ACCOUNTING PROCESS BUDGET

Description	1 Jan	2 Feb	3 Mar	4 Apr	5 May	6 Jun	7 Jul	8 Aug	9 Sep	10 Oct	11 Nov	12 Dec	13 Annual
Salary 1													
Salary 2													
Interest Incm													
Other Income													
TOTAL													
Food Expense													
Clothing Exp.													
Auto Exp.													
Maint. Exp.													
Entertainment													
Utilities Exp.	280	280	200	200	200	150	150	150	150	200	280	325	2,565
Telephone Exp.													
Insurance Exp.													
Education Exp.													
Medical Exp.													
Business Exp.													
Interest Exp.													
Property Tax													
Income Tax													
(Princ. Pmts.)													
TOTAL EXPENSE													
NET INCOME													

Now do the same for every expense on your Income and Expense Statement. Some expenses will probably be pretty much uniform. For these, you can put the same number in every column across the page. Other expenses, like property taxes, will probably only occur once or twice during the year. The rest of the months for these items will be left blank.

Go ahead now. Complete an annual projection of your expenses. Don't forget to do the totals in column thirteen, and don't rush. To do the job right should take you awhile. Don't worry, I'll wait, even if it takes you several hours (or days!). The example on the following page should prove useful.

Finished? Okay, now total the monthly columns from top to bottom and write them down lightly in pencil at the bottom of the page. Don't forget to skip the rows you left for additional expenses.

Let's see what we've done so far. You've totaled the rows from left to right, putting the totals in column thirteen. You've totaled the columns from top to bottom, putting those totals on the next-to-the-bottom line of the work sheet. The totals you get at the bottom of the twelve columns are the totals of each month's projected expenses. The totals in column thirteen are the annual totals of each individual expense. Be sure to total column thirteen and put that total at the bottom right hand corner of the worksheet. That is the total of all your expenses for the year.

I hope all of these totals are written lightly, and in pencil, because they're subject to revision.

Don't do anything about recording your income yet, but make a guess at this point, from your expense projections, as to whether you'll make it on your projected income or not.

Even if you expect you're probably already over your budget, continue along with me. Before we finish up with the expenses, let's put in two more entries. First, think about one or more special things you would like to have or do during this year.

For example, let's pretend you'd like to take a week's vacation to Tahiti. Or, how about a new couch for the living room? How much will it cost? Figure first class on the trip, and top of the line on the couch. Don't worry about whether you'll have the money or not. It's not costing you anything at this point, so go ahead, be a big spender.

The Park Avenue Money Diet

PERSONAL ACCOUNTING PROCESS BUDGET

Description	1 Jan	2 Feb	3 Mar	4 Apr	5 May	6 Jun	7 Jul	8 Aug	9 Sep	10 Oct	11 Nov	12 Dec	13 Annual
Salary 1													
Salary 2													
Interest Incm													
Other Income													
TOTAL													
Food Expense	350	350	350	350	350	350	400	350	375	375	375	375	4,350
Clothing Exp.	90	90	90	100	90	90	200	1,000	90	90	90	90	2,110
Auto Exp.	125	400	100	100	100	100	100	100	250	100	100	100	1,675
Maint. Exp.	60	75	75	75	1,500	75	75	75	75	75	75	75	2,310
Entertainment	285	300	300	300	300	400	1,500	300	300	300	300	300	4,885
Utilities Exp.	280	280	200	200	200	150	150	150	150	200	280	325	2,565
Telephone Exp.	49	55	35	35	35	35	35	35	35	75	75	75	574
Insurance Exp.	185			500									685
Education Exp.					350								350
Medical Exp.	25	25	25	25	25	25	25	25	25	25	25	25	300
Business Exp.	250	250	250	250	250	250	250	250	250	250	250	250	3,000
Interest Exp.	1,645	1,640	1,635	1,630	1,625	1,620	1,615	1,610	1,605	1,600	1,595	1,590	19,410
Property Tax				900								900	1,800
Income Tax				3,500									3,500
(Princ. Pmts.)	220	225	230	235	240	245	250	255	260	265	270	275	2,970
TOTAL EXPENSE													
NET INCOME													

Decide what special thing or things you'd really like this year, and decide in which month or months you'd like to make the purchase or spend the money. Then, make the entry for this expense on your chart. Remember, this is just a worksheet, so take a chance.

Second, if you haven't already done it, put down the amount of the down payment on the real estate investment you want to purchase, and in what month. In the months following your projected investment purchase, put down your estimates of any negative cash flows which will have to come out of your pocket to cover your investment's expenses.

Note 1: Negative cash flows are just those amounts of cash required to be taken out of your pocket (if need be!) after the income the property produces has been used up.

Note 2: In the example that follows, I assume that the down payment is borrowed. Therefore you will see an entry, when we get back to the income section, called loan proceeds. This balances the investment down payment amount. The monthly expenses following the investment purchase include a little extra for the principal and interest payments on this loan. (Instead of doing it this way, you could divide the payment into principal and interest and enter them under the interest expense and principal payment categories.)

Now total your expense figures for these items in the rows from left to right, putting the totals in column thirteen. Finally, retotal all your expenses in the twelve columns for each month and the thirteenth column for the year. Again, put the totals on the next-to-the-bottom line of your worksheet. Draw a single line right above and another one right below these totals.

PERSONAL ACCOUNTING PROCESS BUDGET

Description	1 Jan	2 Feb	3 Mar	4 Apr	5 May	6 Jun	7 Jul	8 Aug	9 Sep	10 Oct	11 Nov	12 Dec	13 Annual
Salary 1													
Salary 2													
Interest Incm													
Other Income													
TOTAL													
Food Expense	350	350	350	350	350	350	400	350	375	375	375	375	4,350
Clothing Exp.	90	90	90	100	90	90	200	1,000	90	90	90	90	2,110
Auto Exp.	125	400	100	100	100	100	100	100	250	100	100	100	1,675
Maint. Exp.	60	75	75	75	1,500	75	75	75	75	75	75	75	2,310
Entertainment	285	300	300	300	300	400	1,500	300	300	300	300	300	4,885
Utilities Exp.	280	280	200	200	200	150	150	150	150	200	280	325	2,565
Telephone Exp.	49	55	35	35	35	35	35	35	35	75	75	75	574
Insurance Exp.	185			500									685
Education Exp.					350								350
Medical Exp.	25	25	25	25	25	25	25	25	25	25	25	25	300
Business Exp.	250	250	250	250	250	250	250	250	250	250	250	250	3,000
Interest Exp.	1,645	1,640	1,635	1,630	1,625	1,620	1,615	1,610	1,605	1,600	1,595	1,590	19,410
Property Tax				900								900	1,800
Income Tax				3,500									3,500
(Princ. Pmts.)	220	225	230	235	240	245	250	255	260	265	270	275	2,970
NEW COUCH								1,200					1,200
NEW INVST.		10,000	275	275	275	275	275	275	275	275	275	275	12,750
TOTAL EXPS.	3,564	13,690	3,565	8,475	5,340	3,615	4,875	5,625	3,690	3,630	3,710	4,655	64,434
NET INCOME													

When you're satisfied that you have entered all of the expenses you expect to have this year, go ahead and project your income across the page in the same manner as you did with the expenses. Don't forget to make allowances for pay increases, overtime, interest income, etc. Enter each item in the month in which you expect it to occur. Total the rows from left to right. Put the totals in column thirteen. Then add up each of the monthly income columns, including the thirteenth column. (The thirteenth column is your total annual figure for each income source.) Put the totals lightly in pencil in the space between the single and double lines which you have already drawn.

PERSONAL ACCOUNTING PROCESS BUDGET

Description	1 Jan	2 Feb	3 Mar	4 Apr	5 May	6 Jun	7 Jul	8 Aug	9 Sep	10 Oct	11 Nov	12 Dec	13 Annual
Salary 1	2,100	2,100	2,100	2,100	2,100	2,100	2,100	2,100	2,100	2,300	2,300	2,300	25,800
Salary 2	1,950	1,950	1,950	1,950	1,950	2,100	2,100	2,100	2,100	2,100	2,100	2,100	24,450
Interest Incm	90	90	90	90	90	90	90	90	90	90	90	90	1,080
Other Income	50	50	50	50	50	75	75	75	75	75	75	75	775
Loan Proceeds		10,000											10,000
TOTAL	4,190	14,190	4,190	4,190	4,190	4,365	4,365	4,365	4,365	4,565	4,565	4,565	62,105
Food Expense	350	350	350	350	350	350	400	350	375	375	375	375	4,350
Clothing Exp.	90	90	90	100	90	90	200	1,000	90	90	90	90	2,110
Auto Exp.	125	400	100	100	100	100	100	100	250	100	100	100	1,675
Maint. Exp.	60	75	75	75	1,500	75	75	75	75	75	75	75	2,310
Entertainment	285	300	300	300	300	400	1,500	300	300	300	300	300	4,885
Utilities Exp.	280	280	200	200	200	150	150	150	150	200	280	325	2,565
Telephone Exp.	49	55	35	35	35	35	35	35	35	75	75	75	574
Insurance Exp.	185			500									685
Education Exp.					350								350
Medical Exp.	25	25	25	25	25	25	25	25	25	25	25	25	300
Business Exp.	250	250	250	250	250	250	250	250	250	250	250	250	3,000
Interest Exp.	1,645	1,640	1,635	1,630	1,625	1,620	1,615	1,610	1,605	1,600	1,595	1,590	19,410
Property Tax				900								900	1,800
Income Tax				3,500									3,500
(Princ. Pmts.)	220	225	230	235	240	245	250	255	260	265	270	275	2,970
NEW COUCH								1,200					1,200
NEW INVST		10,000	275	275	275	275	275	275	275	275	275	275	12,750
TOTAL EXPS.	3,564	13,690	3,565	8,475	5,340	3,615	4,875	5,625	3,690	3,630	3,710	4,655	64,434
NET INCOME													

Now, take the monthly expense totals at the very bottom of each column, and the annual expense total in column thirteen, and subtract them from the monthly gross income totals in each respective column, including the annual gross income total in column thirteen. Enter the figures across the very bottom line of your chart. Draw a double line under this figure. That figure, whether positive or negative, is your projected net income. At the bottom of column thirteen, you have your net income for the year.

PERSONAL ACCOUNTING PROCESS BUDGET

Description	1 Jan	2 Feb	3 Mar	4 Apr	5 May	6 Jun	7 Jul	8 Aug	9 Sep	10 Oct	11 Nov	12 Dec	13 Annual
Salary 1	2,100	2,100	2,100	2,100	2,100	2,100	2,100	2,100	2,100	2,300	2,300	2,300	25,800
Salary 2	1,950	1,950	1,950	1,950	1,950	2,100	2,100	2,100	2,100	2,100	2,100	2,100	24,450
Interest Incm	90	90	90	90	90	90	90	90	90	90	90	90	1,080
Other Income	50	50	50	50	50	75	75	75	75	75	75	75	775
Loan Proceeds		10,000											10,000
TOTAL	4,190	14,190	4,190	4,190	4,190	4,365	4,365	4,365	4,365	4,565	4,565	4,565	62,105
Food Expense	350	350	350	350	350	350	400	350	375	375	375	375	4,350
Clothing Exp.	90	90	90	100	90	90	200	1,000	90	90	90	90	2,110
Auto Exp.	125	400	100	100	100	100	100	100	250	100	100	100	1,675
Maint. Exp.	60	75	75	75	1,500	75	75	75	75	75	75	75	2,310
Entertainment	285	300	300	300	300	400	1,500	300	300	300	300	300	4,885
Utilities Exp.	280	280	200	200	200	150	150	150	150	200	280	325	2,565
Telephone Exp.	49	55	35	35	35	35	35	35	35	75	75	75	574
Insurance Exp.	185			500									685
Education Exp.					350								350
Medical Exp.	25	25	25	25	25	25	25	25	25	25	25	25	300
Business Exp.	250	250	250	250	250	250	250	250	250	250	250	250	3,000
Interest Exp.	1,645	1,640	1,635	1,630	1,625	1,620	1,615	1,610	1,605	1,600	1,595	1,590	19,410
Property Tax				900								900	1,800
Income Tax				3,500									3,500
(Princ. Pmts.)	220	225	230	235	240	245	250	255	260	265	270	275	2,970
NEW COUCH								1,200					1,200
NEW INVST.		10,000	275	275	275	275	275	275	275	275	275	275	12,750
TOTAL EXPS.	3,564	13,690	3,565	8,475	5,340	3,615	4,875	5,625	3,690	3,630	3,710	4,655	64,434
NET INCOME	626	500	625	−4,285	−1,150	750	−510	−1,260	675	935	855	−90	−2,329

Surprise _____

You've just completed another test. I call it the Entrepreneur Dream Category
Quiz. All entrepreneurs dream. They imagine things for themselves, and then
they go out and do whatever is necessary to achieve whatever they want. Just
as in handwriting analysis, you've just revealed a lot about yourself, and your
entrepreneurial nature, and your willingness to dream, by the way you filled
out your Personal Accounting Process Budget. You may be about to learn
some things about yourself that you've been unaware of until this minute.

   I've established three arbitrary categories: Entrepreneur Dream Cate-
gory A, Entrepreneur Dream Category B, and Entrepreneur Dream Category
C. One of these three categories describes the Personal Accounting Process
Budget you've outlined for yourself.

   Note: Whatever category you're in, if you've made your own Personal
   Accounting Process Budget, you're way ahead of the average middle-class
   people we've discussed who are prone to meretricious impulse purchasing. At least you've begun to plan your cash flows, positive or negative. That
   puts you out among the leaders in the financial game.

Entrepreneur Dream Category A _____

You've projected a negative cash flow situation.

   You're the winner! You not only want more out of life, you expect it.
Good for you! (You are providing an allowance for investing and for buying a
few of the things you've really wanted for a long time, aren't you?) It doesn't
matter whether you make $20,000 a year or $100,000 a year, it is always
possible to plan your expenses so that you need just a little bit more—or
better yet, a whole lot more.

   You didn't think you were going to get the top grade on this test, did
you? You have the one motivating characteristic of the great entrepreneurs.
Wanting more and getting more are not that far apart.

   Now you simply have to decide what you're going to do, and—if need
be—what you're going to give up to get what you really want. Of course,
what you really want and need right now is more money! Relax! Getting more

money is easy! Believe it or not, the hard part is deciding that you really want it! And you've already done that, haven't you!

Entrepreneur Dream Category B ─────────────

You've planned a break-even situation.

Your life is in balance. You'll be getting by. You're planning a relatively safe, but not an overly motivating situation for yourself. You're not exactly living on the razor's edge, but there's hope. You've got a chance of reaching financial independence. You should expect to experience some slow progress towards that goal. (I'm again assuming, in your case, that your break-even projection includes some allowance for investing and for at least one important personal purchase!)

Perhaps at some point, you'll decide to motivate yourself to project a negative cash flow situation for yourself. It's then that you'll decide to really get down into the economic machine and get your hands greasy. It's then you'll decide to reach for the brass ring! It's only then that you will really commit yourself, body and soul, to your escape from the middle class.

Isn't there something more you would like out of life this year?

Entrepreneur Dream Category C ─────────────

You are projecting a positive cash flow.

Note: If you are projecting this positive cash flow to create a financial basis for investing, or financial risk-taking, skip the rest of the discussion on Entrepreneur Dream Category C people, and go back to Entrepreneur Dream Category B, or Entrepreneur Dream Category A.

You're not very adventuresome, are you? Either that, or you already have a lot of income and/or property; but more than likely, you're just modest in projecting your expenses. If you've projected a positive cash flow and (I'm assuming!) you're not planning on investing or buying something special that you really want, you belong in Entrepreneur Dream Category C. (Technically, we should probably scratch the Entrepreneur and the Dream, and just call it Category C!)

If you're truly comfortable where you are, and that's the reason you projected a positive cash flow, it's going to be hard for you to motivate yourself to climb to the next financial level. If you continue with this average middle-class thinking, you're going to miss out on a lot in your life. You're not planning the financial moves which could carry you to the real security of financial independence.

Are you worried about your security? Let me warn you, the security you seem to be looking for at present is a false security. You will never be able to sock enough away just by saving it to protect yourself the way you'd really like to.

Why not consider a more ambitious financial projection? Try spending some time with a pencil and paper, dreaming about the sort of life you would like to live if money were really no object. Consider setting your goals beyond your present reach. See if that won't motivate you to look at your near term income potential a little more critically. Who knows? You might encourage yourself to find additional sources of revenue.

It's not important to worry about where the additional income is going to come from at this point. Remember, you're just in the dreaming stages. Perhaps you'll demand that raise you should have demanded a year ago. Maybe you'll start looking for a better job. Maybe you'll take a second job. Maybe you'll motivate yourself to invent that better mousetrap. If your financial projection requires that you need more money, and if you want it badly enough, don't worry! You'll get it.

Let's Be Honest ────────────────────────────

If you're not satisfied with your budget, go back now and revise it to the point where you *are* satisfied with it. You're probably going to want to do that sooner or later, anyway. Making changes in your Personal Accounting Process Budget to reflect your current conditions should become standard procedure from now on. You might even want to revise it one more time right after you finish reading the book. Try and make plans that will eventually put you in the Entrepreneur Dream Category A.

When you've finished with all your revisions, stop and face yourself honestly. Ask yourself which category you really belong in. You're either an **A**, a **B**, or a **C**. Categorizing yourself can be a painful task, so get it over with. If it's too painful to say, write it down on a piece of paper, then crumple it up and throw it away.

*   *   *

Make a permanent copy of your Personal Accounting Process Budget. Copy it over in ink, or make a photocopy of it. Put the permanent copy away somewhere. Plan to refer to it from time to time throughout the year.

Continue to work off the original worksheet (not the ink or photocopy!). Each month, after you complete your Income and Expense Statement, you should update this cash flow worksheet with your actual income and expenses. Make changes when and where necessary. Plan to revise this worksheet once a month (twelve times this year).

Note: Be sure to check all of the totals every time you do an update. Whenever you change one number, you'll probably have to change several more.

Compare your worksheet from time to time with the permanent copy you put away. Ask yourself questions about your budget. Are things going pretty much the way you'd planned? Do you need to cut back in some areas? Do you need to figure out ways to make some more money?

Your Personal Accounting Process Budget will last until the first of next year. At that time, you'll start fresh with a new one.

Keeping accurate records and making financial projections are two things most average middle-class people are unaccustomed to doing. If that's true in your case, remember: Self-made wealthy people aren't necessarily smarter, or harder working, or in any other way different from less successful people. They just do some things that unsuccessful people don't want to do. Accurate record keeping and financial projections are two of those things.

It may not be immediately apparent, but simply keeping your Balance Sheet, your Income and Expense Statement, and this Personal Accounting Process Budget up-to-date and accurate will be a powerful motivator. What's more, keeping your own records and making your own projections will give you a sense of security and a sense of purpose unlike anything you may have experienced to date. You will constantly know where you are financially, and what it's going to take for you to stay afloat and keep moving ahead.

CHAPTER 12

YOUR PROSPEROUS MENTAL ATTITUDE

Note: The following does not apply to adventures with the Roulette Wheel, the Irish Sweepstakes, or the stock market!

In recent years, I've learned that the way I think about things directly affects the way things happen. I've discovered that I am well on my way to achieving something when I begin thinking that I really want to achieve it. Like the professional golfer who sees his ball going into the cup before he ever swings his club, I know that if I can first imagine something happening, it's more likely to come about than if I take the passive or fatalistic approach and merely hope that something will come to pass. What's more, if I take a negative approach and assume that a certain thing won't ever happen, it probably won't.

From past experience with clients, I've found that I can't just suggest this idea to you and expect you to give it much credence. I can only point the idea out to you to let you know it's there. The rest is up to you. To really understand this idea, to accept it, and be willing to invest your bottom dollar in it, you must experience it. The sooner you experience it, the sooner you'll embrace it, and the sooner you embrace it, the sooner you'll start achieving those things you want most to achieve.

When I was living an average middle-class life, I was often negative and indifferent about many things, especially those things over which I thought I had little control. This included the idea of trying to improve my financial situation! I did all sorts of wasteful, unproductive things to try to make myself feel better; to try and make myself feel as though I were getting all I could out of life. I was only kidding myself. All I ever accomplished was to aggravate what I've come to know as my average middle-class problem.

It required a change in the way I thought about things to make me take hold of my life and begin to make something of it. It was a change in my mental attitude that sustained me through my transition from middle class to money class.

You Can Do It and You Should Do It

One of the early steps in my beginning to achieve wealth was the simple realization that "I could do it." Another was the determination that one way or another, "I was going to do it." Once I realized and determined those two seemingly obvious things, I needed little else in the way of backup or reinforcement. I was on my way.

There have been mornings in my life, in recent years, when I've had to mentally fortify myself against whatever it was I had to face during the day. At those times I would reassure myself that, no matter what it was I expected to encounter, "I could do it" and "I would do it!" You too will need to develop a similar positive and aggressive attitude.

Now you can't simply say "I can do it" and "I will do it" while you're sitting here reading this chapter. You'll have to prepare yourself so that you'll be ready to face the challenges you'll have to face as you begin your transition. Later in this chapter I'll suggest a set of mental exercises and attitudes to assist you. Using them, along with the ideas that "you can do it" and "you will do it," will help you to make the transition as simple as smiling and "whistling a happy tune." You'll fool yourself and those around you when you adopt an attitude which leaves no room for self-doubt and defeat.

You Have It Within Yourself

What was it that made you buy this book? It was exactly the same thing that got you involved in all those other investment and saving schemes, and encouraged you to suffer through them with such faith and commitment. It was your mind. There's a little voice inside you that told you that you didn't want to be average and middle class any more. It goaded you into taking just one more chance in your search for riches and self-improvement.

That's right, we all have a guiding voice inside us; we just don't always listen to it. But it's that little voice that has finally steered you to a source which can really help you—a source that is providing you with the details of how to succeed.

Make friends with that little voice. It's your motivator. It's the acorn that will produce the giant oak; the seed of what you eventually expect to accomplish. It's the desire to be more than you presently are, to have more than you presently have, to live more prosperously, to achieve more, and to be happier. Listen carefully to what that little voice has to say. It's been quietly telling you all along that it would be both easier and more fun to be wealthy.

You Only Have One Life to Live

To adapt a phrase from that beer commercial, you're only going to go 'round once in life, so why not do it as a successful person? Why not escape the middle class and become a member of the money class? You'll find you'll get a lot more gusto.

Some people believe you can come back into this world a second time, and you can bet they hope that this is true. I don't believe it's ever been done. No one ever gets the chance to come back and say, "Well, I didn't take advantage of all my opportunities the first time around, so I'll try and do better this next time."

You're only going to have one chance at this wonderful experience called living. Take it from me, it's much more fun and exciting to do it with money than without it. All you need to do is start off by following a plan . . . a surefire plan . . . *The Park Avenue Money Diet*. Make use of the Ten Year Real Estate Investment Schedule, the Personal Accounting Process, and your Prosperous Mental Attitude. They will assure your success.

The Six Mind Hooks of a Prosperous Mental Attitude

When a song writer sits down to compose a song, he begins by looking for a hook. A hook is a word, a phrase, or an unusual rhythm or melodic line which will reach out and grab the listener and make him listen.

Like a song writer writing a song, I'm going to try to put six mind hooks into your psyche for you to hang your Prosperous Mental Attitude on. (Don't worry. They're painless!) If I'm successful, you will have these mind hooks to refer to whenever you need them. The six mind hooks of a Prosperous Mental Attitude are:

Concentrated Effort

Positive Thinking

Habit

Desire

Faith

Specific Goals

We'll start with Concentrated Effort.

Concentrated Effort

The first ingredient for a Prosperous Mental Attitude is effort. Naturally, it's going to take some effort on your part to become wealthy. But effort alone is not enough. The guy that drives the garbage truck and picks up all those heavy garbage cans exerts a lot of effort, but you wouldn't normally consider a garbage collector a successful person (unless he owns the company!), would you?

You probably exert a great deal of effort at what you're doing now, but so far it hasn't gotten you where you want to be. Every day you get up, you go to work, you come home, and you exert a tremendous amount of effort in the process. From the time you awaken to the time you go to bed, you are putting forth effort. The problem is that your effort is dissipated over so many activities, most of which are not of any real importance to you personally, that you're not accomplishing what you need to accomplish for yourself. Most of your effort is being spent routinely playing someone else's ball game in somebody else's ball park.

Have you ever met a really successful real estate agent, doctor, lawyer, or steam fitter? The really successful ones all have one thing in common. They can't talk to you for ten minutes without bringing up the subject of their profession. They eat, drink, and sleep their success. They are totally involved in what they do, and that's a large part of the reason for their success.

To achieve your own success, you're going to want to follow their example. Effort alone is not enough. What you need is concentrated effort directed toward the achievement of your own specific goals. Concentrated effort in this context is largely the province of your mind. It's possible for you to concentrate your efforts toward thinking of, talking about, or working at your plan for success at least several hours a day, even while you continue with your present everyday activities.

You can think about it for half an hour when you first get up. You can talk to your family about it at breakfast. You can think about it for another half hour on your way to work. You can talk about it with the people you work with at coffee break and at lunch. You can give it some more thought on your way back home in the evening. You can get in a concentrated hour of study and planning every evening, you can study and work at it on the weekends, and you can think about it for another half hour before you go to sleep.

Let me caution you. As you begin making concrete plans for your personal success, and especially as you begin to see the results of your concentrated efforts, you're going to start having a really good time. You're going to start making more and more time available for your success. Instead of studying and working one hour every evening, you'll begin working all evening. The more success you achieve, the more you will get carried away, as the electric charge generated by your concentrated effort propels you along. Concentrated effort can work wonders. Harness its energy and make it work for you!

You Can Control What You Think About _____

You may not be able to do everything you want to do in your lifetime this instant, but you can think about anything you want to think about, right now. Your thought process is the one thing in your life over which you have total and immediate control. You can think positive thoughts, or you can think counter-productive thoughts. You can react to situations with anger, fear, apathy, trepidation, jealousy, and disappointment; or you can approach the same situations with a sense of challenge, acceptance, approval, understanding, appreciation, and wonder.

Your thoughts are personal things. It doesn't matter if people around you are thinking entirely different thoughts. It is of no consequence to you whatsoever if others you associate with are prone to wishful or negative thinking. It's reasonable to assume that the people you presently associate with are middle class and will probably not be thinking the same prosperous thoughts that you are thinking. Don't let it bother you. And don't let their thoughts steer you away from your plans for achieving wealth.

It's absolutely true that you can think any thought you want to think. You can't think any thought someone else wants to think, and you normally can't control what other people think. But you can control your own thoughts. You can think positively all the time . . . if you want to!

Of the six ingredients in your Prosperous Mental Attitude, positive thinking will probably sound the easiest. In reality, it's the one thing you will have to work the hardest on. You've spent much of your life learning to analyze and criticize everything you come in contact with. As a member of the middle class, you've been taught the conscious or unconscious habit of thinking negatively . . . even pessimistically. This has got to stop! You must begin to believe in your potential for achieving prosperity and starting today, begin to see yourself as a prosperous person.

You will accomplish exactly what you think you are going to accomplish in life. If you've already said to yourself, "I can't do the things outlined in this book," then you're absolutely right . . . you can't do them. If, on the other hand, you've already said, "I can and will do them," your prosperity is guaranteed.

An element in thought control suggests that, "All prosperous people have positive mental attitudes." Hearing this, the average middle-class person is going to say, "Of course they have positive mental attitudes, they've got money. If I had their money, I'd have a positive mental attitude, too." They refuse to see the absolute truth, which is, prosperous people, those who achieve prosperity on their own, started out with a positive mental attitude to achieve their prosperity . . . not the other way around. Really now, how far do you expect to get when you start out following the ideas in this book if you don't believe they're going to work? Remember, the attitude comes first.

This evening, as you finish up this book, you're going to begin a new life. Tomorrow morning you're going to arrive at your job and you're going to be a different person. It won't matter what the weather is like, it's going to be a beautiful day. Smile, have a spring in your walk, have good words for everyone. Beginning tomorrow, nobody's going to hear about your hangups. Nobody's going to hear about your personal problems or your family's problems. They won't hear about your debts. From this moment on, all of those things are just temporary. So far as those around you are concerned, you don't have one problem. Your mind will be opening itself up to discovering and accepting the challenges of profitable moneymaking opportunities all around you. You never know when one will pop up. You are the happiest, most enthusiastic, creative, and optimistic person on the job.

Of course you're right, you'll be playacting. You'll be putting on a facade, because you haven't accomplished the things you plan to accomplish yet. The trick is, you know that you *will* do them. Because you know you *will* do them, you can have the Prosperous Mental Attitude you'll *need* to do them.

You can begin tomorrow to live the life of a person who has escaped the middle class.

Start of the Day Exercises

If you'll take the time now to learn and practice several mental exercises, you'll begin to get the idea. You can train that little voice inside of you to help guide you through the portage from middle class to money class. With these mental exercises, just like with physical exercises, you must keep at them. If you quit, or start skipping days, you'll remain the loser—and your middle-class mind-set will never be replaced with more useful Prosperous Mental Attitudes. If you quit, or start skipping days, the doldrums will stay around you. You'll be followed relentlessly by a big black cloud. Learn these mental exercises and put them to work for you. They will work. You need them. You will be astonished at how keen your mind will become.

Prosperous Suggestion Exercises

As the first thing you do when you get up every morning, right before bathing and brushing your teeth, look in the mirror, and say:

"Today I'm going to be alert to moneymaking opportunities."

"I'm going to be in an up, positive mood."

"I expect to be successful today."

These statements are not to be used as threats or commands. You don't have to threaten yourself in any way. Threats are counter-productive. They've been used on you all your life, and they only work to beat you down. Instead, what you're going to do is plant positive thoughts in the conscious portion of your brain. After a while these suggestions will move into your subconscious and become a part of you. They're very obvious, calculated thoughts, but they work. Wherever you go and whatever you do during the day, those thoughts will remain with you . . . just as *you* will remain with you.

You need to be a good salesman when you're talking to yourself in front of the mirror every morning. You must look yourself right in the eye and be convincing. Only then will those positive suggestions start replacing the counter-productive patterns in your subconscious.

By the way, you can share your goals and dreams with others. This isn't a secret plan you're following. You can have the support of friends and family members, if they're willing to give it. Once they understand what you're up to, they may be quite helpful. Be careful, though. They might make remarks like "You shouldn't be wasting your money on stuff like that," or "You could set better goals for yourself." Statements like that, while meant to be helpful, might seem negative to you unless you are ready to accept them in the positive spirit you must assume they'll be given in.

End of the Evening Exercises

You began your day with a little positive pep talk. End your day, before saying your prayers and going to sleep, with some self-motivating words and some positive self-criticism.

This time, instead of looking in a mirror, sit by yourself in a quiet room for five or ten minutes. Go through your day while it's fresh in your memory. Was it, over all, a good day or a bad day? Did you get angry today? Did you come up with any new ideas? Were you resentful towards anyone? Could you have done anything better? Is there anything you need to follow up on tomorrow? Discuss the good and bad times with yourself.

If it was a good day, cherish it. If it was a bad day, give it a moment's thought, learn from it, and then forget about it. No one is perfect and no day is all good or all bad. Never pout or give up on yourself. Look at yourself honestly and say to yourself:

"My goals are realistic."
"I will bring my ship in."
"Today was a valuable day."
"Tomorrow will be even better."

If you confront yourself with yourself, every morning and every evening, every day, you will reinforce the love and respect you should have for yourself. Your mind will start rejecting the average middle-class habit patterns which made you reject your own self-interests in the past. Your mental exercises are instrumental to the success of your *Park Avenue Money Diet*. And this brings us to the third mind hook for your Prosperous Mental Attitude.

Habit

You have to form the habit of directing your effort towards your own self-interests, as well as towards promoting your Prosperous Mental Attitude. A lot of people resent thinking of themselves as creatures of habit. That statement tends to make us all think of Pavlov and his salivating dogs. But if you want to get rich, you've got to accept the fact that there is nothing wrong with forming good habits.

To a greater extent than most people will admit, that is what we all are anyway—the sum and total of our accumulated habits. Failures are failures because of their habits, average middle-class people are the way they are because of their habits, and successful people are successful because of their habits.

Habits aren't things that just happen to you. You create your habits, both good and bad. You can concentrate on a habit until it becomes a part of you and you don't have to think about it anymore. Research has shown that most people can create any new habit they want by repeating a behavior pattern for approximately two months. Many people can form habits even faster. But we can say that in a maximum of two months, your subconscious will take over and you will not have to think consciously about it after that time

Let's take one of your habits: sitting down in a quiet room in your home after dinner and working on your finances. You might be studying an investment analysis. You might be reading a book on tax shelters, real estate investments, or wealthy people. Or you might be doing your personal accounting.

Hold on! You say this isn't your present habit? Oh, that's right. Your present habit is sitting down in the family room, watching five hours of TV. Sorry!

We're going to have to change that!

The first evening you try your new habit, you'll have to walk to a different room in the house—a new habit. You'll sit down with a real personal challenge in front of you in the form of a book, a calculator, a pencil and paper, a property analysis, or some accounting forms—a new habit. Think about it. It's peaceful and quiet. Telephones aren't ringing. Laugh tracks from the situation comedies aren't insulting your intelligence. There's no one bothering you. And best of all, you'll be starting to accomplish something for yourself.

Suppose you do that every evening for sixty evenings in a row. For sixty evenings, you make the conscious effort to walk away from the TV room for just one hour after dinner. Around the sixtieth evening, you will end up in your study room and amazingly realize that it didn't take any concentrated effort on your part to do it. A year from now, and for the rest of your life, you will have this habit. You will be devoting at least one hour a day to learning about money, real estate, taxes, and accounting. You will be doing the things you need to do to improve your financial situation.

By the way, everything you pick up out of this book can be a new habit for you to learn. Everything you allow yourself to take out of this book will require you to make a concentrated effort to change old habits. If you do not change, you will remain as you are — average and middle class. If you do not change, you will go nowhere. To change, you will have to develop new habits.

If you have the guts to change, if you do the things I've outlined for you, after doing them for several days they will become much easier. After two months, you will have developed the habit of doing them, and that's all you're going to need to do. Form money-class habits and you will eventually become a member of the money class. Habits will create your future. Understand how important that word *habit* will have to become in your life.

The next mind hook necessary to your success is desire.

You Have to Want It

You have to want to escape the middle class. I don't mean you will dream about escaping the middle class. I don't mean that you wish you were wealthy. You've got to want it with every bone and fiber in your body. Your desire must burn white hot and it must, at times, consume your every thought. You must ache for it until it becomes more painful for you to sit and do nothing than to work towards achieving what you desire. You must have a resolve to get from where you are now to where you want to be. Then you must start doing the things that are necessary for you to get there.

Are you aware that you have everything you've ever wanted, right now? That's right, absolutely, positively everything. True, you haven't got all the things you've ever *dreamed* of, or *wished* for; but *you've gotten everything you've ever really* **wanted.**

To prove the point, answer this question or one like it for yourself. Do you have a college diploma or an advanced degree? If not, the explanation is simple. You didn't want one badly enough. Don't tell yourself that you did want one, but that you never had the time to get one. You could have taken one or two courses a semester. You might have gone to night school. It might have taken a long time to get, but a college diploma or an advanced degree was within your reach. If you don't have one, you just didn't want it badly enough. And that's all there is to it. Other priorities that you wanted more took precedence.

That's what I mean when I talk about wanting something. You will get everything in this world that you want, providing what you want is within the bounds of desire and accomplishment. You will get it if you want it badly enough. Trouble is, most ordinary people don't want very much very badly, and isn't that a sad state of affairs? You must believe that whatever you want is available to you.

Faith

I know your fears! Yes, I do! I've been there! I know that the things I'm suggesting to you are frightening. Like all average middle-class people, you are frightened by the prospect of stepping outside of the confines of your present situation.

You'd like to avoid risking the uncertainty of venturing out into the grit and grime of the world of chance—the place where you could make some real money! There is a real battle going on inside you now. You're not sure if you want to try to follow my advice, or if you're going to try to continue to maintain your illusions of middle-class security. This is a serious problem, and it requires a serious answer. The answer is *faith*.

Taking a chance is an act of faith. You will seldom experience, accomplish, or create anything new if you don't take a chance. At the same time, you'll never have all the information you're going to need to see into the future. If you really want to escape the middle class, someday you're going to have to stack up all your plans, get up off your backside (the place where you're at right now!), and start doing those things you know you're going to have to do if you really want to become wealthy. There is little point in waiting until the fog lifts completely, or until you've verified that the road is paved and free of chuckholes. The fog never does, and the road never is.

You've heard that old saying, haven't you? The one that says you should "look before you leap"?

Well, I hesitate to attempt to discredit an old saying, but there are times when you'd be better off if you would leap before you look . . . or at least, if you'd leap before you tried to see everything with perfect clarity. Those who occasionally leap before they look are often the ones who come up with the really new and creative ideas . . . and they are the ones who are rewarded accordingly.

If you must wait until you gather all the statistics to confirm your choice, or until the market is proven beyond all doubt, your venture is probably doomed to mediocrity. The perfect plan is always a myth. Precise investment projections are almost always wrong. The more detailed a plan is, the less useful it is for accurate forecasting.

Planning is always necessary and useful, but it is seldom adequate. At best, it will give you a rough estimation of the final outcome. Your best plans will seldom come to actual fruition in exactly the form you foresaw them. Most successful investments and ventures diverge drastically from the ideas and plans that originally created them. This is a fact, and it will be as true of your Ten Year Real Estate Investment Schedule as it was of Columbus' plans to sail around the world.

"So why should I make plans at all? Why even worry about setting up a Ten Year Real Estate Investment Schedule? Why study investment analysis?"

Don't misunderstand me. I'm not saying don't plan for the future. What I am saying is, don't expect to get all the details right. The detailed plan is important even if its only purpose is to beguile you into believing that all your problems have been anticipated and that all the solutions to those problems are known. This is because if it doesn't beguile you, you may never go ahead and make your move. It's the plan, the analysis, and the projection which will convince you of the correctness of your decisions. This is true even if you totally overestimate the benefits and underestimate the costs and difficulties your venture will encounter.

Most really successful moves are often no more than on-the-spot responses to totally unexpected situations. That is why faith is so important. You have to have faith in your decisions, faith in the future, and faith in your ability to deal with whatever you encounter there.

In making your plans, think of the past and the present as the fantasy worlds. Whatever has happened in the past or is happening in the present will almost certainly happen differently in the future.

It has been observed that gross miscalculations or extreme ignorance were the key factors responsible for the launching of many of the world's most profitable enterprises. This was true of the building of the American railroad system, the invention of the telephone, and the digging of the

Panama Canal. It was certainly the case with my cattle ranch. Faith in your decisions, and in your abilities to tackle unforeseen obstacles and problems, is the element in your program for achieving wealth which will often allow even folly to bear fruit.

"But what if my decision is wrong?"

What if it is? The fact that you made the decision will weigh heavily on the side of its being the correct decision. It will tip the scales in your favor, tending to make even the wrong decision the right decision. Once you've made a decision, you're going to commit yourself to seeing that it will work, right? (Shake your head up and down!)

Once you're involved in something that you decided to do for yourself, you're going to do everything in your power to see that it is successful. By taking that all-important first step beyond the realm of your present activities and into the world of chance, you'll create for yourself the necessity for a commitment. That very commitment will establish its own confirmation.

It will be your willingness to plunge into the unknown, and to deal with whatever is found there, that will create your greatest returns. You must have faith in your ability to deal with the unexpected, good or bad.

Problems and obstacles should not be avoided. They should be sought after and highly prized. The solutions you find will confirm your faith in your abilities and in yourself. Problems and obstacles are the source of new approaches and new knowledge, which are the stuff that dreams of wealth "come true" are made of.

All answers to the future must be found in faith. There is nowhere else to look for them! You must experience the thrill of taking a chance; the challenge of searching out problems and conflicts and attacking them head on. You must experience the satisfaction of finding solutions. It's the solutions you'll find that will stimulate your new investment ideas and moneymaking innovations.

Of course you will not always be triumphant; but even your failures will be the source of new knowledge and increased energies for creating wealth.

Finally, you must have the faith to allow room for the random events and incalculable opportunities to effect your life. To do anything less will continue to force you to live with the lowered expectations common to life in the middle class.

*   *   *

This brings us to the last and possibly the greatest mind hook in your Prosperous Mental Attitude formula. To the extent you know precisely what you want to achieve, decide to achieve it, and believe you will achieve it . . . you will achieve it.

Goals

At the beginning of this book, I compared most average middle-class people to rudderless vessels twisting and turning on the ocean. They turn, twist, and float through high school, through college, through their first job, from one job to another, and from one husband or wife to another. They drift aimlessly through life, wishing for the day when they will arrive at a safe harbor.

As you approach the end of this book, I want you to join me in the process of taking command of your ship. I want you to chart your own course. Once you take command, your twisting, turning ship will be transformed into a beautiful three-masted clipper. You'll have a rudder, a chart, and your sails will be unfurled into a gentle west wind. You'll know where the safe harbor is and how you're going to get to it. A fine sailing ship like the one you captain will find its safe harbor ninety-nine times out of a hundred.

If you set your goals, and plan to do whatever is necessary to achieve them, how can you do anything but accomplish what you set out to do? Once you have your goals established, you will begin implementing the other five mind hooks. Your efforts will be concentrated. You'll form the right habits. You will have a positive outlook on your life, because you'll know where you are headed and what you want out of life. You will get caught up in your passion to succeed, and you'll have the faith, making the commitments required to accomplish that success. Your life will become a magnificent achievement and a fabulous experience.

There are three goals which you will want to achieve. All three are fundamental to your escape from the middle class.

The first goal is financial independence. Most middle-class people never achieve it. They reach retirement age, if they're lucky, with only the equities in their homes, a pittance in outside income, plus Social Security and some meager pension benefits. They work their entire productive lives and never achieve real financial independence. I think that's a tragedy beyond description, knowing, as I know now, that an entrepreneur in the free enterprise system has so many opportunities.

You should start your journey to financial independence by investing in income-producing residential rental investment properties. Most present-day fortunes were either built in or are being held in real estate. As you begin, don't allow yourself to be distracted by other less worthy investments or endeavors. There is no need for you to look anywhere else right now. Specialize in real estate investing. It's a field from which you'll be able to draw every reward you want, including financial independence. You can eat it, drink it, sleep it, and fall in love with it. Then, if after a period of time, and if after careful study and research, you decide you want to do something else . . . start a hobby shop, or launch a super tanker . . . you'll have the financial strength in your real estate holdings to make your move successfully.

In addition to financial independence, you also need two shorter range goals. The first one we'll call your carrot goal. You've probably seen cartoons where a mule is walking along pulling a cart and trying to get to a carrot which is dangling from a pole strapped to his back, always just beyond his reach. Every time the mule moves, the carrot moves.

Likewise, if you dangle a carrot that's appealing to you out in front of your life, you're going to do something to get to that carrot. When you think of a carrot goal, think of something that is fun to do or have.

How about a vacation? Not just an ordinary vacation out in the backyard with a can of beer, like usual, but something really special. Take a jet to Switzerland, Hong Kong, Rio, London, or the Bahamas. Go some place where other money-class people go. Spend the extra money it will cost you to go first cabin and stay in first class accomodations. See what it's like to be wealthy.

Start planning for that vacation. Find out how much it's going to cost, and then begin looking for ways to earn or set aside the amount you will need. Once you've left for the vacation, spend the money you planned to spend and don't worry about it. This is part of your success plan. Once you see what it's like to experience first cabin, you'll begin looking for ways to continue the experience.

The vacation should cost you at least several hundred (or thousand) dollars more than you would normally plan to spend. It will be well worth it. First, it will be fun. Second, it will help strengthen your resolve to become wealthy.

From this point on, you will want to have a constant succession of carrot goals established to keep you moving in the direction you want to go. Each should be attainable, only slightly extending your ability to reach for them. Carrot goals might be almost anything that's fun to do or have. They should always be first class, and they should never be bought simply on impulse, the way much of the meretricious junk you've bought in the past has been.

A carrot goal could be an expensive suit or outfit, or an entire new wardrobe, dinner out at a really first class restaurant, a special vacation, a new car, a new house, an airplane, a gold watch, or a diamond ring. As you continue to move towards your ultimate goal of financial independence, your carrot goals should keep moving also, becoming more exciting and expensive. If they don't, you're liable to get too comfortable at one level or another and quit reaching.

Part of the fun and the benefit of setting these carrot goals is that it will force you to imagine things for yourself that you never considered as being within your reach before. Imagining them is the first step towards getting them.

I've been using this carrot goal technique for several years now, and my goals are becoming quite exciting. On the succeeding pages, I've included a few pictures of my most recent carrot goals that I've already achieved. Those are followed by a few of the next series of carrot goals, the ones I'm striving for now.

Remember, I said there were three goals you needed to have. The first is financial independence; the second is the carrot goals; and we'll discuss the third one now.

Your third goal is to live every day of your life in a way that will make it a profitable experience. Every good day you have will lead you to the next good day. Commit every day to the eventual achievement of your ultimate success. Totally dedicate and commit yourself to your escape from the middle class and your eventual acceptance into the money class. You know how to do it. It's all right here in the pages of *The Park Avenue Money Diet*.

You now have everything you need to escape the middle class, but you will not achieve the success you want until some time after you've set some definite goals. Write them down. Set time frames around when you expect to achieve them. Hang pictures of them on the wall of your study. There is always the element of "chance" or "luck" involved in achieving success, but even "chance" or "luck" is often the result of an absolutely predictable set of planned circumstances. If you do the things you've learned in this book, you will escape the middle class, and you will be successful.

Present home in winter

Present car and Joshua tree

Present airplane, Mooney 231

Our Texas cattle ranch

Country estate *(future goal)*

Rolls Royce "Corniche" *(future goal)*

Cessna "Golden Eagle" *(future goal)*

Corum $20 gold piece watch *(future goal)*

CHAPTER 13

BEGINNING NOW

I wish it were possible for me to jump right out of the end of the book and help you follow through on your own *Park Avenue Money Diet*. Of course I can't, but I know that my words and ideas can guide you.

You have suffered silently, perhaps even unknowingly, through average middle-class purgatory, but it's not necessary for you to suffer any longer. Fair is fair. You were not born to suffer through life. Remember, all it really took for me to change my life was one event to wake me up to the world of money. Then I went out to begin getting all of the things I ever wanted. It's time for you to do the same.

We've toured your past and your present. We've studied some things you've already known, some you haven't known, and other things you haven't considered for a long time. We've looked into your future. We've discussed ways for you to make the most profitable use of the rest of your life.

You should now be ready to address your average middle-class problem and come out the winner. You read this book to help you change your life forever. Now it's time. Go out and do it.

In the next several days, I want you to go back through *The Park Avenue Money Diet* with a highlighting pen. Mark those ideas or passages that seem to apply directly to you. Study the charts and accounting forms. Go over them several times to reinforce them in your mind. You can't just read this book once and expect it to work for you. Careful research has shown that people retain only 20 percent of what they read the first time through. You can increase that percentage to 40 or 50 percent by rereading once, 70 percent by rereading twice, and so on.

Think and believe "you can do it" and "you will do it" . . . then do it. I wish you the best!

THE CALF PATH

> One day, through the primeval wood,
> A calf walked home, as good calves should;
> But made a trail all bent askew,
> A crooked trail as all calves do.
>
> Since then two hundred years have fled,
> And, I infer, the calf is dead.
> But still he left behind his trail,
> And thereby hangs my moral tale.
>
> The trail was taken up next day
> By a lone dog that passed that way:
> And then a wise bell-wether sheep
> Pursued the trail o'er vale and steep.
> And drew the flock behind him too.
> As good bell-wethers always do.

And from that day, o'er hill and glade,
Through those old woods a path was made;
And many men wound in and out,
And dodged, and turned, and bent about
And uttered words of righteous wrath
Because 'twas such a crooked path.
But still they followed—do not laugh—
The first migrations of that calf,
And through this winding wood-way stalked,
Because he wobbled when he walked.

This forest path became a lane,
That bent, and turned, and turned again;
This crooked lane became a road,
Where many a poor horse with his load
Toiled on beneath the burning sun,
And traveled some three miles in one.
And thus a century and a half
They trod the footsteps of that calf.

The years passed on in swiftness fleet,
The road became a village street;
And this, before men were aware,
A city's crowded thoroughfare;
And soon the central street was this
Of a renowned metropolis;
And men two centuries and a half
Trod in the footsteps of that calf.

Each day a hundred thousand rout
Followed the zigzag calf about;
And o'er his crooked journey went
The traffic of a continent.
A hundred thousand men were led
By one calf near three centuries dead.
They followed still his crooked way,
And lost one hundred years a day;
For thus such reverence is lent
To well-established precedent.

A moral lesson this might teach
Were I ordained and called to preach;
For men are prone to go it blind
Along the calf-paths of the mind
And work away from sun to sun
To do what other men have done.
They follow in the beaten track
And out and in, and forth and back,
And still their devious course pursue,
To keep the path that others do.

But how the wise old wood-gods laugh,
Who saw the first primeval calf!
Ah! many things this tale might teach—
But I am not ordained to preach.

Sam Walter Foss
(1858—1911)

ABOUT THE AUTHOR

Ten years ago, Dan Baumgartner earned a modest living as a part-time music teacher. Through a fluke, he inherited an oil well and suddenly found himself catapulted out of the middle class. But then the oil crisis forced a shut-down of the well and Baumgartner found himself right back where he started—and worse. To meet his staggering mortgage payment, he devised THE PARK AVENUE MONEY DIET. Today, the personable millionaire owns a Cadillac, a Mooney airplane, a home in Lancaster, California, property in Texas and Oklahoma City and a beautiful 400-acre cattle ranch. Of course, Baumgartner isn't satisfied to leave it at that. He still yearns for a Rolls Corniche and a Cessna Golden Eagle airplane. There's always the next ten years...